DUET IN DIAMONDS

DUET
IN DIAMONDS

The Flamboyant Saga
of Lillian Russell and Diamond Jim Brady
in America's Gilded Age

BY JOHN BURKE

G. P. Putnam's Sons
New York

927.92
BURK
1972

CONTENTS

(Illustrations appear after page 128.)

INTRODUCTION

Lobsters! Rarebits! Plenty of Pilsener beer!
Plenty of girls to help you drink the best of cheer!
Dark girls, blonde girls, and never a one that's true,
You get them all in the Tenderloin when the clock strikes two.

AS the popular song whose chorus is quoted above would indicate, the quality of American life has never been so well larded as during the years before and after the turn of the century. By then the industrialization of America had spread its benefits widely and evenly enough for a large share of the population to enjoy a measure of the continent's abundance. It was a period variously known as the Gay Nineties and the Naughty Noughts, more precisely as the late Victorian and Edwardian eras, more critically as the *fin de siècle*. In any case, it was characterized by a tumescence of red plush, an outbreak of bric-a-brac, a shower of good things previously denied the masses. Above all, it was marked by the self-confidence of a generation priding itself on having conquered a continent, lulled by a quarter-century of peace, which could enjoy lashings of food and drink without social guilt, without moral or physical inhibitions, without a nervous counting of calories. Cholesterol, for all anyone knew, might have been a tropical disease. A double jowl, a bulging paunch, a Percheron-like haunch were all the attributes of a citizen in good health, of a man in good standing with his creditors.

7

Looking back on that heyday of our immediate ancestors, examining the artifacts of the period, reading the often denigratory accounts of social historians, it is easy to deplore the excesses of a time which seems to have abounded in vulgar display and in overstuffed stomachs and understocked consciences. We have learned that not everyone was frolicking in the lobster palaces or riding around on bicycles built for two; that there was grinding poverty in the big-city tenements and unremitting hardship for the hundreds of thousands of immigrants who were passing through Ellis Island annually. We know that agitation for social reform was reaching the feverish stage even as much of the population seemed to be standing at the mouth of an open-ended cornucopia; that thousands of the unemployed, a boxcar army, would march on Washington before the century ended, and that meanwhile the country itself took the first long stride on the road to an overseas empire.

Still, in the popular mind, the period stands for a carefree abundance, a sunlit time of clanging trolleys, hourglass figures, Horatio Alger millionaires, ten-course dinners, Floradora girls, bumper harvests, and ragtime music that seemed to set the tempo for a country determined to outdo, outbuild, and outproduce all others. Never was the nation more confident of its mission, more assured of a glorious future, more satisfied with its record of accomplishments (slavery ended, the West conquered, the country covered by railroads from coast to coast, all in a quarter of a century). John Jay Chapman was a well-born New York intellectual, a nonconformist, a social and civic reformer, and a malcontent by the prevailing standards, yet even he was confident of the American ability to reshape itself in more desirable forms. In a letter to a friend he conceded that his generation was different from the preceding ones, but "the extent to which we are different will take care of itself. It is sane not to worry over it but to deal with the world unconsciously—to trust our own nature. . . . That's why the *fin de siècle* talk makes me irritated."

Certainly there was nothing of *fin-de-siècle* resignation, of

8

the lassitude and world-weariness that supposedly comes with decadence, about the Columbian Exposition of 1893 in Chicago. Ostensibly it was to celebrate the discovery of America; actually it was the announcement of American purpose to shoulder its way to the front rank of the world's nations. It was a national set piece, the physical embodiment of the period and its hopes for the future. It showed off America to the world, and the world was impressed. Karl Baedeker, the German guidebook publisher, assigned a young Englishman named James F. Muirhead to provide a new book in his series for the European traveler to America. The first thing any European had to understand, Muirhead emphasized in the Baedeker volume, was that American democracy was more than a slogan, that the foreigner "should from the outset reconcile himself to the absence of deference or servility on the part of those he considers his social inferiors. . . ." Several years later, in a book titled *The Land of Contrasts,* in which he could express himself more freely, Muirhead reflected with delight on the openness and equality, the exuberance of the country he had explored for Baedeker. It really was something new in human experience, he believed; the almost explosive informality of the American way of life was incredible to an Englishman of settled habits. He wrote of transcontinental trains he rode on which the engineer shot rabbits from the locomotive and the fireman jumped off to pick up the trophies, then caught the last car on the train. He also noted the difference in British and American habits: "If an Englishman has a mile to go to an appointment he will make his leisurely way twenty minutes to do the distance, and then settle his business in two or three dozen sentences; an American is much more likely to devour the ground in five minutes, and then spend an hour or more in lively conversation not wholly pertinent to the matter in hand." For all the lustiness of the American character, for all its pride in being blunt of speech, there was still an indelible imprint of the Puritan ethic. "It is in America that I have over and over again heard language to which the calling a spade a

9

spade would seem the most delicate allusiveness; but it is also in America that I have summoned a blush to the cheek of [many people] by an incautious though innocent reference to the temperature of my morning bath."

It was still the "age of innocence," which would end only with the brutal realities of World War I. And it was that innocence, along with a naïve satisfaction with all that America had accomplished, which was on display on the shores of Lake Michigan when the Columbian Exposition was officially opened by President Grover Cleveland pushing the button of a golden switch. When the plaster-of-paris "White City" sprang up seemingly overnight in Jackson Park, America announced her technological genius and commercial superiority to the world. It outdazzled the Paris Exposition of 1889, in all but French opinion, not only with its display of machinery (including Krupp's newest and biggest cannon) but with the garish architecture of the so-called American Renaissance, Daniel Chester French's sixty-five-foot statue of the republic, sculptures by Augustus Saint-Gaudens, the paintings of John La Farge, Mary Cassatt, Kenyon Cox, and others. *Beaux-arts* classicism was most evident in the Transportation Building designed by Louis Henry Sullivan, in the mirrorlike pool of the Court of Honor, in the imitation Greek temples. There were lagoons on which gondolas drifted, immense columns topped by carvings of acanthus leaves, massive domes, and reflecting pools in which all that plaster-of-paris magnificence was duplicated for those strolling thousands who grew weary of craning their necks.

The acerb Henry Adams was not easily impressed by bumptious manifestations of the American spirit, but he proclaimed that "As a scenic display Paris has never approached it. . . . Here was a breach of continuity—a rupture in historical sequence! Was it real, or only apparent? One's personal universe hung on the answer for, if the rupture was real and the new American world could take this sharp and conscious twist towards ideals, one's personal friends would come in, at last, as winners in the great American chariot-race for fame. . . ."

Some of the Europeans who came to see the wonders of the new world, their Baedekers in hand, were less favorably impressed. All those gleaming white buildings, those towering columns and fluttering flags, those endless displays of American ingenuity in industry and diligence in agriculture, those lagoons glittering at night under Edison's new light bulbs seemed an ominous forecast of a New Rome. They saw an overpowering vulgarity where Americans proclaimed evidence of greatness. The White City was not a representation of America but an excrescence; the exposition itself was a fantasy created to conceal tenement streets, reeking stockyards, and smoking factories, and if this was the future, Europe would be wise not to partake of it.

This view was taken by C. S. de Soissons (*A Parisian in America*), who believed he had caught a glimpse of a new barbarism on the shores of Lake Michigan. "At the Columbian Fair in Chicago, in the midst of the whiteness of this *carton-pâte* city, where the imitations of Greek and Latin antiquity were mingled with those of the Italian Renaissance—a curious gathering of columns, porticoes in severe lines with rococo *campanillas*—a fantastic construction attracted us; its walls covered with vermilion appeared to the eye as a bloody spot upon the field of snow. It was architecture of a primary character, of studied roughness; a cyclopean and barbarous conception, but certainly not a common one. One could see in it a seeking after the strange and enormous, a dream of new forms which would harmonize with the tumultuous and brutal genius of the human collectivity acting in Chicago, that monstrous city, forced as a precocious vegetation upon the marshes of Lake Michigan."

To ordinary people without the professional sensitivity of the intellectuals or the jaundiced outlook of envious Europeans the Columbian Exposition was simply something to

11

marvel at, to be exalted by, to encourage self-congratulation. The mother of one of the many architects and artists who had collaborated on creating its transitory illusion said it offered a "vision of the New Jerusalem," solid evidence of how Americans could work together and bring to pass a miracle of beauty.

By the hundreds of thousands those ordinary Americans— men with handlebar mustaches, women with billowy leg-of-mutton sleeves—wandered through the exposition grounds during the spring, summer, and fall of 1893. They rode in wicker "rolling chairs" or in gondolas when they became footsore. Whenever they could slip away from their womenfolk, the men hurried to the Streets of Cairo, where a sinuous Little Egypt writhed to the accompaniment of drum and flute. In more educational exhibits, genuine natives from various parts of the world lived in mock-ups of their homeland villages, Turkish, Chinese, German, African, Indian; there was also an ice railway, a Japanese bazaar, a Moorish palace, a Bohemian glass factory, and an Irish lace factory to astound the outlanders to whom a grain elevator was the only exotic feature of the prairie landscape.

Among the ordinary folk, too, there walked the celebrities and publicity-seekers of the time, equally amazed by the gigantic passenger-carrying wheel constructed by George Washington Ferris for the exposition. Henry George watched an exhibition staged by Apache Indians, the storming of a stockade, and wondered aloud what it had to do with modern art. Mrs. Potter Palmer appeared in the Court of Honor with a retinue of lesser society ladies. Elbridge T. Gerry convened his Purity Congress in a building at the exposition and declared that prostitution existed in the United States, which made a mockery of the White City's pretensions. There was a considerable brouhaha raised, in fact, by the quantities of white female skin on display in the exposition's various concessions, and not only by the wriggly Little Egypt. Anthony Comstock, the old sin-killer himself, always on the scent of anything that might be considered pornographic by his own tetchy standards, trumpeted that the nudity on display at the exposition was a prevision of the new Babylon. Susan B. Anthony and Frances Willard also showed up to make propaganda for, respectively, women's suffrage and the Women's Christian Temperance Union—both causes which men could still afford to guffaw over.

There were more legitimate celebrities, less eager for attention, who were trailed by reporters hopeful of catching a quotable remark on the fly. They asked Mark Twain what he thought about one of the concessions at which women disported themselves in the sketchiest of costumes under the direction of a New Orleans madam, and he naughtily replied that most men would rather see a "nekkid" female than General Ulysses S. Grant in full-dress uniform. Another front-page name was J. Pierpont Morgan, who took leave from his banking house despite the fact that Wall Street had recently taken a disastrous tumble. The purple-nosed Mr. Morgan's principal interest was the Palace of Fine Arts, where a collection of French paintings was on display. Asked what he thought of the collection, he told reporters, "They might just as well have been chosen by a committee of chambermaids."

The most powerful American financier and the most famous of contemporary writers were not, however, the most effulgent celebrities who attended the exposition.

Either on the grounds of celebrity or notoriety, the two visitors most fascinating to the crowds on the Midway Plaisance were James Buchanan Brady and Lillian Russell—the former better known as Diamond Jim, the supersalesman, the walking jewelry store, the biggest eater in a land of plenty, and the latter the star of the musical stage who would serve as America's love goddess until the "vamps" of the silent screen made their appearance.

They had met from time to time in New York, were casual acquaintances until then, but their reunion in Chicago cemented what became a famous and enduring friendship, a partnership in high living, a dual career in getting and spending millions of dollars on food and frolic that would serve as the paradigm of their pleasure-loving age.

What drew them together was a newly discovered affinity for corn on the cob. Lillian was an Iowa girl, and when corn was in season she lunched and dined on corn drenched in melted butter and followed by crepes suzette. Every day she and Brady met in a restaurant, either in the Loop or out on the exposition grounds. Usually they favored Charles Rector's Café Marine, with such friends and acquaintances as George M. Cohan, Stanford White, and Richard Harding Davis at adjoining tables.

Their arrival was the signal for waiters to start carrying in trays of corn on the cob. Between them, that summer, Brady and Russell must have devastated several Iowa cornfields by themselves. Their gastronomic feats attracted almost as much attention as Little Egypt or the Transportation Building. The newspaper sketch artists, capturing them at table behind a barricade of denuded corn cobs, began labeling them "Beauty and the Beast." They were the star attractions of Exposition Summer.

Fleshly arm in arm, plump shoulder to shoulder, they toddled together into the social history of their time.

J. B.

DUET IN DIAMONDS

1

STAR QUALITY

HER first theatrical billing read "Miss Lillian Russell, the English Ballad Singer."

In that brief announcement there were two errors of fact. Her real name was Helen Louise Leonard, and she was no more English than the corn-covered plains of her native Iowa. She was called plain Nellie, in fact, until a theatrical producer decided that there was star quality about the lissome, golden-blond girl whom he renamed Lillian Russell.

Almost from birth, however, there was little of the plain Nellie about the girl who would become the most durable sex symbol American theatrical history has known. As the starting impetus of a highly unconventional life, in which she had more than the contemporary quotient of husbands and lovers and a thundering herd of admirers, she could hardly have chosen her parents better herself. Her mother was a fiery feminist at a time when women's rights were regarded as ridiculous, and her father made himself notorious by publishing the works of the foremost American atheist.

Helen Louise Leonard and her four sisters were all born in Clinton, Iowa—Helen in 1861. Her father was Charlie Leonard, then an easygoing newspaperman who published the weekly

Herald. It was from her strong-willed mother, the former Cynthia Van Names, who married Leonard in 1852, that she inherited the trait of hardheaded independence which would make Lillian Russell the cigar-swallowing despair of theatrical producers from London's West End to San Francisco. It was Cynthia Leonard's first principle that being a female didn't mean one was destined to be crushed into whimpering conformity in a man's world.

She was a handsome, talented, ambitious young woman who blamed most of her frustrations, perhaps rightly, on masculine dominance. The stupidest man was legally and morally responsible for his womenfolk, no matter how superior they might be. A woman, regardless of how clever and talented, was condemned to the holy trinity of her allotted tasks: children, church, and kitchen. Mama Leonard would raise her five daughters beyond the toddling stage, but then she would make her own mark in the world, goaded on by the infuriatingly indulgent smile of Charlie Leonard.

It was a wonder that Cynthia Leonard had any time at all to spare for her daughters. She was constantly in furious communication with the other scattered, beleaguered women who were just then banding together to campaign for their full emancipation; they were something like the Committees of Correspondence which had started an earlier revolution. And Cynthia Leonard yielded to none of her comrades in the composition of fiery prose that threatened American manhood with Biblical destruction if it did not accord womanhood its equality. "Oh, unhappy, grasping, power-loving man," she apostrophized the overbearing Victorian male in one of her broadsides, "how long will you continue in your blindness? For more than two hundred years my ancestors have been born in America—I had two greatgrandfathers in the Revolutionary Army, and yet I am not a full-fledged citizen. Why? Because man chooses to disinherit me. Because he loves to tyrannize over me. Because (alone) he is incapable to administer justice. Verily, men are bringing down upon themselves and upon us the flood of Noah, the destruction of Jerusalem! Truly masculine rule is a total failure. Your might is not right!"

She found outlets for her energy in establishing new schools and temporary churches in the growing town, performed on the violin and guitar, and sang the solos in a fine contralto at the Baptist church. After the Civil War broke out, she busied herself in providing care for the convalescing wounded Union soldiers and founding the first soldier's home in Iowa. But Clinton wasn't large enough to provide the necessary scope for her ambitions to uplift, and occasionally outrage, her fellow citizens. At her urging Charlie Leonard sold the Clinton *Herald* and transported the family to Chicago in 1863. Helen, their youngest daughter, was then two years old.

Leonard set himself up as a printer, while Mrs. Leonard expanded her activities as a social reformer and women's rights crusader. Imperious as she was energetic, she became the leader of a group of women with "progressive" interests which met weekly at an ice-cream parlor called the Maison Doree. In this vanilla-scented salon Mrs. Leonard rallied her colleagues for assaults on the established order. The enemy citadel was City Hall, the stronghold of big-bellied Irish and German aldermen who, by national tradition, were especially antipathetic to the theory that women should share political power. Those political barons, with ethnic constituencies in the tenement districts of the North Side and the stockyards, rumbled with coarse laughter over the spectacle of a bunch of women meeting in an ice-cream parlor and threatening to "clean up" Chicago.

Aldermanic scorn was soon to be converted to dismay, the penalty for having underrated the collective fury of women, even though denied the privilege of voting, on the warpath for civic and moral betterment. With Valkyrian fury, the ladies of the Maison Doree learned one early afternoon that the Chicago Common Council at its meeting that evening intended to sneak over an ordinance which would license houses of prostitution. Cynthia Leonard, with the meeting less than six hours away, whipped up her fellow activists to go out and shanghai their husbands—however reluctant—plus whatever other relatives they could round up, to join a protest march on City Hall. At eight o'clock that night Mrs. Leonard and her cohorts, bearing a lengthy petition, appeared in the Common Council chambers and threatened to pull down the city if the proposed ordinance was passed. The aldermen, shaken to their boot heels, quickly agreed it wouldn't be such a good idea to legalize the redlight district. Another way of looking at the problem, of course, was that prostitution would continue in any case, except that the "fallen women" would have to walk the streets looking for clients rather than living in some degree of comfort, with a measure of protection from pimps and Jack the Ripper types, in a decently run whorehouse.

Mrs. Leonard did not stop at her victory over the aldermen in her concern for the city's prostitutes. The great fire of October, 1871, dispossessed most of the streetwalkers. According to reports reaching Mrs. Leonard and her coworkers, they were being harassed by the police. With characteristic determination and energy, she announced the formation of the Good Samaritan Society. Respectable people tended to avert their gaze from such problems, believing that soiled doves were God's business, but Mrs. Leonard raised a clamor that would not allow them to neglect the plight of the streetwalkers. She reaped so much publicity in the Chicago newspapers through a series of meetings that a wealthy German came forward with the offer of a forty-room mansion to shelter the prostitutes. Mrs. Leonard took charge of the shelter and rehabilitation work herself, found what would later be called foster homes for the younger girls, and bullied a number of the others into agreeing to take up housework or candy-dipping at four dollars a week rather than continuing on the more lucrative but socially undesirable primrose path.

Cynthia Leonard might have finished cleaning up the city had she not been diverted by literary aspirations. For several years she had relieved this itch by writing letters to the newspapers, usually taking up the most unpopular positions she could think of. Now she busied herself writing two novels which the presses at Charlie Leonard's printing establishment were commandeered to publish, with dismal results for his balance sheets. The first was titled *Lena Rouden, or the Rebel Spy*, in which the authoress somehow managed to work in the great Chicago fire, removed as it was in time and distance from Confederate espionage. Her second and last literary effort was *Failing Footsteps, or the Last of the Iroquois*, which did little damage to the literary standing of James Fenimore Cooper.

Very well, if her own artistic tendencies couldn't be satisfied by literary overreaching, she would turn to the promise exhibited by her youngest daughter. Cynthia Leonard was a born stagemother. Helen Louise, called Nellie, was a beautiful child with what her teachers proclaimed to be an extraordinary voice. The child had been educated at the Sacred Heart School, where the nuns discovered her singing and acting talents and placed them on exhibit in school entertainment programs. She attended a West Side finishing school, the Park Institute, where her talents were further remarked. At fourteen, angelic in sight and sound with her clear, high, bell-like soprano, she appeared in a concert at the Kimball Music Hall. The reception of that maiden effort convinced her that she was born for a career in grand opera.

"Our family was a musical one," as she later related. "We sang and danced and played, and all of my sisters had exceptionally fine voices, which were carefully trained. So it was natural that when I heard my first opera—*Mignon*, sung by the Clara Louise Kellogg Opera Company—I should decide to become a grand opera singer. I had no doubt of my success. I awaited with impatience the day when I should burst upon the world in all my effulgent splendor and show it what it had been missing during the years it had taken me to grow up. Our favorite game at home was Opera. I borrowed my mother's dresses and shawls and made trailing robes for myself and stalked about in them and sang until my parents were obliged to ask for interludes of silence."

In 1878, when Helen Louise had reached the age of seventeen and male heads turned with metronomic regularity as she tripped down the street with her dimity dresses clinging to a figure that aroused thoughts of statutory rape, Mama Leonard decided it was time to make her break for freedom and emancipate herself from the thralldom of domesticity. Perhaps if Charlie Leonard just once had raised his fist . . . but no, his indulgent smiles, his wincing acceptance of her various essays into social reform and literature, his maddening *tolerance* were the mark of a passive man who would never satisfy her ambitions. Mrs. Leonard also wanted to escape the second-rateness of Chicago, always in New York's shadow. Besides, the feminist movement was beginning to gain momentum and Cynthia Leonard wanted to take her place beside Susan B. Anthony and other leaders of the suffrage crusade.

The most talented, beautiful, and promising of her five daughters was Helen Louise, so she decided to take the seventeen-year-old with her to New York and launch her on a singing career. The four other girls would be left in Charlie Leonard's care; it was time he shared the responsibilities of parenthood in full.

What did easygoing Charlie Leonard think of this arrangement, which he was not called upon to ratify, merely to accept? He always kept his own counsel on the subject. Undoubtedly, though, it was a vexing, even a heartbreaking situation. Helen Louise had always secretly been his favorite, the most vivacious of his daughters as well as the youngest, whom he called "airy, fairy Nellie." She would never again live under his roof. Many years later Marie Dressler, her best friend, would write that Charlie Leonard was the only man who understood the glamorous creature known to the world as Lillian Russell. He kept in touch with his youngest daughter as best he could and, according to Miss Dressler, "would sit up all night in a day coach, if necessary, and travel a thousand miles to hear her sing three songs." His feelings about his wife may be divined from the subsequent turn his career as a printer and publisher took.

Evidently he felt that, having endured almost a quarter century of domination by Cynthia Leonard, it would be intolerable to consider an afterlife under the stern dictates of the God envisioned and promulgated by the Baptists. Charlie Leonard gained sulphurous renown as the publisher of agnostic and atheistic works, particularly those of Colonel Robert G. Ingersoll, whom their generation regarded as the devil's plenipotentiary on earth.

Cynthia Leonard and her principal asset in carving out a life independent of masculine interference arrived in New York early in 1878. Properly managed, Mrs. Leonard believed, her daughter would achieve stardom on the lyric stage, and her first step toward that goal, after they established themselves in an apartment in Brooklyn, was to place Helen Louise in the studio of the noted voice teacher Dr. Leopold Damrosch, with a career in grand opera as the ultimate objective. Helen Louise was willing enough, though Marie Dressler later wrote that by disposition she was more domestic than thespic. "Temperamentally," said Miss Dressler, "she was cut out for a bungalow apron, a kitchen smelling of ginger cookies, roses climbing over the back fence, and a yard just big enough to hold a clucking hen and a brood of biddies. Instinctively she was the most domestic of women. . . ."

Instead of being allowed to follow her own inclinations, young Helen Louise's tip-tilted nose was pointed firmly in the direction of theatrical success by her mother.

And that success, if not instant, came with astonishing ease and swiftness. As the noted impresario Florenz Ziegfeld exclaimed after first seeing her on stage, "Destiny and the cornfields of Iowa shaped her for the stage." What he meant was that Helen Louise Leonard was enveloped by an aura of sexual magnetism that melted the wax in the mustachios of every able-bodied male. She was then slender but paradoxically voluptuous, with a small waist and jutting breasts and (later to be revealed) shapely legs. She was a golden blonde with what fancy writers then called a *retroussé* nose and a complexion that seemed to partake of rose petals and fresh cream. And there was something provocative in her blue eyes, the swing of her hips; there was a hint of the coming opulence of her figure and just that touch of vulnerability essential to every love goddess, which was also visible in such successors as Jean Harlow and Marilyn Monroe. American-style Venuses must convey a suggestion of accessibility, of earthiness, even a touch of pathos, a sense of being ill-used by men, which thus makes them appealing to women. The girl who became Lillian Russell had those qualities innately, they did not have to be developed, and that presumably was what Mr. Ziegfeld meant by the imperatives of destiny.

But it was not those budding nympholeptic qualities that riveted her voice teacher. Dr. Damrosch was transfixed by the quality of her voice, a true if slightly metallic soprano which could effortlessly, repeatedly, and without evident strain hit high C. A voice in a million, ten million. Several years of intense study and practice could make her a young diva to rival Melba and Madame Nordica.

Dr. Damrosch and Mrs. Leonard agreed that she should be trained for grand opera. The girl herself disagreed, and after all, Mama had taught her to be independent. Helen was not willing to spend years in Dr. Damrosch's atelier, followed by years of small roles and constant study, practice, and instruction. Her assets were marketable immediately if she was willing to lower her sights from grand opera to light and comic opera. The wife of Colonel William Sinn, who managed the Park Theater in Brooklyn and was a neighbor of the Leonards', suggested that she approach a theatrical manager named Edward E. Rice, who was casting for the American production of *Pinafore*. The musical stage in America was just beginning to boom, having progressed from *The Black Crook* to Jacques Offenbach's *The Grand Duchess*. Untroubled by any international copyright laws, because they did not then exist, Rice simply lifted *Pinafore* for presentation on the American stage.

One look at the eighteen-year-old Helen Louise Leonard, and Rice engaged her for the chorus of *Pinafore*.

And once plunged into the distractions of a professional theatrical company, Helen Louise cast off her mother, not financially but as guide and preceptor, quite as briskly as Mrs. Leonard had disencumbered herself of Mr. Leonard. There may have been an element of daughterly revenge. In any case, Helen Louise no longer took maternal advice.

From the moment she pranced onstage with the *Pinafore* chorus at the Boston Museum on November 15, 1878, she was on her own and on her way, free to make her own mistakes and pay for them. *Pinafore* was a huge success; soon there were more than ninety companies trouping throughout the United States in pirated versions of the Gilbert and Sullivan operetta, and the whole country was whistling its jaunty piping tunes. Helen Louise Leonard was only a small part of that success, professionally speaking, but personally she was attracting more than her share of the attention. Her sexual magnetism seemed to radiate over the footlights, and knowledgeable males in the audience found themselves watching the bouncy blonde in the chorus line rather than meditating on the affairs of the Queen's Navy. A handsome and well-born young man named Walter Senn was reserving a front-row seat at virtually every performance and sending flowers backstage. She was also being courted by Harry Braham, the leader of the orchestra in the pit. The rivalry between Senn and Braham became a matter of theatrical gossip, with most of the betting in favor of young Mr. Senn, because millionaires outweighed musicians on practically anyone's scale of values. Everyone's but Helen Louise Leonard's, whose emotional history would record a fateful weakness for musicians.

Mother Leonard strenuously objected to the match but, or therefore, Helen Louise went off and married Harry Braham early in 1879, shortly before *Pinafore* ended its run at the Brooklyn Academy of Music.

It was a short and tragically terminated marriage. A son was born to Helen Louise before the first year of marriage ended, but she refused to abandon her career. A nurse was hired to care for the infant. One afternoon Braham came home to find the baby dead. The young and inexperienced nurse by accident had stuck a diaper pin into the infant's stomach and he died in convulsions. The couple had not been getting along too well before the baby's death, largely because of a conflict of careers and a sizable age difference, but now they were bitterly estranged. Braham blamed Helen Louise for leaving the baby in a nurse's care. Undoubtedly, secretly she blamed herself. Her mother stepped in and made things worse by accusing Braham, as he later recounted, of having caused her grandson's death by giving him an overdose of paregoric. The couple separated and were soon divorced.

Whatever sorrow and guilt she felt over the death of her baby and the breakup of her marriage she proceeded to erase in hard work. No matter what Harry Braham alleged about maternal neglect, it was also true that they had been short of money and needed her paycheck.

About this time she caught the knowing eye of Tony Pastor, the star-maker of his day, who presided over the Casino Theater on Fourteenth Street near Tammany Hall (show business was years away from coagulating around Broadway above Forty-second Street). The short, round, and rubicund Pastor, with his impeccable taste in popular entertainment, had provided a showcase for the talents of the Four Cohans, Montgomery and Stone, Weber and Fields, Maggie Cline, Nat C. Goodwin, and Eddie Foy. His obituaries would justly credit him with being the "father of vaudeville."

As she later told the story in her autobiography, she was "discovered" by Pastor when the impresario heard her sing at the home of a friend. On the spot he offered her $75 a week to sing at his variety theater. Lillian, as she recalled, protested that her mother would object to her appearing in an "unrefined" music hall like the Casino.

"We will give you a new name," Pastor replied, "and not tell your mother until we see how it goes."

Pastor then supplied her with a list of suggested stage names, and she chose Lillian Russell because "I loved all the l's in it."

Thus she stepped up a notch from ex-chorus girl to "English ballad singer," as Pastor billed her. On the evening of November 22, 1880, just two years after she made her first stage appearance in the chorus, Tony Pastor was introducing her from the stage of the Casino Theater as "a vision of loveliness and a voice of gold." With her rose-petal complexion, her splendidly curved figure, and her silvery soprano, she brought down the house with her first number. Just past her nineteenth birthday, by the alchemy of innate talent she had the presence of a Byzantine empress, she commanded the attention of her audience, she possessed the invaluable trait which actors define as "authority."

Within a few days Lillian Russell, in a voile dress with a big blue bow tied in the back of her hair, became the talk of the town. A newspaperman, who lodged at the same house as Mrs. Leonard and her daughter, told the former that "There's a girl singing at Pastor's who looks exactly like your daughter. Why don't we go over to the Casino tonight and find out why she slips away from the house every evening?"

After Lillian completed her first number that night, as she later wrote, she saw her mother stand up in the audience and heard her shout, "That's my Nell!"

From then on, after an apprenticeship of only a few months in the theater, she knew all the prerogatives of stardom back when the theater was the unchallenged medium of entertainment, when millionaires by the platoon played stage-door Johnny, and really dashing fellows drank champagne out of actresses' slippers.

The remarkable thing is that she was relatively unspoiled by success. Her fellow actors, jealous of their own share of the

spotlight, regarded her as a generous woman who never up-
staged a lesser player, never indulged in temperamental displays, and was always on time for rehearsals. Though she came
from a middle-class background herself and had not been
forced to struggle very hard for success, she seemed to understand and empathize with those less fortunate. Her dressing-
room door was always open to chorus girls in trouble and
actors down in their luck. Her impulsive generosity was, in
fact, legendary.

No one could better testify to that than her dressing-room
maid, a girl named Maggie. One of Maggie's duties was to
collect Lillian's pay envelope nightly after the curtain fell. In
the years when Lillian was the top box-office attraction of the
American theater she insisted on being paid in cash, no checks,
after each performance, since she had acquired a low regard for
managerial honesty. After several years Lillian learned that
Maggie had been deducting twenty or thirty dollars from each
pay envelope as a sort of pioneer form of social security and
had built up a bank account of five thousand dollars. Maggie
was discharged but allowed to keep what she had stolen. "It
was all my fault," Lillian explained. "I had no right to expose
her to that temptation and I never scolded her. I told her that I
thought we had been together too long and I believed she
understood why she was being dismissed." Several years later
Maggie, having collected a dowry, found herself a prospective
husband and sent Lillian a wedding invitation. Lillian replied
with a silver coffee service. . . .

Inadvertently and indirectly, Gilbert and Sullivan provided
her with her next boost up the theatrical ladder. Rather than
allow American producers to continue pirating their works,
William S. Gilbert and Sir Arthur Sullivan, with their manager D'Oyly Carte, brought over their next opus, *The Pirates
of Penzance*, and presented it themselves at the Fifth Avenue
Theater. They reckoned without American ingenuity, particularly that of Tony Pastor, who announced that he was putting
on a show called *The Pirates of Penn Yann*, which would be a

travesty of the Gilbert and Sullivan operetta, in effect a satire of a satire.

One of the leading roles was assigned to Lillian Russell in a cast which also included Flo and May Irwin, John Morris, and Jacques Kruger. It was a hit, and Lillian was a smashing success. Gilbert, Sullivan, and D'Oyly Carte went down to the Casino to inspect it and came away raving over the talents of Lillian Russell. The trio decided to do a little pirating themselves, proposing that she jump her contract with Tony Pastor and assume a leading role in their own show.

Lillian wisely and honorably turned them down and was soon rewarded when Pastor gave her a showcase role in his tabloid production of *Olivette* opening March 7, 1881. Costumed as a cabin boy, she sang "In the North Sea Lived a Whale" and danced a hornpipe at the end of each verse. Several days later she got her first rave notice in the *Dramatic Mirror*, whose usually hard-nosed critic remarked, "Miss Lillian Russell as Olivette gave additional proof of her adaptation to the requirements of *opera bouffe*. She acted and sang most charmingly, and was faultlessly costumed. If the young lady does not allow adulation to conquer her ambition and elevate her too high in her own esteem, she will become a bright and shining light on the lyric stage."

Tony Pastor evidently agreed with the critic that a swelled head was Lillian's greatest danger at the moment, and instead of sending her on tour with *Olivette*, he farmed her out to the celebrated comedian Willie Edouin, who was taking a company to San Francisco to present *Babes in the Woods* and *Fun in a Photograph Gallery* in repertory. With Edouin, said Pastor, Lillian would learn the art of timing and other requirements for a comedienne.

On the transcontinental train journey to the Coast Lillian also learned to play poker and pinochle with members of the company and became a rabidly enthusiastic card player, despite the Baptist indoctrination that playing cards were the devil's pictures. From then on Lillian would drop everything, except

possibly the prospect of a good meal, to sit in on a poker session
—whether with stagehands or millionaire playboys it made no
difference.

The San Francisco engagement, aside from teaching Lillian
the joys of filling a straight flush and how to wait for a laugh,
was an exhilarating experience. San Francisco, far less blasé
than New York, was a great theater town, an actor's heaven on
earth. For a beautiful girl it was even more celestial. The city
on the hills was booming, with most of the fortunes made in
the Comstock Lode and the profits from the rich agricultural
hinterland being expended in its marketplaces, and it supported, with lavish enthusiasm, a dozen legitimate theaters.
The town was vibrating with new money and new ways to
spend it. Men who had worn long red underwear in the foot-
hills a few years ago were trussing themselves up in evening
dress glittering with diamond jewelry. Magnates barely able to
read and write were signing approximations of their names at
the bottom of six-figure checks. Their ladies, who had recently
rubbed their knuckles raw on scrubbing boards or had been
liberated from the city's many parlor houses, were learning to
extend their pinkies when drinking tea and to walk down
marble staircases at a stately pace.

These newly rich were absorbing culture in large doses and
dutifully patronized the opera and Shakespearean repertory,
but they went wild over a troupe like Willie Edouin's with the
ravishing Lillian Russell in leading roles. For *Babes in the
Woods*, furthermore, she pulled on purple tights and exhibited
her legs—a shocking and titillating sight in the 1880's, when
lechers would spend hours on windy street corners straining for
a glimpse of feminine ankles. Existing photographic evidence
indicates that, for the modern connoisseur, Lillian's legs were a
trifle on the sturdy side. But to the Comstock millionaires risk-
ing their necks by leaning out of the boxes for a closer look,
they were perfection.

Babes in the Woods and *Fun in a Photographic Gallery*
alternated at the Bush Street Theater, formerly the Alhambra,

which was regarded as the most luxuriously appointed theater in the United States, the playhouse in which Lawrence Barrett, Edwin Booth, Helena Modjeska, E. H. Sothern, and other gilded names had exhibited their talents.

In booming and pleasure-loving San Francisco Lillian Russell learned the meaning of the phrase "toast of the town." Nightly, after her performance she was swept off to supper parties by a swarm of admirers. At the Poodle Dog, the Maison Riche, and the Maison Doree, in the plush-covered private dining rooms, surrounded by the biggest wine-buyers in town, she gorged herself on the French cuisine on which San Francisco prided itself. The delights of the table would add lamentable poundage to her striking figure, but that was a concern for the future. While rough-hewn compliments from the hard-rock magnates fluttered around her golden head, she smiled graciously and plied her beestung lips with *caviar sur canane, paupiettes de basse, raye à la Normandie, poulet de grain aux cresson,* and a few discreet sips of vintage champagne.

And there was a more substantial tribute paid her beauty and talent one night late in the San Francisco engagement. A bearded and gorgeously uniformed admirer tossed a bouquet over the footlights. Nestled in it, as she discovered back in her dressing room, was a sapphire and diamond ring and a note reading, "Tomorrow I leave for Russia and probably will never get a pleasure to see you again. . . . Believe me, Madame, a Russian bear can be pleased with great talent." The resounding signature read "Anatol Royal Ivanovsky, Lieutenant Commander, SS *Moskva,* Imperial Russian Navy."

From that San Francisco success Lillian swept on to a higher crest back in New York that fall when John A. McCaull starred her in *The Snake Charmer,* a performance which drew from the *Dramatic Mirror*'s critic the statement that "Lillian Russell's looks, costumes, singing and acting create a furore. A year ago we noticed this little lady at Tony Pastor's; now she is a bright particular star of *opera bouffe.* There is nothing to compare with her in this country. Paris will have to beg her of

Manager McCaull if D'Jemma [Lillian's role in *The Snake Charmer*] is ever to be ideally represented there." For all the money she was bringing in at the box office, Lillian was receiving only $60 a week, but soon enough she would learn how to deal sternly and successfully with theatrical managers.

In any case, there were fringe benefits to stardom: flowers, baskets of fruit, jewelry, even cash gifts delivered to her dressing room by admirers who, undoubtedly, looked for more than a gracious smile as a reward for their generosity. Such gifts she always returned. It was more difficult to deal honorably with an anonymous admirer who, as Lillian revealed in her autobiography, showered her with gifts totaling $100,000 over a three-month period.

Every week she received expensive jewelry imbedded in hampers of fruit or bouquets from the unknown admirer. At Christmas he sent roses entwined with ten $100 bills tied in a ribbon. A short time later she received two sealskin coats, one for Lillian and one for her mother. Before long she had accumulated a ruby and diamond bracelet, a pair of ruby earrings, a ruby ring, diamond earrings, and a pearl and diamond chain all from the same anonymous source.

Lillian, of course, tried to find out who her shy benefactor was, but the matter wasn't cleared up until one evening months later when she met a wizened little man of indeterminate age and undistinguished bearing who introduced himself at a dinner party as Jack Duncan and invited her to view the paintings at the Metropolitan Museum of Art.

Next day, among the old masters, he revealed himself as the person who had sent all those gifts. "My name is not Jack Duncan," he told her. "I shall never speak to you again. But I sent you the jewelry because I knew you are good as you are beautiful. You should have the things you want without temptation. So this is good-bye." The little man sidled away, and she never saw him again. Looking back on the episode in her autobiography, she confessed she had always been deeply touched by it. "There is much reward," she philosophized, "for unselfish love." Her benefactor needn't have worried about Lillian being tempted by a yearning for material things. If and when she "went wrong," it wouldn't be for a lack of cash or jewelry. For her temptation would always assume an emotional rather than a material guise. The incident, however, illuminated one of the more striking facets of her public personality. Robust though she was in physique and disposition, the prismatic quality of stage lighting somehow transformed her into a Dresden shepherdess, something as fragile as a porcelain figurine, and brought out the protective instinct of the males in the audience.

The women were undeceived, and so through bitter experience were theatrical managers, who came to realize that dainty Lillian was one of those iron butterflies who have shortened the lives of so many producers. Generous as she was with fellow actors and everyone else who worked in the theater, she regarded producers as fair game—even Tony Pastor, who had discovered, promoted, and groomed her for stardom. Her last show for Pastor was *Billee Taylor*, in which she wore a clinging blue sailor suit and won the praise of one critic, who wrote that she "sings music like a transmigrated nightingale, acts like a materialized grave, and looks like Venus after her bath." Somehow she became convinced that Pastor didn't have enough class for her and quit the cast of *Billee Taylor* after three weeks. Furthermore, when she jumped into a New York production of Gilbert and Sullivan's *Patience*, she was able to boost her salary from the $60 a week she received from Pastor to $250 a week. Subsequently she sang the role of Aline in John A. McCaull's production of Gilbert and Sullivan's *The Sorcerer*, which opened October 17, 1882.

Money poured into McCaull's box office at the Bijou Opera House, largely through the presence of Lillian Russell, who once again began quarreling with the management over money matters. One night she failed to appear at the theater, and Producer McCaull immediately decided that she was holding out for more money, though word came from the Russell camp that Lillian was suffering from a low-grade fever "with typhoid symptoms" and that her mother had assumed charge of her care. Not only that, but militant Mama Leonard wrote a letter to the *Dramatic Mirror* in which it appeared that the malady had transformed itself from typhoid to bronchitis. "Lillian Russell has been dangerously ill two weeks and yet no announcement has been made through the press," Mrs. Leonard wrote. "This fact has created some unkind criticism and much unpleasant curiosity. It is not unusual for singers to be troubled with bronchial affection, and Miss Russell is subject to trouble of this kind in damp, unwholesome weather. . . ." Whatever the nature of Lillian's illness, it was only complicated when Mrs. Leonard insisted that her allopathic physician be replaced by a more esoteric practitioner of homeopathy. Lillian survived both methods of treatment, thanks to a robust constitution.

Perhaps her convalescence was hastened by an urge to get Mother Leonard back in the women's liberation movement and away from cudgeling managers and the press on her behalf. The relations between Lillian and her mother were also complicated by the fact that Lillian had fallen in love again, and again it was a musician, and again Mrs. Leonard strenuously objected to the romance. With her career blossoming, with managers fighting for her services, what did Lillian want with a husband? Harsh words were exchanged on the subject, and Lillian moved to a hotel to get away from her mother's ultrafeminist arguments.

The new man in Lillian's life was Edward Solomon, an Englishman with dark, soulful eyes, who had composed the music for *Billee Taylor*. More ominously, in the light of Lillian's past experience with the species, he was an orchestra leader.

The development of that romance, as described by Lillian years later in her autobiography: "After my long illness the first one to come to see me was Edward Solomon. While I was convalescing, he would sit at the piano and play for me. He had the peculiar gift of expressing in a melody the serious and the romantic as well as the ludicrous incidents happening in a room where many people were congregated. While various individuals were talking or laughing he would quietly play a bit of music which accentuated their peculiarities and appealed to my sense of humor. Naturally, when I was quite well again, I fell in love with him."

During the spring of 1883 she returned to McCaull's management in the leading role of Offenbach's *Princess of Trebizonde*. In the orchestra pit was Edward Solomon, waving his baton and soulfully staring up at Lillian.

When that engagement ended, Solomon was doing his best to persuade her that she should break four or five American contracts she had signed to appear in various cities and instead accept an offer to play the lead in his operetta *Virginia and Paul*, for which H. P. Stephens had written the libretto, at the Gaiety Theater in London. The only catch was that she would not only face lawsuits by the American theater managers but would have to run out on various creditors. Musicians are always broke, and Solomon was no exception. Whatever liquid assets Lillian possessed would be required to pay her own passage to England plus that of Mr. Solomon, his collaborator, Mr. Stephens, and Mrs. Stephens. On the whole it was a thoroughly bad idea; aside from running out on debts and contracts, she needed to build up her popularity base with American audiences before venturing abroad. But Lillian's head for business, sound enough when it came to tangling with tightfisted producers, would always be overruled by glandular urgencies.

So one morning in October, 1883, she and Solomon, with Mr. and Mrs. Stephens, took a hansom cab over to Jersey City and later that day sailed for England aboard the *Lydian Monarch*. Behind her she left writ-brandishing lawyers (including the formidable Hummel & Howe), seething managers, and wailing creditors. As her former supporter the *Dramatic Mirror* put it, Lillian had embarked for England "dishonoring her contracts, deceiving her friends, family and creditors, and leaving behind as unsavory a reputation as the most reckless female could desire."

Her sole defender was her mother, outraged as she was by Lillian's elopement. Cabled word from London a short time later that Lillian had married Solomon did nothing to soothe Mrs. Leonard's maternal concern, but she sat down and wrote a letter to be published in all the New York newspapers simultaneously defending her daughter's reputation and lashing at Solomon's.

As Mrs. Leonard explained it, Lillian had become disillusioned with the dishonesty and double-dealing around her:

> Every attempt was made to try to blackmail her by men who claimed to be of great importance. Diamond frauds were undertaken, and almost everyone who came to her seemed bent on extracting money. She came at last to look upon the commercial world as a legalized swindle. After leaving home she was soon convinced by Solomon and Stephens that there was no money in paying debts, and much in sailing for England, especially as she had to defray the expenses of the entire party over.

Mother Leonard also paid her respects to Lillian's former producer, John A. McCaull, and went on to berate the musical talents of her new son-in-law:

> Most of the men whom he [McCaull] calls dudes, who frequent the Casino, are stockholders in the McCaull opera company . . . the dividend returned being an introduction to the women on the stage, and a promise to make them solid with the same; consequently those whom he cannot manage easily he pronounces fractious and unmanageable.
>
> Miss Russell's popularity did not depend upon the young or old men of New York. She had as many admirers among women as well as men, and while she was ill last winter many of the baskets of fruit, flowers and wine came from ladies— some of the finest ladies in the city. . . .
>
> I am not surprised, however, that she is underrated now,

as she has done herself the injustice to sing nothing but Solomon's trashy music since her return to the stage, particularly in concert, where she should have rendered her best efforts to the public. She will probably see her mistake soon. . . .

Lillian would indeed repent her elopement to England. Meanwhile she was hearing echoes of the journalistic tirade launched against her in New York. *Music and Drama*, for instance, defended McCaull against Mrs. Leonard's allegations and countered: "If anyone has been guilty of lack of modesty in this company it is Miss Lillian Russell herself, whose flirtations from the stage during the performances with her admirer, the young Haitian Negro prince, who nightly occupied a stage box, became a matter of public scandal." (Lillian did not find room for the Haitian prince in her memoirs.) Furthermore, *Music and Drama* took a good-riddance attitude toward Lillian's departure:

> The stage is burdened by far too many Lillian Russells, who usurp places of better artists and more estimable women. It is to be sincerely hoped that she will achieve so great a success there that she may never deem it advisable to afflict us with her presence again. There is something of the eternal fitness of things in paying our indebtedness to England by sending her our Lillian Russells in return for her trashy theatrical people sent over of late.

Obviously Lillian would have a public relations problem on her hands if she ever returned to the American theater, not to mention arranging a reconciliation with her mother. Mrs. Leonard was so indignant over the way women were misled in a man's world that she took direct action by running for the office of mayor of New York in the 1884 election. She was buried under a landslide, but at least she learned how many men in New York sympathized with feminist aspirations. Only eighty-four votes were cast for the first women's candidate in a New York municipal election.

Lillian opened in *Virginia and Paul* in a West End theater

with Solomon waving his gold-tipped baton in the pit, but the critics detested Solomon's music, Stephens' lyrics, and even found fault with their star. Lillian's voice was splendid, they agreed, but her manner was "too American" and her figure was too buxom for dainty English tastes.

After *Virginia and Paul* quickly closed, Solomon learned that Gilbert and Sullivan were still infatuated with Lillian's possibilities, and their manager, D'Oyly Carte, quickly agreed to give her the leading role in *The Princess Ida*, opening at the Savoy. Difficulties soon arose. It seemed that William S. Gilbert had become enamored of Lillian the woman as well as Lillian the performer. As imperious as he was bad-tempered, Gilbert sent word to her that he wanted her to "rehearse" initially at his London *pied-à-terre*. Lillian knew all about private "rehearsals," which were all too often conducted horizontally.

She simply failed to show up at the appointed time at Gilbert's apartment. Next day he stormed into her dressing room at the Savoy where the *official* rehearsals were being conducted. The ensuing dialogue had little of the sprightly quality of the lyrics for which Gilbert was justly celebrated:

> GILBERT: Why didn't you come to rehearse with me last night?
> RUSSELL: I think I am sufficiently prepared to play the part.
> GILBERT: (roaring): You beard me! You dare to beard me! Send your solicitor to me at once. Someone else will play your part.

Lillian stormed out of the Savoy, and her solicitor stormed in a few hours later with a suit charging breach of contract and demanding 5,000 pounds sterling in damages. Later, like most theatrical lawsuits, growing as they do out of combustible temperaments, it was quietly dropped.

Until then her career had been on a rocketlike trajectory; now she learned the bitter meaning of the phrase "at liberty." The word had gone around that La Russell was hard to handle, broke contracts quicker than an inexperienced maid in a china closet, and was dominated by the Svengali-like Edward Solomon—and a stage husband was a more virulent nuisance than a stage mother. Actually the last rumor wasn't quite true. Solomon was more or less managing, but not actively interfering in her career. He was training her voice in hour after hour of practice and coaching, while they were both at liberty. And he taught her how to bring out a wider range, a richer tone, a greater depth of expression. She was a far better singer and a wiser woman for the sabbatical she took in England for two years.

She and her husband may not have missed any meals during that period following her dismissal by Gilbert, but they were forced to reduce their style of living to the proletarian level. By then, too, Lillian was with child. Under the stress of poverty, evidently, the fabric of the marriage was fraying. From what Lillian told her later, Marie Dressler wrote that Lillian "complained bitterly of his [Solomon's] stinginess. Her chief grievance seemed to be that he forced her to wear made-over clothes while he boasted a wardrobe of sixteen suits. She never forgave him for this affront to her pride."

By the time her daughter, Dorothy, was born, late in the summer of 1884, her husband had finished work on a new operetta titled *Polly, the Pet of the Regiment.* He made the rounds of the producers' offices with the score, and despite Lillian's later strictures on his "stinginess," he was sufficiently generous to insist that if and when *Polly* was produced Lillian must sing the leading role. It worked out fine. *Polly* was produced at the Novelty Theater, opening early in October, 1884, and had a successful run. Lillian was back on her feet professionally and went into the title role of *Pocahontas* immediately after *Polly* closed.

Thus, early in 1885 she was able to return to America in a semblance of triumph. Mama Leonard had forgiven her and was waiting on the dock. The managers who had been suing her withdrew their suits and were bidding for her services. And when she appeared in the New York production of *Polly*, at the

Casino, she was fervently welcomed back by the public and the critics. *Polly* was given fifty-five performances, then a respectable run.

Both her career and her marriage seemed to be working out when, late in 1885, her husband announced that he had to go back to London on business. Her next news of Edward Solomon came on the front pages of the New York newspapers. Solomon had been arrested the day he returned to London on a warrant charging bigamy. Some years before he had married a girl named Jane Isaacs, and what with the distractions of composing operettas, leading orchestras, and fighting with managers and collaborators, he had forgotten to divorce her. He had also forgotten to tell Lillian that he had been married before.

Lillian immediately went into seclusion, her only word for the clamoring press an announcement that she would have her marriage to Solomon annulled. She never saw him again or communicated with him; the fact that he hadn't even sent her a cable when he was arrested or any other word of explanation or contrition made it seem advisable to write him off as just another mistake. She had the kind of ebullience—often found in show business, where it is a highly desirable quality—that allowed her to rise above such personal disasters. That does not mean an actress is heartless or unfeeling, simply that personal emotions tend to be smudged over in a constant conflict between private reality and public role-playing. It was *unreal* that Lillian Russell, the American Beauty, as theatrical advertising proclaimed, should have contracted a bigamous marriage; therefore it was to be dismissed. The public, equally unable to conceive of its golden girl as merely another betrayed woman, also dismissed the matter. It was more appropriate to think of Lillian Russell as gloriously unfettered, her life divided between the theater and the cafés where her entrances inevitably caused a commotion, her career a glamorous surrogate for all those whose lives were so much drabber and meaner.

Following the humiliations of her second marriage, she trouped to the Coast in *Iolanthe*, appeared in Newport's marble halls, and enjoyed a long New York run in *The Queen's Mate* at the Broadway Theater. In the spring of 1888, the management of that hit decided to take the show on the road, with Lillian continuing in the leading role. Once again she became embroiled with the front office. Producer James Duff insisted that she appear in tights in one of the scenes, as she uncomplainingly did in the New York production. Lillian demurred on the grounds that the theaters in the hinterlands were drafty and she might catch cold. Another consideration, perhaps, was that people in the smaller cities were easily outraged by the spectacle of an actress exposing her legs. A third, possibly the overriding factor, was that motherhood and a growing appreciation for the pleasures of the table had added a lot of pink and white flesh to the most celebrated female figure in America. She now weighed in at 165 pounds, well distributed though they were on her five feet six inches. Corpulence, of course, was then an essential ingredient of sex appeal; an hourglass figure, with a jutting bosom, a solid haunch, and a tiny waist, achieved and reinforced by whalebone corsets, was the ideal. A *thin* Lillian Russell would have been an affront to well-upholstered American manhood. Still, it was possible to overdo, and Lillian had become just a little worried about the amount of flesh she was displaying.

Producer Duff took the issue of whether she would wear tights to court and not only lost the case when a gallant judge observed that Lillian's figure was a national asset and had to be protected from all hazards but had to do without her in the touring company.

That triumph of justice was celebrated in a verse composed by the resident poet of one of the New York newspapers:

> There was a young lady named Russell
> Who wouldn't wear tights 'neath her bustle
> 'Cause it gave her a cold
> Where it cannot be told

And she and Jim Duff had a tussle.
Then Jimmy, the young man, he sued her,
Rather tough for a person who'd wooed her.
But you can't quite explain
The regrets in the brain
Of a man who finds out he don't suit her.

The judge was a sort of Golightly,
And treated the matter politely;
Made a speech against tights
And gave Russell her rights
While Jimmy went home very quietly.

Certainly the publicity did her no harm. It did nothing to discourage Rudolph Aronson, the manager of the Casino Theater, from offering her a contract to become the resident prima donna of his troupe, for which she would receive a startling $20,000 for the season.

The Casino, at Thirty-ninth Street and Broadway (the theater was finally encroaching on Longacre Square, later renamed Times Square), was the temple of light opera in America. Six years in the building, it was the number-one showhouse of the eighties, the haunt of the city's gilded youth who turned out for first nights in the new tailless evening coat called the tuxedo. Connoisseurs of female flesh maintained that the Casino's chorus line, the statuesque Casino Girls, were the most beautiful young women in America. Its stage door was besieged nightly by the foremost lechers, the most indefatigable skirt-chasers in Manhattan, who whisked their prey around the corner to the bar of the Normandie Hotel. Its productions were mounted in the lavish style for which Florenz Ziegfeld later became celebrated. Almost every first night was attended by such *bon vivants* as the theater-loving Civil War hero General William T. Sherman, Abe Hummel, the craftiest criminal lawyer of his time, the playboy brothers Herman, Charlie, and Harry Oelrichs, and the prince of big spenders, Diamond Jim Brady himself. Grand dukes and industrial magnates competed for the privilege of occupying its boxes.

Lillian, too, was no stranger to the scene, having allegedly ogled a Haitian prince seated in one of the Casino's boxes. The theater was her touchstone and made her what the critics called "the Queen of Light Opera." With her pull at the box office, *Nadjy* ran for 256 performances, and she was equally triumphant in *The Brigands*, despite the fact that the lyrics she sang were composed by her old enemy William S. Gilbert. Some years before Gilbert had collaborated on *The Brigands* with Offenbach, his partnership with Sir Arthur Sullivan having been disrupted by the latest of their frequent quarrels.

In February, 1890, she scored a tremendous success in *The Grand Duchess*, which was her all-time hit. For this, too, the music was composed by Jacques Offenbach. Later it was said that Offenbach wrote it specially for Lillian, but this was nonsense. Offenbach died in 1880, ten years before the *Grand Duchess* was imported, and he had never heard of the blond American singer whose career he unwittingly promoted. Anyway it was a happy, though posthumous, mating of talents. Offenbach, his partnership with Sir Arthur Sullivan having logne synagogue, so immensely talented that Wagner proclaimed that if he had turned to heavier themes, "Offenbach could have been a Mozart." For all the wit and tremendous vitality of his music, he was a frail and sickly man who weighed only ninety pounds. In 1877, three years before his death and several years before Lillian began creating a stir in the theater, Offenbach had visited the United States and been given an enthusiastic reception, with 50,000 persons gathering outside the Fifth Avenue Hotel and cheering until he appeared on a balcony. *La Grande-duchesse*'s first production in Paris had delighted the French because it caricatured life in a petty German court and pointedly satirized the Prussian soldier. Prince Otto von Bismarck, though the chief Prussian totem of his time, had attended the premiere performance in 1867 and roared with delight; the reason for his amusement became apparent several years later when those satirized Prussians goose-stepped along Paris boulevards.

In its American manifestation, Producer Rudolph Aronson, who was superbly reckless with his Wall Street backers' money, contrived a spectacular entrance for Lillian in *The Grand Duchess*. Draped in ermine, topped by an enormous fur hat, she drove a sleigh onstage through a fake snowstorm. The opening night brought her an ovation, which was only slightly marred when an overwrought Italian staggered down the aisle under a huge bouquet, hurled it over the footlights, and knocked Lillian over on her well-upholstered bottom.

Still on the sunny side of thirty, she was the most famous, perhaps the most notorious, and certainly the most lusted-after woman in America. *Town Topics*, which retailed scandal and pioneered the gossip column, rarely had anything nice to say about anyone, but its editor-publisher, Colonel William d'Alton Mann, was one of Lillian Russell's most fervent admirers. Colonel Mann, who had led a cavalry regiment at Gettysburg, had invented the railroad sleeping car, and had divined the possibilities in combining blackmail with journalism (the most interesting stuff written for *Town Topics* never appeared in print because Colonel Mann had shown the galley proofs to his prospective victims and been paid to suppress the more damaging items), usually covered Russell openings in person. He ululated over Lillian in love-sick prose: "If Lillian Russell does not cease to take on new phases of beauty every month or so, there will be no reason why the flowers of spring should bloom, for the resplendent lady will crowd the neighborhood with all the tint and tenderness that can safely be withstood. In *The Grand Duchess* she fills the eye like the splurge of roses, and amazes the ear with an abundance of melody equal to a virgin wood at a summer sunrise." Lillian Russell was one celebrity who did not have to make the sorrowful and expensive trek up to Colonel Mann's office on Fifth Avenue to keep any of her misadventures from being described or hinted at in the columns of *Town Topics*.

Her fame was so certified, so integral a part of American life that no one was surprised when her voice was chosen for the first public tryout of Alexander Graham Bell's long-distance telephone line between New York and Washington. President Grover Cleveland would be at the receiving end, in the White House, and obviously the dulcet voice of Lillian Russell would be more caressing to the Presidential ear than the hoarse bellowing of a Tammany Hall politician. The telephone line was laid from the New York exchange to Lillian's dressing room at the Casino Theater.

During the intermission after the first act of *The Grand Duchess*, Lillian made her debut as a long-distance singer, the first performer anywhere to become a link with the new technology. And when she sang the "Sabre Song" into a large metal funnel, it was the first glimmering of the mechanization of show business. Television, unperceived, was rearing its frowsy head. At the other end of the line to Washington was another funnel about which President Cleveland was grouped with the comedian De Wolf Hopper, the New York politician Bourke Cochran, and Francis Wilson.

A few days later the New York *World* reported that Thomas Alva Edison, who was busy developing other bits and pieces of the technology which would revolutionize the theater and magnify an actor's personality into Golem-like proportions, was going to call on Lillian Russell at her apartment to "bottle up her voice in a phonograph. This has been a pet idea of Prof. [*sic*] Edison's for a long time. He will send her a piece of her preserved voice in the shape of a roll of foil."

For the time being, in an age when people were privileged to be entertained by flesh-and-blood human beings instead of six-inch shadows on a glass screen, Lillian Russell didn't really need the amplification of the growing technology. Her salary as prima donna of the Casino Theater troupe kept rising steadily, not without some gentle pushing from Lillian, as Producer Aronson would ruefully recall in his memoirs. And when she went on the road, every hick town turned itself inside out and momentarily became a Venusberg to celebrate the presence of America's own corn-fed love goddess. Even a university town like New Haven, which prided itself on a certain amount of sophistication, stood on its ear, according to the recollections of Clarence Day when he was a Yale student and Lillian appeared with the road company of *The Grand Duchess*.

Her attractions, as the author of *Life with Father* later analyzed them in his maturity, were incomparable in a time when Captain Billy Watson's Beef Trust—a thundering herd of bovine burlesque beauties who weighed about 180 pounds on the hoof—were a great attraction for the lower orders. Lillian couldn't offer quite the avoirdupois of one of Captain Billy's amazons, but the quality of her near-classical voice made her respectable for the sophisticates and the college-town intellectuals, and as Clarence Day noted, "there was nothing wraithlike about Lillian Russell; she was a voluptuous beauty, and there was plenty of her to see. We liked that. Our tastes were not thin, or ethereal. We liked flesh in the Nineties. It didn't have to be bare, and it wasn't, but it had to be there."

Day and some of his classmates, lacking even the price of a gallery seat, managed to obtain a closeup view of their idol by hiring out as supers, or spear carriers, during *The Grand Duchess'* engagement in New Haven. They had a choice of filling in the background as French soldiers or Russian muzhiks. Day was cast as a muzhik. "For the sake of seeing Lillian Russell," he related, "I put on a greasy gray wig, a pair of broken boots, a fur hat, a smock and a long set of dirty whiskers. Many men of all kinds had been wearing those whiskers for months, but most of them had been paid something for doing it. I did it for love."

Before he made his own humble debut, he watched her in rehearsal and was enthralled. "She threw back her golden head and caroled coquettishly when the hero made love to her, she caroled severely at the villain, and she danced till the old Hype stage shook." His own part in the proceedings opening night was close to disastrous. The first scene in which Day and three classmates also pretending to be muzhiks appeared was, unfortunately, Lillian Russell's sleigh-borne entrance. Visually it was the highlight of the production. As the curtain rose on the scene, a snowstorm of confetti made from the New Haven *Register* was falling. Day and his three comrades, holding up lanterns to light the Grand Duchess' way, were stationed along the sloping wooden ramp down which Lillian rode in her sleigh. Just as the sleigh started its descent, Day, fearing he was going to be run over, stepped back off the ramp. So did the other muzhiks. It produced a curious stage effect not visualized by the producer. Day and his three friends had tumbled off the ramp and only their whiskered faces were visible to the audience, making it appear to the audience as though they had been decapitated.

There was a roar of ironic applause, which at first puzzled Miss Russell and the stage manager. As the applause continued, and was mingled with some boos and catcalls, the stage manager found out what had happened and started in pursuit of Day and his three friends. Day recalled that they "fled from the theater, four amazingly agile old graybeards, sprinting across muddy Chapel Street. The other fellows brought our clothes to us later and took back our costumes. They said that Miss Russell had sent for the tall man [the stage manager] to ask if any of us were hurt, and that he had screamed at her, 'Not yet.' "

Following *The Grand Duchess*, Lillian appeared in *Poor Jonathan*, which was almost as successful and ran for 208 performances in 1890. The continuing prosperity of the Casino, though often endangered by Rudolph Aronson's insistence on mounting each production as lavishly as possible, obviously owed much to the lustrous presence of Lillian Russell. Her salary had shot up phenomenally to $35,000 a year.

At the end of each season, until her final one in 1891, she conducted negotiations with Aronson for her salary for the following season. She always asked for an increase, not an exorbitant one, and the matter was settled without rancor. "Her last observance of this custom was the occasion of our very slight disagreement," as Aronson recalled in his memoirs. "We had arranged for the usual increase which brought her salary up to, I believe, seven hundred and fifty dollars a week; and she left me, saying she would call on the following Thursday to sign the contract, which I was to have ready at that time.

"On the day agreed, Miss Russell called at my office and said: 'Mr. Aronson, I have signed.' Not entirely understanding what she meant by this remark, I told her the contract was ready for her signature. She continued then rather nervously: 'I have signed with Mr. T. Henry French for twelve hundred dollars a week and a share in the receipts above a certain amount every week.' To this I made the only reply possible for me to make, that if she signed a contract on such terms she was to be congratulated."

If congratulations were in order for Lillian, however, commiserations would soon be extended to T. Henry French. The theater, like the rest of the American economy, was booming in the early nineties, but it could not afford to meet all the demands of superstars like Lillian Russell, as French would learn to his dismay. Her guaranteed earnings put her in the class of steel company presidents and Wall Street brokers. Not only did she receive a base salary of $1,200 a week but also a percentage of the box office and a fifteen-percent share of theater concessions, including sheet music, photographs, and hat checking. In her autobiography she reported that the contract with French brought her a minimum of $2,300 a week and often more.

With that kind of money rolling in, just before the stock market crash and a depression that sank less fortunate citizens to the soup-kitchen level, Lillian could afford to splurge. She had lived out of steamer trunks in flats, apartments, and hotel rooms long enough; and she wanted to provide a more home-like atmosphere for her daughter, who would always live in her mother's sizable shadow. Her New York base from then on would be a brownstone house on West Seventy-seventh Street near West End Avenue, a section which was beginning to rival Fifth and Park avenues as a fashionable address, close to a riverside park in which her daughter and governess could stroll.

The press was invited to inspect the premises when they were refurbished and newly decorated early in 1893. On the first floor the parlor was furnished in the prevailing style, Late Victorian Monstrosity as later generations would regard it; heavy mahogany furniture, divans built for hefty figures, a rosewood and brass table of surpassing inelegance, a collection of souvenir spoons under a glass dome, another collection of snuffboxes, a beveled mirror extending from floor to ceiling. She had also yielded to the contemporary craze for the Turkish cozy corner, a huge divan littered with pink pillows, surrounded by an incredible array of bric-a-brac (miniature musical instruments, china, medallions, more snuffboxes), taborets with mother-of-pearl inlaid, and to add the final genuine Oriental touch, an incense-burner exuding a sickly scented smoke. Visiting journalists with sharp eyes could also note a collection of jeweled cigarette holders, which gave rise to the rumor—true this time—that Lillian Russell was a secret cigarette smoker, that most criminous of vices for a Victorian female, which all but certified that she was a fallen women. Not even the most unconventional women—except for streetwalkers leaning against lampposts—dared to smoke in public.

The drawing room was similarly filled with elephantine furniture, its centerpiece a grand piano, its floor covered by two outsize tigerskin rugs, which Elinor Glyn would soon reveal as likely to encourage libidinous activities not usually conducted in drawing rooms. The dining room, also on the first floor, carried out the theme of conspicuous display and included leather-covered walls, red velvet hangings, a Chippendale sideboard, palm trees in tubs, and a fireplace suitable for roasting wild boars. Near the fireplace was a barrel with a silver inscription politely inquiring, "What will you have?" which opened up to reveal a row of decanters.

The second floor was taken up by a sitting room, where

Lillian trilled through her practice exercises, a bedroom, and a bathroom which a Roman proconsul would not have scorned. Lillian's bed was a huge brass affair draped with multicolored satin ribbons and surrounded by mirrors. Whoever shared it with Lillian, after lolling in the Turkish cozy corner downstairs, half delirious from incense, must have felt like a particularly well-favored pasha.

The third floor was reserved for her daughter, Dorothy, and also contained several guest rooms, and the servants' rooms were on the fourth.

To the house on West Seventy-seventh Street, which to Lillian represented the recompense of a decade's hard work and far-flung trouping from London's West End to San Francisco's Market Street, came such fellow luminaries of the theater as Francis Wilson, Digby Bell, Leo Dietrichstein, Florenz Ziegfeld, and John Drew, such men of affairs as the orotund Chauncey Depew, and such classical opera stars as Madame Nordica, Ernestine Schumann-Heink, and Nellie Melba. Lillian had little of the sense of rivalry which makes the backstages of opera houses such small hells of clashing temperaments. She simply admired those whose sound boxes and training in the classical disciplines made them eligible for the statelier roles of grand opera, the designation of artiste rather than performer.

Most intensely she admired Nellie Melba, the Australian-born diva with the Roman profile who lived and loved in the grand European tradition (her great romance was with Philippe, the Duc d'Orléans, pretender to the French throne).

When it came to relations between Lillian and her voice and her public, however, she would not take advice even from the esteemed Nellie Melba. One night Melba went backstage at the Casino after Lillian had finished a performance of *The Grand Duchess*. In her enormous plumed hat and pearl-encrusted costume, Lillian looked like a Gainsborough painting and retained something of the ducal manner from her performance; it must have been like the meeting of two queens.

Melba complimented Lillian on the proficiency with which she managed her cadenzas and effortlessly hit her high notes. Her virtuosity would make her the envy of any grand opera star, Melba added.

"By the way," she said, watching Lillian's reflection in her dressing-room mirror, "have you ever taken count of how many times you reach high C during a performance?"

"Sure," Lillian replied with a modest shrug of her dimpled shoulders. "Eight times."

"Eight times," said Melba reflectively. "And how many performances a week?"

"Seven. That's, ah, fifty-six times I hit high C every week, not counting those in practice at home. Not bad, is it, Nellie?"

"Not bad!" Melba almost shouted. "It's an outrage! No prima donna in grand opera would think of straining her voice in such a manner." Her tone was that of a master craftsman addressing an overeager apprentice. "The public never values anything that comes to them so cheaply. Take my advice and give your audience just *two* high C's a night. You'll be far more appreciated."

It was sound advice, but Lillian didn't take it. A performer, unlike an artiste, had to give her all every time the curtain went up. The public could tell when you held back from it. If she was capable of eight high C's a night, she would continue giving out. She was a trouper before anything else.

2

WERE ANY OF HORATIO ALGER'S HEROES FAT?

LITTLE wonder that the boy born over a saloon on the West Side of Manhattan grew up the most omnivorous eater in the nation's history, grazing over whole oyster beds and feedlots, decimating the wildfowl population, and laying waste to whole flocks of spring lambs, before he finally laid down his knife and fork.

Practically the first words that young James Brady heard were recollections of famine and the flight from a stricken island, and all around him were the tenements inhabited by hundreds of thousands of Irish and German immigrants clawing for a living in the new land.

The boy was born August 12, 1856—the summer that James Buchanan was contesting for the Presidency of a divided nation —in a bedroom on the second floor of the saloon at the corner of Cedar and West streets. He was better off than most infants born that day on the lower West Side of Manhattan because his father owned that saloon.

His father, Daniel Brady, and his mother were both immigrants who had fled from Ireland in their youth, the Ireland of the 1840's in which a million and a half of their countrymen died and from which another million emigrated, those lucky

53

enough to survive the Atlantic crossing in "hell ships" aboard which often half the passengers succumbed to disease or starvation.

The boy christened James Buchanan Brady, after the Democratic Presidential candidate the year of his birth, heard tales of the Irish Diaspora at his mother's knee and in the saloon downstairs, where he crawled and toddled in the sawdust. Not Mother Goose but the horrors of the famine, not fairy tales but the deviltry of the English overlords formed the legend of his childhood. The Irish famine was less than ten years in the past when he was born. The Irish longshoremen who patronized his father's saloon, who raised families in the surrounding tenements on less than ten dollars a week and worked six twelve-hour days to get it, talked of little else than the gut-hungers which still afflicted them.

A bright child, if rudely raised, young Jim could see all around him the need to surmount his environment. If Ireland was a green hell during the famine decade, the slum sections of New York City were anything but the environs of a promised land. His boyhood was spent in one of the toughest waterfront districts, a few hundred feet from the piers and stringpieces of the North (Hudson) River: a section of brick tenements, warehouses, street gangs, saloons in which there were hourly brawls, slaughterhouses, and vegetable markets. To the north there was more of the same, only worse, in the human wasteland known as Hell's Kitchen. Everywhere he looked in the years just before and during the Civil War, young Jim Brady could find evidence that his native cobbled streets were a place to fight your way out of. The first Irish-American writer of sizable talent, Fitz-James O'Brien, who lived in those West Side streets before dying in a Civil War battle, provided a graphic description of them: "This tract of land is perhaps the most melancholy and mysterious spot in the whole city. The different streets that cross the Island pull up, as it were, suddenly on reaching this dreary place, seemingly afraid to trust themselves any further. The buildings that approach nearest to its confines are long, low ranges of fetid slaughterhouses, where on Sunday bloated butcher boys lounge against the walls, and on weekdays one hears through the closed doors the muffled blow, the heavy fall of oxen within, the groan and the hard-drawn breath; and then a red sluggish stream trickling from under the doorway and flowing into the gutter, where hungry dogs wait impatiently to lap it up. The murderous atmosphere, those streamlets of blood, seem appropriate, however, as one approaches the desolate locality...."

Young Jim and his brother, Daniel, Jr., who was two years older, and later the sister born a year or two after Jim, attended the public school at North Moore and Varick streets, where they absorbed the homilies of McGuffey's Reader and of a former Baptist minister who served as the schoolmaster. The theme of their schooling, which educators in the slum districts deemed singularly appropriate, was that the meek shall inherit the earth. The corollary was that it behooved the downtrodden to stay meek and patiently await their rewards. Young Jim, as he would later recall, was disinclined to accept that doctrine. He listened more receptively to the men who gathered in his father's saloon. Every saloon was a political center, and every saloonkeeper an aspiring politician, and every Irish saloon-keeper a Democratic politician. To the immigrant Irish it seemed that wealth was as poorly distributed as in the "old country," only here it was the Anglo-Saxon Protestant Americans who lapped up all the gravy, while in Ireland it was the Anglo-Saxon Protestant British. The only difference here was that the poor were allowed to lick the plate.

Yet young Jim Brady, by the time he was tall enough to reach the free-lunch counter, began to see things differently. You couldn't wait for the meek to inherit the earth. Nor could you sensibly waste your time ranting in saloons about injustice and placing your hopes in politicians' promises. You couldn't lick the rich, so why not join 'em?

Even as a boy—a fat boy who didn't care much for fighting in a neighborhood where you learned to swing your fists or take your lumps—young Jim was something of a loner. He kept away from the street gangs which dominated lower Manhattan: the Gashouse Gang, the Little Plug Uglies, the Tenth Avenue Gang, the Hell's Kitchen Gang (led by a teen-ager named Dutch Heinrich, who specialized in heisting banks and brokerages), the Whyos, and the Little Dead Rabbits.

Violence of any kind always appalled him, though his boyhood should have conditioned him to the almost casual breaking of heads and smashing of jaws that went on all around him. When he was only seven years old, the Draft Riots broke out in the immigrant-packed sections of the West Side. The worst of the rioting from July 13 to 17, 1863, occurred outside the lower West Side, but the whole island was terrorized by mobs totaling more than 50,000 men and boys, mostly Irish, who revolted against the Conscription Act of 1863 and tore the city apart. Before order was restored by a larger force of Union infantry, cavalry, and artillery brought into the city, more than 2,000 lives were lost, 8,000 to 10,000 were wounded or injured, and the West Side streets looked as though a major battle had been fought there.

There was no rioting in Jim's neighborhood, but he could hear the gunfire and see the flames shooting up over the skyline during those anxious nights in which his fellow Irishmen almost destroyed the city. The aftereffects of that worst riot in American history lingered for years; they marked Jim and all other Irishmen as dangerous, animallike members of a violent underclass it would take generations to Americanize. The process of making their fellow Americans see that the Draft Riots were a symptom of utter desperation rather than a Neolithic tendency toward violence and anarchy would take many years of counterpropaganda, at which the Irish were adept, and not a little of the credit for building a new Irish-American image would fall to Diamond Jim Brady and the geniality, the generosity, the vast fat-man's amiability which emanated from him.

In more ways than one, the year 1863 was a tragic turning

point in the boy's life. Shortly after the Draft Riots his father died (of natural but unspecified causes). His mother was a lively and attractive woman, still young, who did not intend to wither away in Victorian widowhood or assume the responsibilities of keeping a saloon and raising two sons and a daughter without a husband. Before a year of widowhood had elapsed, in fact, she married a man named John Lucas. And that, in effect, was the end of Jim's childhood. His new stepfather insisted that Jim and his older brother, Dan, help out around the place by swamping out the sawdust, cleaning the spittoons, and washing the glasses after school hours.

Jim no longer hung around the saloon, especially since Lucas slapped his hand whenever he reached for the free lunch, but escaped to the streets and in the early evening hours, after the horse-drawn drays had gone to their stables, playing baseball with the other neighborhood boys.

In 1867, when he was eleven years old and his brother thirteen, he and Dan decided that they would run away from home as soon as they could find some sort of employment. Dan Brady's Saloon had gone rapidly downhill under their stepfather's management. Lucas lacked their father's political talent and mine-host geniality; the longshoremen no longer patronized Brady's, and the place had become something of a dive. Sailors and drifters and down-and-outs hung around and waited to be victimized. Lucas had entered into an arrangement with various shipmasters whereby Brady's Saloon became an unofficial and involuntary hiring hall for brutal sea captains unable to muster a crew through the usual methods. Lucas would slip knockout drops in the drinks of able-bodied patrons, and the next thing they knew they were lying half drugged in the stinking forecastle of a tramp bound for a guano port—shanghaied was the trade name for their plight.

Dan was the first to break away from the rooms over the sailor's dive that Brady's Saloon had become. He found a job as bellhop at the St. James Hotel, the first large and luxurious hotel to be built north of Madison Square. Three months later

Dan hung around the corner of Cedar and West one night until his younger brother appeared outside, and told him he had persuaded the St. James management to hire his kid brother.

At the age of eleven, without much coaxing from his older brother, after whom he had tagged along since he was old enough to walk, Jim Brady simply strolled away from home and became a wage-earner. Because of his heft, and perhaps the street-wise shrewdness in his blue eyes, Jim could have passed for fifteen; anyway, that was a period in which child labor had not yet been stigmatized as a social evil. Thus began a four-year career as a bellboy at the St. James, during which he studied the manners, morals, and customs of the big-bellied, silk-hatted men who had made good in the big city. In between hopping bells at the hostelry, he put his experience in Brady's Saloon to use as a helper in the bar in which the gin rickey was concocted in honor of a devoted patron, Colonel James K. Rickey of Missouri. No doubt his observations in the hotel bar only reinforced the lessons learned in Brady's Saloon that liquor was a good thing to keep away from; Jim himself never touched a drop in his life, a true saloonkeeper's son. But the St. James bar and the lobbies and other public rooms of the hotel provided his secondary schooling. Dropouts were not then pursued by truant officers, and in any case Jim had learned to read, write, and do arithmetic. If his diction and syntax would always resemble that of the dockwallopers he left behind him on the lower West Side, even when Ivy League graduates were hailing him as the "statesman of American salesmanship," he still absorbed enough as a bellboy to get him by in fairly polite society.

What he learned at the St. James was how to conduct himself as a hail-fellow businessman in the expansive style popular in the booming postwar years when the United States was industrializing at an incredible pace. If you wanted to be successful in that grossly materialistic era, you wore a heavy gold watch chain, you flashed and sparkled with diamonds, you spoke in a loud, self-confident voice, and you ordered drinks for the house in a splendidly carefree manner. You were, in a word, a sport. Out West you never asked a man where he came from; here you never asked where he got his money, because all too often his seed money came from selling obsolete rifles, leaky ships, cardboard-soled shoes, rotten beef, or shoddy cloth for the armed forces of the glorious, somehow victorious Union.

Jim grew up, bright and impressionable and adaptable, in what became known as the Flash Age. The designation was both apt and precise; the vulgarity of the New York profiteers was rivaled only by the crassness of Washington during the Johnson and Grant administrations, the corruption of which was so widespread that reformers and idealists were all but incoherent in their despair. The fashionable St. James was a tributary to a society in which James Gordon Bennett, Jr., the son of the publisher of the New York *Herald*, would celebrate New Year's Day by urinating openly into the fireplace during a party in his fiancée's home, a matter for mild reproof. Historians of a few years later were going a little too far—but not much—when they compared the late sixties, the Flash Age in America, to France under Louis Napoleon. "In its endeavor to keep pace with the Second Empire," as *Valentine's Manual*, the social history of nineteenth-century New York, observed, "the Flash Age took note only of the superficial and, like all imitators, failed in the matter of good taste, a quality inherent in the French. The march of Prussian troops through the Arc de Triomphe brought New York's era of false prosperity and extravagance to its close, but it staggered on for two years without a guide, then collapsed with equal suddenness."

The Tweed Ring, headquartered at Tammany Hall, was looting the city with hardly an outcry of protest, certainly not from the dozen daily newspapers. Its figurehead mayor, the elegant A. Oakey Hall, philosophized that "This population is too hopelessly split up into races and factions to govern it under universal suffrage, except by the bribery of patronage, or corruption." Amen, said most of the ruling powers. The New

York *Post* was receiving $5,000 a month from the Tweed Ring. The ring also controlled magistrates and judges who sold writs of habeas corpus, and the city's jails were well stocked with men put there only because they had offended someone with more juice at City Hall. As Edward Crapsey, a journalist who believed there must be something more enlightened than government by clout, wrote in *The Nether Side of New York*, the greatest city in the country was ruled by admitted thieves "rioting in suddenly acquired wealth" who "constantly exhibited themselves to the public gaze loaded with diamonds and guzzling costly wines, like the vulgar knaves they are. . . . Men who are fit to be ushers at minstrel shows were made State Senators, and the keepers of gin-shops were manufactured into legislators for the great state of New York. Among the police magistrates were the meanest of political tricksters, and a man who had been brought back from a distant state to answer for a felony was made Auditor of the public accounts. There was not only general acquiescence in this government, but general desire to share in its booty. It came to be accepted as a matter of course that all governments were corrupt, and that of New York was no worse than others."

It may seem that a boy like Jim Brady, a runaway, only a nominal communicant of the Catholic faith into which he was born, with nothing to guide him but the precepts of Boss Tweed and the example set by the men who drank at the St. James bar and never lifted an eyebrow at the way their city was being despoiled, was likely to be recruited into one of the criminal arts and crafts. For a boy without education the underworld was, despite the preachments of Horatio Alger, a more alluring prospect than clerking in a counting house downtown and hoping to catch a millionaire banker's runaway horse, thereby winning the millionaire's daughter and a vice-presidency.

No one was surprised when the Reverend Henry W. Bellows informed a public meeting in 1871 that there were 30,000 professional thieves, 20,000 "lewd women and harlots," 2,000 technically illegal gambling establishments, and 3,000 un-licensed grogshops in the city. If he did not succumb to the attractions of crime, there was equal danger that a runaway boy like Jim Brady would be snared by the Children's Aid Society. In its early history that worthy organization functioned as a press-gang for employers of child labor, and its agents scoured the streets for waifs who were sent to what they claimed were "good homes in the west." Actually they were indentured to farmers who worked them from sunup to sundown without pay until they were old enough to escape. As Charles L. Brace, who served as president of Children's Aid for many years, explained in *The Dangerous Classes of New York*, its adoption system guaranteed that such children would not "fall into habits of dependence."

Jim escaped the net of such benefactors because he could claim that he was employed. No child-labor procurer, in any case, would have pounced on him after noting his girth and his fat-boy appetite. Jim began his career as a gourmand at the free-lunch counter of the St. James bar, where the viands on display were sumptuous enough to tempt the city's most jaded palates. On Sundays, his day off, he grazed farther afield. The St. James' patrons were generous tippers, and Jim would take the money he accumulated during the week for field trips to a seafood fanciers' paradise along the docks of lower Manhattan.

On Catherine Slip, near the Fulton fish market on South Street, there was an outdoor eel market where eels captured on the Canarsie mud flats were sold by the yard. Nearby were specialty restaurants called eel pots. You could dine alfresco off the carts of merchants who sold fried eels and eel pies. After the eel market had taken the edge off his appetite, Jim would stroll along South Street to the wharves where the oyster boats unloaded their catches. The oysters were sold fresh from the sea at one cent apiece. Jim would manage to ingest twenty-five oysters with pilot crackers to keep them tamped down—a prom-ising start for a seafood connoisseur who would order six dozen oysters when he reached his full stride.

Judging from Jim Brady's boyhood, there must have been some element of reality in Horatio Alger's uplifting tales. Jim, who was always eager to please, who, in fact, made a career out of catering to other people's pleasures as well as his own, caught the eye of a regular patron of the St. James named John M. Toucey, an executive of the New York Central. Toucey offered him a job with the railroad in the baggage department, with the understanding that he would go to night school and be given an opportunity to advance himself. It meant taking a cut in pay, but young James Buchanan Brady could see there was more future in railroading than bellhopping.

At the age of fifteen he went to work in the baggage room of the Grand Central Terminal, an occupation then known to disgruntled travelers as baggage smashing. He also attended night sessions at Paine's Business College on Canal Street, where he took courses in bookkeeping and chirography (a fancy word for penmanship). At that time a man's signature, complete with curlicues and flourishes, was as much an indication of his stature as was clean linen or well-polished shoes.

About the time he entered a railroad career he and his brother were reconciled with their mother. During their absence from home they apparently had kept in touch with domestic affairs through their younger sister. The decline of Brady's Saloon both as a social center and a source of revenue had disillusioned Mrs. Brady, a woman of uncertain temper in the best of times, with her second marriage. Their stepfather had "gone West," a portmanteau phrase in those days, and would be seen no more. Mrs. Brady had sold the saloon and bought a house at 391 Washington Street in which she established a hostel for young Irish girls who had just migrated to find servant work; the hostel served as a way station until they obtained employment. Both Dan and Jim contributed to her income from their paychecks. Given half a chance, Jim would always be a dutiful son, and Mrs. Brady not only believed in the Irish matriarchal system but considered that motherhood gave her a permanent lien on her offspring.

Jim's diligence in shifting baggage at Grand Central resulted in his promotion in less than two years. Not quite seventeen, he was appointed station agent for the New York Central at Spuyten Duyvil, which for a native New Yorker was practically in the wilderness. Spuyten Duyvil was a flag stop in the Bronx, just across the Harlem River from Manhattan. As a further step in his self-improvement program, Jim learned telegraphy, which also improved his rating with his patron in the executive suite at Grand Central.

He always prided himself on his honesty—whatever genial corruption he fostered as a supersalesman being outside his moral code—but in later years he would admit to reporters that he was guilty of one misstep while station agent at Spuyten Duyvil. On a Sunday morning, counting the previous day's receipts, he discovered a 95-cent shortage in his accounts. While he was brooding over this, the leader of a German brass band going up the Hudson on a picnic stepped up to the ticket window and asked for five round trip tickets. Jim gave him five one-way tickets but charged for round-trips and thus made up the shortage. Late that afternoon the bandleader stopped by to complain that he had been bilked, but Jim pretended he couldn't understand the man's heavily accented English, and the German finally went away grumbling to himself.

He was only eighteen years old in 1874, when his patron, John M. Toucey, by then general manager of the New York Central, decided to bring him back to Grand Central as a clerk working in the general offices. Three years later Jim was promoted to chief clerk at a respectable salary of $50 a week. He then proceeded to make a serious mistake. He had always looked up to Dan with a kid brother's half-concealed admiration, had credited Dan with rescuing him from their home over the waterfront dive, and wanted to return the favor. Dan was slim, handsome, glib—everything Jim wasn't. He also had a wise-guy fondness for shortcuts, ethically speaking. Not quite aware of certain flaws in his brother's character, Jim got Dan a clerkship in the New York Central offices.

Before nepotism resulted in sidetracking his career, Jim luxuriated in his position as right-hand man to the general manager. He studied and tried to imitate the glossy style of Toucey and the elegant Chauncey Depew, who was president of the New York Central as well as the city's leading orator and after-dinner speaker. A good part of his income went into clothes, the frock coats and silk hats with which fashionable New Yorkers adorned themselves, even though his corpulent figure was hardly a tailor's delight.

In his confidential position Jim also learned the railroad business down to the last detail, everything from the time and cost exacted by locomotive repairs and the reliability of the new air brakes to the performance of electrical equipment under adverse weather conditions. More important, he learned how great corporations maneuver against each other, the public, and the various forms of government. With his aptitude for collecting information and storing it for future use, he soon learned as much about the inner corporate life of the New York Central as Toucey, Depew, or any of the Vanderbilts who owned the controlling interest in the system.

But that didn't mean he had turned himself into a drudge. At least several nights he went out on the town, an aspiring *bon vivant*, with his boyhood friend Jules Weiss, who later became a tailor and got all of Jim's business. The theater was his passion, next to food. He fell in love with Lotta Crabtree when she appeared in an adaptation of Charles Dickens' *The Old Curiosity Shop* at Wallack's Theater. The theater was moving uptown from the Bowery, and Jim would be its most faithful patron in the years when Broadway became the Gay White Way. He was permanently stagestruck, a one-man fan club for everyone from Edwin Booth to Fritzi Scheff.

He had held down the chief clerkship for less than two years when a scandal erupted in the general offices. His brother had gotten into trouble, probably some minor speculation or petty-cashbox raiding, and was discharged. Dan, in a viperish display which he was to repeat some years later and cause Jim even more embarrassment, blamed his troubles on Jim.

General Manager Toucey decided that Jim, for the sake of discipline and morale, would also have to be sacked. It was a decision most reluctantly arrived at. Jim Brady, in brief, knew too much. With the recent death of the founder, Commodore Cornelius Vanderbilt, the New York Central management was involved in various problems and difficulties, some of them traceable to the take-over by the Commodore's son William Henry Vanderbilt. Despite the latter's slogan ("The public be damned"), the railroad was trying to fend off a threatened investigation by the New York State Legislature, some of whose upstate members had always been irked by the New York Central's political and economic power. The fact that it had been averaging net profits of ten million dollars a year for the past decade also attracted the attention of social and political reformers. It was not difficult to imagine ex-chief clerk Jim Brady taking the stand as star witness and spilling everything he knew about the railroad's corporate maneuvers. On the other hand, Jim would also make a valuable employee for one of its rivals—Jay Gould, for instance, who was demanding a chance to buy large blocks of stock, threatening that otherwise he would use other Eastern roads for the traffic from his Western termini. There was also talk of establishing a new railroad which would all but parallel the New York Central's lines to the West; that outfit could certainly use Jim's talents and his inside information.

No, John Toucey decided, his wilted protégé could not simply be thrown out on Forty-second Street. Another job would have to be found for him. Toucey's decision, which was also urged by a genuine affection for young Brady and a belief that he was innocent of any wrongdoing, resulted in Jim's conversion into the greatest salesman of his time, perhaps of all time. Thus Jim found his natural role by accident.

One of Toucey's close associates was Charles A. Moore, a

partner in the railway supply firm of Manning, Maxwell & Moore. Moore was looking for a salesman to handle a new item in the firm's line, a patented handsaw which could cut the steel rails and fit them to size while they were being laid. Until then rails were cut in a foundry, and if a certain length was required the standard-sized rails had to be shipped back to the terminal. The handsaw promised to save considerable time, money, and labor, but considering the conservatism of railroad practices it would probably take a persuasive salesman to bring the device into wide use.

Jim was excited by the prospect of becoming a handsaw salesman. Constant travel was no problem for a twenty-three-year-old bachelor. And he liked the style of the salesmen who came into the New York Central offices, their expansive manner, their free spending on expense accounts, their fancy tailoring and flashing display of jewelry. In the American business credo it was the salesman who kept the economy under a full head of steam. A salesman could be a seedy drummer peddling forty-rod whiskey, a red-nosed veteran of the smoking cars bemoaning the prospects which had narrowly escaped him, or he could be a lordly fellow who brushed aside purchasing agents and strutted into presidential offices. There was no doubt in Jim's mind which type he would be.

The first obstacle was Charles Moore, who had to be persuaded that James B. Brady, without any selling experience, could cut the mustard.

At their interview Moore initially was not too favorably impressed by the young man John Toucey had sent him with the highest recommendations. Not that there was anything wrong about a young fellow being a trifle stout, but Jim in addition had rather small eyes that carried out the porcine theme a trifle too closely. He also had the lower-class New Yorker's dem-and-dose accent, and despite careful tailoring he lacked polish. Jim was the rough-diamond type, all right, but then so were many of the Western railroaders. Perhaps, Moore decided, it was

66

more important that the young man seemed to know everything about railroad operation and equipment and that after spending an hour with him Moore found himself liking the man more and more. His geniality was natural, unforced, and seemingly limitless. If he lacked a touch of class, that was something he could acquire through association with his social betters.

Jim was hired by Manning, Maxwell & Moore before he left Moore's office that afternoon.

Before he went out on the road for the first time, Jim planned his campaign as carefully as Robert E. Lee mounting an invasion across the Potomac. "If you are going to make money," as later he often told aspirants in his profession, "you have to look like money." Jim used up all his savings to "look like money" when he hit the road for Manning, Maxwell & Moore. First he had his old friend Jules Weiss, who now owned a small tailor's shop of his own, make him three black suits of the most conservative cut to go with the Prince Albert he had bought as chief clerk, his stovepipe hat, his detachable cuffs, and his fur-collared overcoat. As a final touch, he bought a one-carat diamond ring for $90; without a diamond on at least one finger, he knew, a hotel clerk would assign you to a broom closet, and a headwaiter would put you at a table next to the kitchen door.

Jim Brady was an instant success. From every railroad center in the country big enough to have a roundhouse came a blizzard of orders for the new Manning, Maxwell & Moore handsaw. On that first swing through the country Jim saw that there was no point in selling only the handsaw but other items of railroad equipment—brake rigging, draft gear, switch stands, undercarriages—as well. The handsaw became merely the lead item in his portfolio.

He was determined to make himself the number-one salesman in America, and during those first years on the road he devoted all his energy to that program. There was more to it than merely walking in on a general superintendent or purchasing agent, oozing charm, and getting out the order book. You had to know so much about each company's affairs down to the track-gang level that you could tell the buyer what he needed or would need in the near future. So Jim did not reach the top drawer of salesmanship merely through the exercise of his manly charm but through intense calculation and extensive leg work. Instead of going to the company's equipment buyer at once with his wares, Jim reconnoitered, conducted his own inventory of its requirements.

He quickly made friends with the men who really ran the railroads, the section foremen, the master mechanics in the roundhouses, the track-laying bosses, the stationmasters, and the gandy dancers. This was easy enough, because he talked their language and after working hours entertained them in his hotel suite with beer binges (orange juice or root beer for the teetotaling Jim) and poker parties. Sober and alert, he gathered all sorts of inside information.

One of the more spectacular sights of American railroading in its prime was Jim Brady and one of his section-foreman friends out on a field trip. They would board a handcar, which in those days had to be pumped manually, Jim in a plug hat with the tails of his Prince Albert coat flying, the foreman in his overalls. It was a hard way to make an honest dollar, pumping away mile after mile at the bar of a handcar, but using that means of locomotion Jim was able to visit every tool shack along the right-of-way and determine just what equipment and supplies the company needed, down to the last spike and coupling.

Only after doing all that exhaustive research would Jim Brady, immaculately barbered and dressed, exuding good cheer and detailed information, present himself at the office of the man who bought equipment for the railroad. As his legend grew in pace with his girth, as he became known as the princeliest of wine buyers and hosts, most New Yorkers believed

Brady made his fortune as a salesman simply by outdazzling the competition socially. But the groundwork he laid far from the cabarets and lobster palaces was his trade secret.

Even all those traits and attributes, however, did not make up the entire composite of what *Fortune* magazine, almost fifty years after his death, called "the greatest capital goods salesman of them all."

He could also demonstrate a mastery of psychology which broke almost as many barriers as his diligence and admiability. Some tycoons, he came to realize, could not be handled with the ordinary methods of salesmanship. One was George Baer, the terrible-tempered president of the Reading Railroad, who hated salesmen even more than he detested labor unions. To break down Baer's resistance, Brady camped in Baer's outer office for five days. Finally Baer couldn't stand the silent siege any longer, came out, and demanded to know why Brady was sitting there day after day, impassive as some rough-hewn Buddha, when he was manifestly unwelcome.

In the most pleasant tone, Brady replied, "I've been waiting to tell you, Mr. Baer, that you can go straight to hell."

Baer was so charmed that he immediately invited Brady into his office. An hour later the latter left the Reading offices with a contract for five million dollars' worth of freight cars.

Luck was with him, too. He had started selling railroad equipment at the apogee of the Age of the Iron Horse. During his first decade as a salesman, from 1880 to 1890, the railroad industry was literally expanding in all directions. The total trackage doubled in that decade; the railroads extended from the main trunks to hundreds of offshoots, branch lines, and feeder routes designed to tap the mineral wealth of the Rockies and bring in the bumper crops from the wheat plains to Eastern ports, from which much of the harvest was shipped to Europe. Starting up a new railroad was almost a weekly occurrence. During the eighties 70,000 miles of new track were laid. All that expansion signified a snowballing business for railroad equipment suppliers and multiplying commissions for Jim Brady.

* * *

To become a super salesman—somebody elevated above the ruck of mere order-taking, somebody whom chief clerks and secretaries would bow into their superiors' offices the moment one sailed into an anteroom—would take more than hard work and incessant travel in Pullmans and handcars. A supersalesman had to create an aura of legend. His name and presence—it was a daring thought, not to be voiced in hearing of tycoons with monumental egos—had to be more resounding, more impressive than the products he sold.

With the same dogged persistence with which he had worked his way up from the lower West Side, with the same gusto he exhibited in gorging himself on eel pies and oysters on the half shell, Jim Brady set about creating a personal legend. Essentially it was his purpose to outflash everyone else. If a successful salesman wore a diamond ring and accessories, Jim would glitter with precious stones in his fingers, at his cuffs, on his chest, even the ferrule of his cane. If it was necessary to spend money on entertainment, he would be the most lavish host on the business scene. He would further enhance his persona by always being seen in the evening surrounded by beautiful and, if possible, complaisant women—which in the eighties meant actresses and chorus girls who didn't have to be too fussy about their reputations. It also meant low bows from grateful head-waiters, grabbing checks whenever they appeared on a silver salver, buying champagne, and popping corks in a constant fusillade.

It meant, above all, artful self-advertisement.

His fame was secured the day a fellow salesman fastened the sobriquet "Diamond Jim" on him. It happened, according to Parker Morell, a biographer of Brady's, one day in Cincinnati early in 1884. Jim was then only twenty-eight years old, an early age for the encrustation of legend. A number of salesmen had agreed to gather in Cincinnati and spend the weekend in a marathon poker game.

They were hanging around the lobby of the Burnet House when a salesman named Markie Mayer began taking the roll-call.

"Has anyone here seen Diamond Jim?" he asked his colleagues.

"You mean Jim Brady," asked one of them, "the big fat guy who doesn't drink?"

"That's him," Mayer replied. "Diamond Jim Brady, the pawnbroker's curse."

Diamonds are a boy's best friend, as Jim had learned in his first four or five years on the road. They were not only a man's portable signboard, testifying to his credit rating and sporting instincts, overawing hotel clerks and impressing headwaiters, and half blinding impressionable girls. They were a portable bank account. Banks could fail, stocks could shrink in value, but diamonds were forever.

Jim became a collector soon after going on the road. In each city he would take time out from selling railroad equipment to make a tour of the pawnshops, where bargains might be struck after hard-headed negotiations. Jim knew all about jewelry store markups. Thus the foundation of his collection, which would rival those of European royalty and the temporary hoards of courtesans, came from pawnbrokers. After his death the collection would be broken up, and since diamonds never wear out, many a dowager has sported diamonds on her tiara which once emblazoned Jim Brady, once nestled in pawnshop trays, and once graced some rambling, gambling man in the mining camps of the West or possibly the madam of a Denver whorehouse.

His colleague and accidental publicist, Markie Mayer, wasn't indulging in hyperbole when he called Brady the "pawnbroker's curse." Many a pawnbroker was tempted to draw his blinds and bolt his doors when he saw Jim Brady's stout figure approaching his establishment. Jim bargained as ferociously, as persistently as any rug peddler or horse trader, and when he walked out with his newest buy his opponent was usually left with a very small profit on the transaction. On top of that, he always insisted that the stones be removed from their mountings and the gold bought back by the pawnbroker for melting.

In a few years he accumulated so many stones that he had to carry them around in a money belt, which he would frequently take off to display the contents to his traveling companions on the long Pullman rides from city to city. Occasionally some cynic would examine the James Buchanan Brady collection and scoff that they were fakes, paste imitations. Jim was always delighted by such challenges because they provided the opportunity for further self-advertisement. He would grab one of the stones, walk to the nearest window, and using the diamond as a nib, scrawl on the pane of glass JAMES BUCHANAN BRADY.

The crowning touch, though, to the early phase of his self-glorification as the biggest sport of them all—a bit vulgar, perhaps, but possessing a certain princeliness—came when he bought a three-carat diamond and had it imbedded in the ferrule of his cane.

What later became known as Expense Account Society owes a considerable debt to the pioneering efforts of Diamond Jim Brady. He saw that salesmanship was a continuing process, not merely scuttling in and out of purchasing agents' offices, which had to be cemented by bonhomie, nights on the town, and a constant rendering of favors. After several years on the road, he persuaded Manning, Maxwell & Moore to give him an unlimited expense account. This would allow him not only to lavish hospitality on his customers while traveling from city to city but to entertain them when they came to New York.

A railroad president or general superintendent coming to New York, whatever the more legitimate reasons for his visit, was likely to account his mission a failure unless he had been given the Diamond Jim Brady treatment: champagne and cigars in his hotel suite, dinner in one of the better restaurants, much wassail in the cabarets, topped off (if the visiting fireman was sportive and spry enough and could get away from his wife) by a tour of the Tenderloin, also known as Satan's Circus, or some of the raunchier joints farther downtown. If he had any taste for the theater, Brady would also see to it that he saw the best plays and musicals.

It was generally agreed that no one could show you a better time than Diamond Jim. He could always find a pretty girl of amiable disposition and no excessive prudishness to drape on your arm. He became uproariously indignant if anyone else tried to pick up a check. His jovial personality seemed to envelop you from the beginning to the end of your visit, and you went back to Omaha or Chicago or Council Bluffs, possibly with a slightly damaged liver, a flawed conscience, and a skull-busting hangover, but also with some lively memories. You may have broken a bottle over a waiter's head or waked up one morning with a strange woman in your bed, but you knew that Jim Brady was the soul of discretion and no one back home would ever learn of your capers. Naturally when good old Jim appeared in town on his next selling trip you did your best to prove that you, too, were a jolly good fellow.

Jim had made himself a prominent figure in New York night life with the underpinning of his Manning, Maxwell & Moore expense account and the lavish spending he did out of his own pocket. During the eighties the headquarters of sporting life was Harry Hill's, a complex at Houston and Crosby streets which included a music hall, a restaurant, and a number of bars. A number of important boxing matches were held in the music hall, and among those who frequented the place were Thomas A. Edison, James Gordon Bennett, Jr., P. T. Barnum, and Richard K. Fox, the publisher of the *Police Gazette*, which in its day was a combination of *Playboy* and *Sports Illustrated* and had very little to do with the constabulary. One expert on the after-dark scene of New York in the eighties wrote of Harry Hill's:

For a quarter of a century, until the distinction had been usurped by the offices in the new *Police Gazette* Building, Harry Hill's was the sporting center of the United States. Every important match was made here and Harry usually officiated no matter where a contest was held on this side of the ocean; and often, if the affair was of commanding importance, he traveled abroad. John L. Sullivan was first brought here by William Muldoon to make his New York debut in the ring at Hill's place, and made himself so nationally famous by knocking out Steve Taylor in two rounds that less than a year after this feat, the Boston Strong Boy was privileged to beat Paddy Ryan for the heavyweight fistic championship of America. Herbert Slade, the Maori, boxed here and married one of Hill's sweet-faced waitresses. Jack Dempsey, the Nonpareil [not the later heavyweight champion of the same name], was among the many who exhibited his skill of fist on the Hill stage; and William Muldoon, then a strikingly handsome young athlete, wrestled all comers.

It was at one of Harry Hill's bars that Jim formed a long friendship with the hard-drinking John L. Sullivan, who was the number-one hero of Irish-Americans. Sullivan's respect could be won either through a demonstration of superior skill with the fists or an ability to knock back drinks in pace with himself. At their first meeting the bartender served Sullivan tall seidels of Pilsener while Jim drank root beer. Each had disposed of fifteen seidels when John L., not knowing then that Brady's strongest drink was root beer, complimented him on his capacity, shook his hand, and proclaimed, "By God, you're a man, and I'm proud to call you my friend." The friendship endured even after Sullivan learned that Brady was a teetotaler.

During those years in which he spent about nine months on the road and three months refurbishing his reputation as a man about town, he also gained renown as a first-nighter and an unrivaled theater buff. His free-spending and winning, if somewhat rough-edged, personality won him entree into theatrical circles, where his boyishly enthusiastic admiration of actors and actresses was certainly no handicap. He was allowed to worship at close range such personalities as Lotta Crabtree and Mary Anderson, who was the most popular singer until she was displaced by Lillian Russell. Lily Langtry also admitted him to her circle of admirers, and he managed to hold a platonic place in her affections by frequent gifts of jewelry. From Brady's standpoint, as well as that of those he adored, there was naturally an element of self-aggrandizement. It didn't hurt his business a bit when he was able to take some visiting railroad tycoon backstage and introduce him to the Jersey Lily.

Jim was also gaining the respect of his contemporaries—who had little use for the lean and hungry type perhaps because it represented a spoilsport—for his marathon endeavors with the knife and fork. When Diamond Jim tucked a large, snowy napkin into his wing collar, the waiters had to begin operating in relays. His capacity at table first attracted considerable attention, including that of prowling journalists, during the two weeks he spent each summer at Manhattan Beach, not having become rich and fashionable enough as yet for such watering places as Saratoga and Long Island. At the Manhattan Beach Hotel he spent the mornings at the beach, the afternoons at the nearby Sheepshead Bay racetrack. That still left him plenty of time for the pleasures of the table.

Watching Jim Brady in action was starting to become an indoor spectator sport. His breakfast, as correspondents for the New York dailies noted, usually consisted of a small steak garnished with several chops, pancakes, eggs, fried potatoes, hominy grits, corn bread, and muffins, all washed down by a pitcher of milk. About 11:30 A.M. he came up from the shore and soothed his hunger pangs by downing several dozen oysters and clams on the half shell. That sustained him until lunch, when he made do with more oysters, a few deviled crabs, a brace of broiled lobsters, roast beef or steak, salad, and half a fruit pie. Dinner was likely to be on a more baronial scale: oysters and clams, followed by a tray of canapes, a tureen of green turtle soup, broiled fresh shad from the then-unpolluted

Delaware River, a columbine of larded fowl, a crown roast of mountain sheep; then a spot of sherbet, while he caught his second wind, followed by an all-out assault on canvasback duck, diamond-back terrapin, and fresh asparagus, and with a dying fall of the mammoth appetite, an hour or so of dawdling over vanilla mousse, fruit, walnuts, bonbons, and mints while watching the nightly fireworks display through the wide windows, "The Fall of Babylon" and "The Destruction of Pompeii." In honor of Jim Brady's dinner they might at least have added a fireworks spectacular titled "Trimalchio's Feast."

As he rounded, literally, into his thirties, he had every reason to congratulate himself on a well-ordered life. Like any good Irishman, he could pride himself on having stayed a bachelor through the dangerous twenties. The money was rolling in from commissions. He had few responsibilities aside from stoking his stomach and sending money to his mother, who was now operating a boarding house. Prosperity had been made permanent, it was generally believed, in an ever-expanding American economy, and James Buchanan Brady was guaranteed more than his statistical share in that abundance.

In 1888 he took the first steps toward advancing from the status of a prosperous salesman to a man of wealth and substance. Once again it was a matter of luck, as well as his reputation for being a supersalesman, that caused his advancement. That summer a short, rubicund Englishman named Sampson Fox, the president of the Leeds Forge Company, one of the lesser but more ambitious of the British steelmasters, arrived in the United States. He hoped to break into the American market with his all-steel Fox Undertruck.

Until then the undercarriages of American railway cars were cumbersome contrivances of wooden beams girded by wrought iron fittings. Much thought and work had gone into designing ornate and luxurious Pullmans and plushy parlor cars, but little effort had been put into body construction. Fox's company had developed a lightweight undercarriage of pressed steel which was in use on all the British railways. For several months Sampson Fox had ranged through the United States trying to sell his product to the American railroads, but their experts objected that his undercarriage was too light to bear up under the American freight cars, which were heavier than the British. In desperation Fox returned to New York and consulted with Charles Moore of Manning, Maxwell & Moore.

Moore told the Englishman his company couldn't handle the pressed-steel truck, but added, "I've got a crackerjack young salesman who might be able to put it across for you. He's returning to the city later today and I'll talk to him about it. If he wants to take your undercarriage on as a sideline, it's all right with me."

That evening Fox and Jim Brady sat down to a twelve-course spread at the Hoffman House and, after glutting themselves, came to a remarkable arrangement. Brady agreed to represent the Fox Undertruck in the United States and develop a market, if possible, while Fox promised to pay him an astounding $33\frac{1}{3}$-percent commission on every piece of equipment he sold.

With a sugarplum like that dancing before his eyes, Brady was determined to put over his new sideline. First he had to find facilities somewhere in the States to fabricate the Fox Undertruck; importing them from England would be too expensive. He located and leased a blacksmith shop in Joliet, Illinois, with space enough to turn out the pressed-steel parts. By that time Fox had sent over a young man named Clem Hackney to take charge of the fabrication. The machines necessary for stamping out the steel components were installed at Joliet within a month. Two weeks later the undercarriages for ten freight cars had been produced, enough for Jim Brady to begin his sales campaign.

As with Manning, Maxwell & Moore's handsaw, which had made his reputation for salesmanship, he perceived that he would have to get around the conservatism of American railroaders. They always had to be *shown*; theories were so much hot air to men who prided themselves on hardheaded practicality. Brady ran into the same objections that railroad executives had presented to Fox. Unlike the diffident Briton, he brushed them aside. His first target was the New York Central, which was the bellwether for all the other roads. Central's motive-power superintendent told Brady the all-steel trucks would take curves only at sharply reduced speeds. Brady responded that if the Central didn't at least give them a tryout he would take the Fox Undertruck to its leading rival, the Pennsylvania, and give the Pennsy first crack at a product which would revolutionize the industry. That jarred the Central executive enough to order a test, provided Brady could supply him with twenty undertrucks in a hurry to make a trial run. The Joliet branch of the Leeds Forge Company went back on overtime and turned out ten more undercarriages, which were shipped to New York by fast freight.

The first twenty cars produced at Joliet were fitted on freight cars in the New York Central shops under Brady's supervision and then were loaded with rock and scrap iron. The test run would be made from New York to Albany and back, a route which offered plenty of curves to prove whether the Fox Undertrucks had the flexibility and tensile strength required for American roadbeds. A special train was made up and sent on its way up the Hudson. It made the round trip in satisfactory time, and Jim's sideline passed all tests. The New York Central immediately ordered a hundred of the steel undercarriages.

To Brady that was only the opening wedge. He wanted every bit of rolling stock converted to pressed steel; his one-third bite of the sales price would make him a rich man, a junior-grade magnate, a fellow who could talk to the Morgans and Carnegies as a near equal. Within a few weeks he had talked the Pennsylvania into getting next in line for 250 of the Fox Undertrucks; then both the New York Central and the Pennsylvania decided to convert entirely to Jim's product. That was the beginning of an avalanche of orders from all over the country. By early 1889 he was selling hundreds of undercarriages every week. And within a year the Joliet plant had expanded to three large buildings housing hundreds of workmen and turning out not only the undercarriages but hydraulic brakes and other equipment.

It was just shifting into high gear on the production line, in fact, when the empire-building of the Pittsburgh steelmaster Andrew Carnegie reached out for the steel plants around Joliet. The American subsidiary known as the Fox Pressed Steel Company had been obtaining its steel from those plants at a price enabling it to make a tidy profit. Now Carnegie engorged those plants and inevitably raised prices.

Once more the entrepreneurial talent of Jim Brady was called upon. Obviously the Joliet plant would have to find its own source of steel, independent of the Carnegie trust's jiggling of the price structure. He learned that the Carbon Steel Company of Pittsburgh was foundering under the pressure of competition from Carnegie's trust and was about to fling itself on the mercy of a referee in bankruptcy. His plan was to find sympathetic parties sufficiently well heeled to take over the ailing Carbon Steel and whom he could trust not to boost prices outrageously. The conventional method would have been to trudge up and down Broad, Wall, and other streets in the financial district looking for venture capital, but Jim preferred to do business in more amiable surroundings. He scouted the Manhattan water holes until, at the bar of the Hoffman House, he found a couple of Wall Streeters named Munson Raymond and Frank Robinson drinking juleps to while away the late afternoon.

Raymond and Robinson allowed they might be interested in joining the ranks of the steel magnates. They were downright fascinated when Brady offered two inducements, provided they were willing to keep their prices down to a reasonable level. One was a promise to take all the steel they could produce, the other the formula for a process (developed by Leeds Forge in England) which produced steel of great tensile strength.

The new company was capitalized at one million dollars,

with Brady taking a chunk of the stock himself. It was an immediate success, producing not only for the Fox Pressed Steel Company but for several of the larger locomotive manufacturers. The demand for its product was so great that a second plant had to be built in Pittsburgh. Meanwhile Jim was collecting commissions from Fox Pressed Steel, Carbon Steel, and Manning, Maxwell & Moore. No wonder people were beginning to call him the "statesman of American salesmanship" before he reached the age of forty.

He was doing so well as an entrepreneur and financial adviser to Fox Pressed Steel and Carbon Steel that Charles Moore once suggested that he might want to quit going on the road for Manning, Maxwell & Moore. Jim regarded this as an affront to his sense of loyalty; the railroad supply house had raised him out of the wage-earning rut and given him his first real break. "Why in hell should I leave you now?" he demanded. "You gave me the chance to make good. You told Sampson Fox about me. And now, just when I've got every railroad eating out of my hand, you want me to resign. Why, hell, don't you know I can get any order for you by promising them to put them at the top of the list for pressed-steel trucks? I'll be God damned if I'll quit now!"

That sort of speech, everyone would agree, was the essential Jim Brady—rough-mannered, profane, but dead loyal to his friends; generous and easygoing unless you crossed him, or one of his friends, or the Democratic Party.

Much as he spent on himself and his friends, he was still in a sound financial position early in 1893 when the panic hit Wall Street. Things kept looking blacker every week as the Southern and Western banks drew twenty million dollars out of the New York banks to meet the demands of their depositors. Mines and factories closed, banks failed, and the overexpanded railroads were harder hit than any other sector of the economy. Within a few years 169 railroads would be in receivership. And those roads that managed to stay out of the receiver's hands had to cut purchases to the bone. As a good Democrat, Brady radiated optimism among his peers at the Hoffman House bar; he was certain that President Grover Cleveland would save the country from financial calamity and the Republicans when he summoned Congress to a special session to repeal the Republican-sponsored Sherman Silver Purchase Act, which had caused an evaporation in the gold supply.

Personally, he was in good shape, with a hundred thousand in three different bank accounts and very little money tied up in stocks endangered by the violent fluctuations of the stock market. He had cut short his last road trip when it appeared that even Diamond Jim Brady wouldn't be able to sell so much as a brake shoe until times got better.

It was time to take the first real vacation of his life and spend the summer at the Columbian Exposition. He settled down in a suite at the Palmer House, mingled with the rubes at the Transportation Building out at the exposition, and formed his lasting friendship with Lillian Russell over mounds of sweet corn. And what balm it was to the Brady ego when the most gorgeous woman in American indicated her preference for his company. J. P. Morgan, the number-one plutocrat and a formidable womanizer, whose conquests outside high finance included the stately actress Maxine Elliott, had made approaches to Lillian, arrogantly assuming that she would prefer his company to that of any other exposition visitor. Lillian, however, had brushed aside J. P. Morgan and made Diamond Jim her favored companion and nightly escort after the theater. He had bested Andrew Carnegie in a business deal and elbowed aside J. P. Morgan as a rival stage-door Johnny. A boy from the lower West Side couldn't hope for much more than that.

3

PRINCESS NICOTINE AND
SIGNOR PERUGINI

EXPOSITION Summer found Lillian Russell at loose
ends. She was neither married nor in love, a worrisome
situation for a woman of thirty-two, especially for one who was
supposed to be the most desirable woman in America. Her
lucrative contract with T. Harry French had resulted in a personal success in *Giroflé Girofla*, but French had found that a
man could go broke paying a prima donna's salary, and the
contract had been terminated.

Therefore, she looked with some eagerness to the engagement at the Columbian Theater on the Midway. For one
thing, it was nice to be returning to Chicago, where she had
been raised, in triumph and high style, and it was even nicer to
be the number-one attraction of the great Columbian Exposition. Lillian Russell's larynx was a wonder to match the Ferris
Wheel, the Manufacturers Building (the largest structure in
the world, with eleven acres of glass in its skylights), and the
greatest electrical display the world had ever seen lighting up
the great white palaces and lagoons. Little Egypt's contortions,
not to mention her diamond-studded garters, may have caused
more talk, but Lillian Russell was a respectable attraction, a
cultural asset, an educational experience.

Still it was rather disheartening that Chicago society, unlike New York and Newport, turned up its collective nose at her as a "theatrical person" not worthy of mingling with the sons of immigrant meat-packers and other one-generation aristocrats. When the Infanta Eulalia of Spain and her consort Prince Antoine swept haughtily into town to inspect the latest manifestations of American vulgarity, Lillian Russell was *not* among those invited by the local society queen, Mrs. Potter Palmer, to meet the snotty young Spanish princess, who snubbed Mrs. Palmer (whose husband owned the Palmer House) as "the wife of my innkeeper" and consented to make only one appearance at the exposition, on occasion marked by the scattering of 30,000 pansies before the disdainful Spaniard. She also appeared at a reception in "sullen unbending silence," then escaped to a yacht sailing around Lake Michigan. Lillian was also not invited to meet the Austrian Archduke Franz Ferdinand, who made a poor impression on the commoners by refusing to visit the Old Vienna Café at the exposition.

It wasn't that Lillian hadn't tried to make a loud enough splash on arrival in Chicago. During her sixteen-week engagement she rented a mansion on a fashionable South Side street and even imported her horses and carriage. Still there were no invitations from Mrs. Potter Palmer, the Armours, the Swifts, the McCormicks, or other nabobs. She soon discovered that the upper echelon of society in her old hometown regarded her as being more notorious than famous. It was all right to visit her backstage, perhaps, out of curiosity. It was all right to stare at her in a restaurant as she made a regal appearance under one of her vast plumed hats. But one really did not want to have "that woman" under one's own roof. That feeling, of course, extended to almost all of the theatrical profession, which was still regarded as a form of vagabondage.

A more determined snub was administered when she announced plans to attend Derby Day at Washington Park. Lillian was a racing enthusiast and would soon be accounted one

of the most ardent track-followers in the country. The Derby
was run on a Saturday, when she usually appeared in a matinee
performance, so she switched the matinee to Thursday. Early
in the Derby afternoon she appeared in one of her dashing
outdoor costumes at the Washington Park clubhouse, serenely
confident that her presence would be welcomed. Instead it
created an uproar. It wasn't the male members who objected—
not at all. But their wives descended on the president of the
racetrack association and demanded that "that woman" be
ejected from the clubhouse instantly. The president pointed
out that Chicago was a city in Illinois, which was a state in a
supposedly democratic nation, and that ejecting Lillian Russell
would make them all look ridiculous. But the wives and
daughters of the members raised such a hullabaloo that he had
to ask Lillian if she would mind watching the Derby from a
box in the grandstand.

Visibly more amused than crestfallen, conscious that the racing program was being held up while the matter was thrashed
out, she made a stately progress to her box while the grandstand erupted with enthusiasm over her presence. The Chicago
Tribune reported that Lillian's box was "one of the best in the
grandstand" and tried to whitewash Chicago of having treated
America's reigning theatrical personality so much shabbier
than foreign princes and potentates. The Chicago *Record* was
franker. It described Lillian as "holding a levee between the
races" and an informal reception in her box for "all sorts" but
mostly "members of the profession which Miss Russell adorns."
Chicago newspapermen, democrats to a man, placed Lillian
Russell at the top of their lists of prominent persons attending
the Derby and thereafter gave her name greater prominence
than Mrs. Potter Palmer's in any similar listings.

She could shrug off the snobbishness of "high" society, a
society still so unsure of itself that it fretted endlessly over
pedigrees, but a matter of greater embarrassment was the ersatz
romance the press concocted by linking her name with that of

Sandow the Strongman. Florenz Ziegfeld had discovered him in Europe when he went over to procure military bands for the exposition. While listening to the oompah-oompah of brass bands, which were in surplus supply in the kaiser's Germany, he had come across young Sandow exhibiting his magnificent musculature and decided he might make a hit at the exposition. His showmanly instincts told him that Sandow's virility and strength might prove a box office sensation in a time when so many Americans were trying to make a virtue out of sloping shoulders, flabby biceps, and sagging chests—and he was right.

The exposition's promoters began publicizing Sandow as a Samson, a Hercules, with a gentle, poetic nature. Publicity, for once, was based on reality. Amy Leslie, the drama critic for the Chicago *Daily News*, took a stroll with Sandow through the Wooded Island and was surprised to find the strong man anything but the type of German who had been flexing his muscles, usually behind a bayonet, back in the Fatherland. On their walk Sandow paused to snip part of a snapdragon blossom and explained to Miss Leslie, "Now, when we were little in Germany, we took these blossoms and pressed them so, and if the mouth of the flower opened, that meant our mothers were calling us to come home." Just then a park guard came up, shouting that Sandow had broken the law by picking a flower. Unwisely the guard grabbed Sandow by the elbow. Sandow simply picked up the guard and held him at arm's length, examining him as some curious specimen of the park's fauna. He put the guard down only at Miss Leslie's pleading.

Sandow was introduced to Lillian as a cocelebrity of Exposition Summer, but she found the rather simple and naïve German something less than overpowering as a personality. Her tastes were more sophisticated. Yet she was seen in his company often enough for the newspapers to report they were romantically attracted to each other. Eugenically speaking, it was pointed out, the robustly beauteous Lillian and the stalwart Sandow would be a perfect match. Underneath all the gossip there was a sexual rather than scientific titillation, particularly when Colonel William d'Alton Mann heard about the supposed romance back in New York and wrote in his *Town Topics*:

> I have tried very conscientiously to trace to its source a rumor at present current in Chicago, to the effect that Miss Lillian Russell is to marry Sandow, the strong man. The giant has given audiences to a number of beautiful Chicago girls within the last week or so, and as he has managed to quite capture most of their hearts, why not the airy and erstwhile fairy Lillian's? I have no comment to make on the match should it come, so to speak, but protest in all seriousness that the couple would look simply magnificent marching up the aisle of the church together.

No doubt the deft hand of Flo Ziegfeld was manipulating the press in its speculations over such a match, which greatly enhanced Sandow's pull at the box office.

About the time all the publicity value had been abstracted, however, Lillian met Diamond Jim Brady, and finding themselves so compatible at the dining board, they were constant companions until the exposition ended.

It was good publicity for Lillian to have it known that Diamond Jim liked to shower her with diamonds. He made few demands on her except to be seen in her company where the lights were brightest. He was understanding about and fascinated by her career. He was always available as an escort whose advances would not have to be fended off in the cab ride home. Underneath all the suet, too, there was a kindly fellow whose generosity and loyalty were legendary. He may have been gross in appearance, an overweight gargoyle, but he could exhibit an almost feminine insight and tact. There was a lot to be said for a platonic friendship which always offered an anchorage when her emotional troubles with other men made her life stormy.

As in the best of all such partnerships, the benefits were of equal if not greater value to Brady. He lived in a constant blare of party-going and party-giving, of endless nights on the town, but essentially he was a lonely man who knew exactly how many of his "friendships" depended on his ability to buy champagne and lift the tab at Delmonico's. His lavish giving, his pressing of presents even on those reluctant to receive them, were symptoms of a private despair over the inner conviction that nobody loved him for himself. To most people he was just a walking stomach, a dispenser of tips and favors.

With Lillian it was different. She was rich and famous and valued him for what he was, for whatever Irish charm still lurked below the layers of fat, for his shrewd, instinctive knowledge of human motives. Having the same utterly sensual nature, she could understand that he literally lived to eat, as men of finer sensibility might live to paint masterpieces, and was not disgusted when he wallowed in food. Far from being disgusted by his compulsion, she wallowed right along with him.

Lillian Russell was the capstone of Diamond Jim Brady's career, the centerpiece of his collection of people and things, the largest and most expensive jewel he could adorn himself with. When he wore her on his arm, basking in the envy of men handsomer, cleverer, more amusing, and even richer than himself, it was better than wearing the Kohinoor for a collar stud. What was the price of diamonds and other trinkets he bestowed on her every time he could find an excuse compared with the radiations of her fame? He found warmth in her reflected glory, consolation when he had been taken advantage of by other people. He often said that "it's fun to be a sucker," but there was a bitter aftertaste to that bit of philosophy. Lillian's friendship somehow proved to Brady that he was more than the Barnum of salesmanship and more than the biggest eater in the United States: that he had an understanding heart as well as a stomach six times larger than the average man's.

Soon after the exposition engagement ended, Lillian would have need of his sympathy and understanding. The events that led to her third marriage—each new venture in that line seemed to be progressively more disastrous—began with the announcement that she would star in *Princess Nicotine* at the

Casino Theater, her lucky showplace, under the management
of Lederer and Canary. George W. Lederer was regarded as
one of the ablest producers and directors in the musical theater. The Canary part of the firm represented a young man with
a large bankroll and aspirations to enlarge it on Broadway.
Colonel Mann almost swooned with ecstasy at the prospect of
once again viewing Lillian Russell from a box overlooking her
magnificent cleavage and droolingly reported in *Town Topics*
that "she will expand and heave, throb, bloom and fascinate
once again in our vicinity. It looked as though we might lose
all that pinkness for a season or so, but a man named Canary,
reputed to have half a million dollars in his hip pocket, twit-
tered at it for a spell and it came back. He can have a brass cage
on my premises any time he wants it, for I shall never forget
that he is the preserver of Lillian, and should that half million
dollars ever dwindle, let him remember that seed and a piece
of cuttlefish await him at my address."

During the rehearsals for *Princess Nicotine*, Lillian and the
amiably pug-faced young comedienne named Marie Dressler,
who many years later would star in such films as *Dinner at
Eight, Tugboat Annie,* and *Min and Bill,* as well as a memorable appearance in an early Charlie Chaplin film, formed the
friendship which endured throughout Lillian's lifetime. For all
her magnitude as the biggest name in the musical theater, Miss
Dressler found her unassuming, "one of the most generous and
gifted women who ever brightened the American scene . . . as
loveable as she was lovely."

Early in their friendship Marie Dressler learned that Lillian
would fight for, as well as cherish, those she cared about. During the run of *Princess Nicotine* Lillian learned that Marie was
receiving only $40 a week, although she was a principal mem-
ber of the supporting cast. She asked her friend what she
thought she ought to be paid, and Miss Dressler replied, "A
hundred dollars a week." Lillian reflected for a moment and
then advised, "Tell George Lederer you want that much or
you won't go on tonight."

A few minutes later Producer Lederer rushed into Lillian's dressing room to complain that Marie Dressler was making an exorbitant salary demand, adding, "She can stay away from the theater forever. I will have a new woman tonight."

"Oh, no," Lillian sweetly replied, as she recalled in her memoirs, "we can't have a new woman tonight. I am not going to have my performance ruined completely. You must get Miss Dressler back somehow, otherwise I can't play. Please remember that my contract states that you cannot discharge anyone without my permission."

Lederer howled with managerial grief but had to give in or close down a highly profitable show. "That was," Lillian later wrote, "the only bit of temperament I ever deliberately displayed, and it worked beautifully. . . ."

Early in their acquaintance Miss Dressler remarked to Miss Russell that "it must be wonderful to be famous."

"La, no, child." Lillian replied. (The "la" evidently was an affectation picked up from her European opera friends.) "You ought to try to eat raw oysters in a restaurant with every eye focussed on you. It makes you feel as if the creatures were whales, your fork a derrick, and your mouth the Mammoth Cave."

The only flaw Marie Dressler would concede having found in her friend was that "she was none too clever about men," a weakness often to be detected in large-souled women.

That blind spot in what was evidently a fairly keen intelligence evidenced itself once again when the cast of *Princess Nicotine* was assembled, and Lillian's big blue eyes fairly melted at the sight of her leading man, the tenor *robusto* who styled himself as Signor Giovanni Perugini. His straight name was Jack Chatterton, and he had been born not in the shadow of La Scala but in the backwoods of Michigan. He had adorned himself with a fiery Italianate manner and could claim to have sung opposite Adelina Patti, and he had all the temperament for which tenors have been credited with sending impresarios to early graves.

Princess Nicotine *and* Signor Perugini

It was Lillian's bad luck that he also had those dark liquid eyes which she found irresistible. Her friends believed that Perugini Chatterton flashed those compelling eyes of his at Lillian because he hoped that through her influence Producer Lederer could be persuaded to elevate him to costar billing. Certainly it was not Lillian's ripely curving body or her famous profile that attracted him. Signor Perugini was in love with himself, and whatever emotion he could spare from self-infatuation was not likely to be wasted on a female. The *signor*, in fact, was alleged in Broadway gossip to have homosexual inclinations. This was probably a canard; he was too self-absorbed for such capers. For the moment the irony of the fact that America's most desirable woman, whose profile even appeared on cigar bands, the ultimate accolade of the time, was smitten by a man whose greatest delight was to stare into a mirror, seemed to have escaped everyone.

Princess Nicotine opened on November 24, 1893, and was a resounding success with the public, but much less so with the critics. Audiences then, with so few other forms of entertainment to distract them, were not particularly demanding when it came to the vehicle in which a star was presented. The dramaturgic qualities of the operettas would hardly have satisfied readers of modern comic books. *Princess Nicotine*'s libretto, for instance, had Lillian pretending to be a Spanish cigarette maker, which seemed to be the favored occupation for light-opera heroines. In this Carmenesque role she was menaced by the provincial governor, who was determined to preempt the nuptial rights of her tobacco-planter bridegroom. Subsequent plot turns involved a series of misunderstandings in which the bridegroom was convinced that the governor had exercised his seignorial rights. There was much popping in and out of closets, in the best traditions of French farce. Act III, of course, was devoted to Lillian's lyrical pleas to her bridegroom, as portrayed by Signor Perugini, that she was intact.

There was something new in *Princess Nicotine*. For once the splendor of Lillian Russell's costuming was rivaled by that of another member of the cast. As the *Dramatic Mirror* reported, "It is Signor Don Giovanni Perugini who divided attention with Miss Russell. The three costumes he wears are marvels of color. His wedding dress, which is white, with gold clocks running up his stockings, is especially brilliant."

All that peacockery, as well as his frequent tantrums, convinced Lillian's friends that there was something a little offbeat, even for a tenor, about Perugini. The Lillian Russell Protective Society rallied around in an effort to keep her from what they delicately called "making another mistake."

Marie Dressler was particularly vigorous in this effort. As she recalled in her memoirs, Perugini was "petty, effeminate, and colossally selfish and conceited," and she tried her best to make Lillian see him as he appeared to others. "I used to get on my makeup in half the time it took the others," she related, "and I often dropped into the star's dressing room to kill time while she was finishing. I had to pass Perugini's dressing room on my way to Lillian's, and I took malicious pleasure in reporting anything I could find to laugh at. I'm afraid I never missed a chance to poke fun at the tenor's mannerisms. Once I caught him tweaking his eyebrows and smirking at himself in the mirror. I could not resist mimicking this absurd performance for Lillian's benefit."

A few months before Lillian had told reporters who sought an interview on rumors that she was about to remarry, "I do not intend to marry until my stage career is over. Someone who does *not* love me started those reports that I was to marry so-and-so and so-and-so. But that is not so."

Now the rumor that she intended to marry Perugini was in busy circulation, particularly in the basement bar of the Hotel Normandie, around the corner from the Casino Theater, where New York's leading womanizers gathered to exchange information on their avocation. In this bourse of the sexual commerce of New York, it was regarded as ludicrous that Lillian Russell could even be considering marriage to a tenor, one of a theatrical breed whom manlier chaps considered "nothing more than a superfluous larynx on legs."

Again the journalists clamored around Lillian's town house on West Seventy-seventh Street for enlightenment on her matrimonial plans. She received them in a gorgeous kimono decked with diamonds. "Yes," she told them, "I did say only a few months ago that I was done with married life, but I've changed my mind. Why? Well, I'll tell you. Signor Perugini is a gentleman; he is a dear, good fellow, and he has asked me to marry him. That would probably be sufficient reason, but in addition to that I am tired of reading these reports of my coming marriage in the papers. I am only a woman, after all, and these rumors—all of which have been false, of course—have both annoyed and hurt me. I hope my marriage will put an end to that sort of thing."

The reporters then descended on the dear, good fellow himself and found Signor Perugini in only slightly less gorgeous dishabille. "I am thirty-nine years old," he told the reporters, "and this is the first time I have been engaged. When a man of my age falls in love, it is the genuine thing. My wife—ah! that is to say she who is to be my wife within two months; I wish it were now!—and I are very happy. We shall devote ourselves to opera comique. I say we, but it is Miss Russell that is the one; I put myself in the background."

Despite that modest disclaimer, the producers of *Princess Nicotine* found that Perugini, for a man supposedly dazzled by the prospect of marrying Lillian Russell, was strangely obsessed by an urge to have his name go up in lights with hers. Costarring rather than cohabitating seemed to be his overriding ambition. But Lederer and Canary fended off the tenor's demands, which did not improve his temper backstage.

There were other complications, largely those raised by the fascinated press. The New York *World*, which was always ready to investigate anything from Standard Oil conspiracies to parish-pump gossip, delved into Lillian's matrimonial record and came up with its several columns of findings under the scare head: WILL IT BE BIGAMY? The *World*'s bird dogs had discovered that Lillian's divorce from her first husband, Harry Braham, had been obtained in the New York Supreme Court and that the decree had included a rider which prevented her from marrying again in the state of New York.

Lillian had a sentimental longing to be married in church, to the strains of Mendelssohn rather than the pounding of reportorial feet, but once again an elopement seemed to be in order. An elopement, in fact, to unromantic Hoboken across the Hudson in New Jersey where she could be married without being arrested, like her second husband, as a bigamist.

On a Sunday morning, January 24, 1894, an informal wedding party conveyed in hansom cabs formed up outside Lillian's house on West Seventy-seventh Street. Included in the party, for once, was Lillian's mother, who had decided that maternal disapproval would never prevent Lillian from following the dictates of a still girlish heart. The wedding party was pursued by a brigade of journalists in other hansom cabs, providing a chase scene of opera *comique* proportions. The marriage ceremony was hastily performed by a justice of the peace, and the wedding party returned to Manhattan for the reception in Lillian's town house.

What happened later was subsequently related by one of the guests at the reception, George Lederer, Lillian's producer. "We had a jolly little supper," Lederer told the late George Jean Nathan many years later, "and then, somewhat to my astonishment—since it was hardly the gesture of a bride on her wedding night—the fair Lillian suggested that we all sit down to a game of cards. It was now about half past one in the morning. We got out the cards and chips and presently were in the midst of a friendly little game of poker. Perugini, along toward two-thirty, got sleepy and retired.

"But, though I made several suggestions that we stop the game, the beautiful Lillian insisted that we continue. She loved cards, and they were her favorite pastime. We kept on playing, playing, playing. I began to think our hostess' habitual politeness prevented her from getting rid of us, so I suggested to her, as politely as I in turn could, that she boot us out bodily. Whereupon she looked at me very sweetly and said: 'Not at all! I wouldn't think of it! I *always* play cards on my wedding night!' "

The marriage was a total disaster, the most distressing and humiliating episode of Lillian's life. Perugini had married her with no intention of consummating the marriage. It was a marriage of convenience—his convenience. His attitude, as Lillian later revealed to her friends, was that she was too much a goddess for a mere mortal to approach with thoughts of physical love. Or as he put it, in the language of the librettists, "I love you too much to defile you." Lillian had been only too eager to be "defiled" but accepted the situation, for the time being, with the shrugging philosophy her various missteps had taught. The convolutions of human sexual behavior were then a mystery most people would rather not think about.

According to Marie Dressler's recollections, the members of the *Princess Nicotine* company were whispering among themselves within a week after the wedding that Lillian was what was then tactfully referred to as a "kissless bride." As Miss Dressler recalled, "As soon as the last curtain fell, Lillian would rush feverishly around, inviting people to go home with her after the show. It was evident that she did not want to be alone with Perugini. I think she was afraid of him even then." Any fear Lillian might have felt undoubtedly stemmed from Perugini's raging frustration, though the weedy tenor would hardly have been a match for Lillian, weighing in at 165 pounds, in a fair fight. He had expected that the day after they were married his name would go up on the marquee of the Casino Theater, and he was outraged that Lillian did not force Lederer and Canary to comply with his reasonable wishes.

95

After all, he had sung in grand opera, opposite the great Patti herself, and Lillian by comparison was a mere comic-opera singer.

If her parody of a home life was miserable, her relations with Perugini onstage were even more unbearable. Perugini, it seems, had declared guerrilla war on his bride. During their scenes together, he would throw her off balance by muttering obscenities and bloodcurdling threats. His treatment of Lillian evidently was encouraged by his status as a matinee idol. Reports of their marital difficulties had appeared in the press, and Perugini's female following, clustering around the stage door, greeted him as a martyred hero who was being maltreated by his overbearing wife. And Perugini played the role of the misunderstood and browbeaten husband for all it was worth.

While *Princess Nicotine* was playing out its run at the Casino, Marie Dressler, a formidable figure of a woman, decided it was time that Lillian was offered a measure of physical protection, onstage at least:

> Once during a performance, Perugini called his wife a name that made me furious. "If you ever say that again, I'll throw you into the bass drum," I told him under the cover of my lines. He knew I would do it too, and he cooled down considerably during the rest of the act.
>
> When the curtain fell, I picked up a stage brace [a persuasive instrument of wood and iron] and he made for his dressing room. He refused to go on again that night until the manager provided him with a bodyguard. It was funny to watch him scuttle from dressing room to stage and back, protected from his stage mother-in-law by a couple of able-bodied scene shifters.

The ferociously loyal Miss Dressler was also enraged by Perugini's female claque, which had taken to hissing Lillian when she made her entrance in *Princess Nicotine*. A few days later, on a Saturday matinee, Miss Dressler found them gathered, as usual, around the stage door:

96

Their chatter made me so sick that I climbed up on a convenient barrel and then and there made my first public speech. In plain, unvarnished English, I told those silly women the truth about their handsome idol. A few booed me at first, but before I finished, the crowd was silent and respectful. After that, there were no more hisses for Lillian.

Perugini had stopped harassing Lillian when they were onstage, but his offstage treatment of her worsened after *Princess Nicotine* closed and they appeared together in a revival of *Giroflé Girofla* at the Casino. He became particularly petulant over the *Dramatic Mirror* (the *Variety* of its day) review of the production, especially since he had always considered that Lillian's soprano served as a mere counterpoint to his brilliant tenor, a drab background for his vocal magnificence. But the *Dramatic Mirror* noted: "It is doubtful if Miss Russell ever sang the dual role as well as she did on Tuesday night, and she certainly never threw more spirit into the acting of it. Signor Perugini was more interesting from mere juxtaposition, as Merasquin, than he was effective either vocally or in acting."

The glorious voice of Don Giovanni Perugini a mere "juxtaposition" for that music-hall soprano? The *signor* was so outraged, as Marie Dressler wrote, that he became "more beastly than ever in private" to Lillian.

Billed as the Lillian Russell Light Opera Company, the *Giroflé Girofla* troupe and its embattled principals took the road, traveling through cities on the Eastern seaboard. By then it was common knowledge that Lillian and her husband were having domestic difficulties, to say the least, and that their passionate scenes behind the footlight were a mocking commentary on the reality of their relationship. During their appearance at Williamsburg, the audience roared with laughter when Perugini delivered the line, "I think it is a proper plan to take a business view of marriage."

In Philadelphia their quarreling took a physical turn. Finding himself unable to outbox Lillian by Marquis of Queens-

97

berry rules, Perugini tried to throw her out of the window of the seventh-floor hotel suite. Only the sudden appearance of a chambermaid prevented him from continuing the struggle.

Lillian then made the estrangement official and public and moved into a different hotel. *Giroflé Girofla* ended its tour in Newark, and Lillian retired to her Manhattan town house. There was so much newspaper speculation over the termination of her third marriage that finally, hoping to quiet the press, she issued a statement to be published in the New York *Herald*.

She began by reviewing her marital record, blaming the collapse of her first marriage on the fact that Harry Braham was many years older, the end of her second on Teddy Solomon's bigamous miscalculations. For eight years, she said, she had stayed single and done her best to please the public. Then along came the *signor*, who seemed to be "so artistic and refined . . . so spiritual and graceful of manner."

The morning after they were married, she continued, Perugini announced that he would decide who her friends were to be and that he intended to discharge all her servants. She would have gone along with that dictatorial program, she averred, if only he had "proven himself a husband worthy of the name."

There were bitter quarrels and "it was during one of these trying scenes that Signor Perugini admitted to me that he had never loved me, but that he had married me for artistic position purely. This proved to be true, as I have ascertained from a few of his most intimate friends to whom he boasted when our engagement was first made public that 'I joined the company to marry her. I played a strong card, and have won. We will be married, and I am sure of a position for life.' . . . Notwithstanding these quarrels, I determined to live with him as a sister and maintain at least the appearance of happiness before the world.

"But when Signor Perugini insulted my friends and used personal violence on me at the Hotel Stenton, in Philadelphia,

I felt that the end had come. I could not stand it any longer. My home is my only resting place. I could not allow him to live with me. I could not sing and be tormented. I have to tell these painful facts to assure the world that it was my desire to be a devoted wife to a man who showed that he had no right to marry any woman."

Lillian's statement sent Perugini into a towering tizzy. His response was to give an interview to a reporter from the *Tammany Times,* who appeared to be sympathetic as Perugini sobbed out his story of mistreatment at the hands of the Amazonian Russell but who went back to the weekly's office and wrote a story that slyly confirmed Lillian's insinuation that he was a poof.

"Do you realize the enormity of this woman's offense—her crime?" Perugini demanded, tears running down his cheeks. "Do you know what she did to me? Why, sir, when we had to share apartments, she took all my pillows; she used my rouge; she misplaced my manicure set; she used my special handkerchief perfume for her bath; she always wanted the best mirror when we were making our toilets, whether for the theater or street, and she usually got it. She's a desperate character, for all her smile is sweet for the public. Once when I became excited because she had moved my bandoline [a jar of pomade used for hairdressing], she threatened to spank me, and she did. With a hairbrush! You can't expect a fellow to take a spanking with equanimity, can you? That was the time she got scratched."

The *signor* was so beside himself, the *Tammany Times* reported, that he was planning to sue Lillian for alimony.

"She told me I'd have a good job, a regular snap," he wailed. "She said I wanted to turn off all her servants the first day of our honeymoon, but it was she who suggested that I might just as well make myself useful around the house while I had nothing else to do. I know her. I'm going to prove she was negotiating for another tenor. She said he was going to be my understudy, but I know she meant for me to stay at home. She once told me she saw no reason why I cared for fame, since I would be sufficiently honored through the applause she would receive."

Signor Perugini really showed his claws at the end of the interview when he remarked, "I want you to say she laces [that is, she wore corsets] and wears false hair and is horribly made up, and is not the least bit pretty off the stage!"

One can only wonder what the public made of those slightly muffled insinuations of homosexuality. Most people had never heard or read of sexual inversion, ancient though its history. Or perhaps that generation was in the position of its professional cynic Ambrose Bierce when he listened to his friends discussing in a Fleet Street pub the trial of a man charged with homosexuality in a London court. "Why," Bierce protested, "I never heard of such a crime before." To which one of his friends replied, "What the gentleman means is this. He never before heard that it was a crime."

Lillian was so disillusioned by marriage that she was almost ready to agree with Mama Leonard that men were unreliable brutes. She did not even bother to sue for divorce. At least her marriage to Perugini would serve the purpose of making it impossible for her to lose her head again. It was Perugini, four years later, who finally sued for divorce on charges that Lillian "abandoned" him. Presumably that charge was based on her refusal to allow him to throw her out of seventh-floor windows.

Yes, as Mama Leonard always said, it was the woman who paid. At least back in the 1890's, when the male was not only supreme but could do no wrong. A woman with three marriages on her record was presumed to be some kind of Jezebel, probably, or insatiable; and the fact that Lillian had simply lucked out on her choice of husbands was not taken into consideration. Besides, she was an actress and everyone knew how "fast" actresses were. Professional moralists rose from pulpits, editorial pages, lecture platforms, and soapboxes to denounce Lillian Russell for carelessly taking and discarding husbands. A Texas preacher won himself front-page space all over the country when he nominated Lillian Russell and Sarah Bernhardt as "the most eminent of fallen women."

At such times Lillian could always turn to Diamond Jim Brady for companionship and consolation, for reassurance that she was the nicest as well as the most glamorous woman on the American scene. Also, his mere existence proved that not all men were cads and bounders.

4

LOBSTER-PALACE ROYALTY

FROM the middle nineties to the end of World War I, as the accounts of the era's survivors and the researches of social historians make evident, New York glittered as never before or since. The lamps would go out all over the world with the coming of the 1914 war, as a British statesman observed, but it took Prohibition to dim the lights of the lobster-palace world. It was a curious irony that Prohibition came about as the direct result of women's suffrage, a movement in which Lillian Russell became energetically involved, and that Lillian herself was the uncrowned queen of that garish little world she helped to dim out.

The Broadway of that day was a compelling legend, a hallucination, a Cockaigne which made impossible promises of sensual delight. It shed a glow, perhaps only the phosphorescence of the decayed morality it represented to Anthony Comstock and other sin-killers, over the whole American scene—a glow all but unimaginable to anyone inspecting its present squalor. The Great White Way from Madison Square to Longacre Square (Times Square after 1903) was a city in itself that lived by night; its lifeblood was the electricity that blazed from Edison's light bulbs. Drably commercial by day, it assumed a frenetic and somewhat specious gaiety once the lights went on and the hansom cabs came clop-clopping from all parts of Manhattan Island.

It was the domain of a "society that flourished through the night but dissolved at dawn," as Lloyd Morris observed. "By day, its members recognized no affiliation; they moved in widely separated orbits. Evening revived their collective unity. They became citizens of Broadway, dwellers in the city of beautiful nonsense. Here they met on common ground—Wall Street financiers, industrial magnates, gilded fractions of the Four Hundred, gaudy playboys, journalists, celebrities from the Bohemia of the arts, the greatest stars of the theater, gamblers, jockeys, pugilists, professional beauties, chorus girls, kept women—notorious votaries of pleasure, the cynosures of a vast, prosperous public."

It was a demimonde, in which people careful of their reputations ventured incognito, even to such a relatively respectable place as Rector's on Longacre Square, where the decorum of the patrons was expected to be as impeccable as the service. "But a lady of fashion went to Rector's 'incognito,' " as a survivor of the era wrote. "If she had attended the theater in a low-necked frock, she must hurry home, change her dress, put on the largest and floppiest hat she owned, and then hope nobody would recognize her during her evening's adventures. Her escort would be bidden to select one of the less illuminated tables in a distant part of the room. If she went to Rector's décolleté, she put herself in a class with the feminine habitués who were not bound by caste or tradition. . . ." One of those habitués whom the slummer in the floppy hat might covertly stare at across the tables at Rector's was the beautiful and bold Anna Robinson, who had come from London bedecked with diamonds appraised at $800,000, which had been given her by an Australian millionaire for services rendered. Later she married an Anglo-Irish nobleman who relieved her of the Australian's diamonds, and in a conclusion satisfactory to the moralists she died penniless in the psychopathic ward at Bellevue.

It was part of a midtown Manhattan newly adorned with huge and luxurious hotels and restaurants decorated in the neorococo nineties style of immense crystal chandeliers, ornate moldings of plaster, gilt trimmings, walls covered with tapestries inspired by Gobelin, thick carpeting, red plush upholstery, an excess of everything but restraint, in an atmosphere of easy money and apparently boundless prosperity.

The entry fees into this world, the record is plain, were plenty of money vulgarly displayed and a reckless disregard of the effect of overeating and overdrinking on the human constitution. A genuine rounder also spent ten hours of his time, from nightfall to dawn, to make sure he touched all the bases. There was no creeping down dawn streets in fear of muggers, but there was a plentiful assortment of pickpockets, con men, prostitutes, panhandlers, and drug addicts. The real damage was done by late hours and overindulgence.

A night on the town, in classic style, was exhaustive. From various memoirs and other palimpsests of the era, it would seem that you started out with cocktails, following a route that began at the Hoffman House bar and continued to the bar of the Knickerbocker Hotel with Maxfield Parrish's celebrated mural of Old King Cole. The Knickerbocker, at Broadway and Forty-second Street, was known as the Forty-second Street Country Club. From there you proceeded to the bar of the new (now demolished) Astor Hotel on the west side of Longacre Square.

For dinner you plunged into the lobster-palace ambience: Louis Martin's Parisian restaurant on the site of the old Delmonico's, with its marble-topped tables, its plush banquettes, and its atmosphere of what one patron called "exotic impropriety"—the latter quality evidently provided by well-groomed women who loitered in the foyer and were rarely known to have refused an invitation. Or you could choose Shanley's lobster palace on Longacre Square, Louis Bustanoby's Café des Beaux Arts over on Sixth Avenue, Rector's palatial establishment on Longacre Square, or Delmonico's down on Madison Square. If you were a trifle less sportive, you might prefer one of the vast hotel dining rooms. The Imperial Hotel, with its Palm Room finished in green marble, was located at Broadway and Thirty-second Street. There was the Holland House just north of Madison Square on Fifth Avenue on which the then-phenomenal sum of $1,200,000 had been spent. Or the Waldorf-Astoria, which was completed in 1897, or the Savoy, on which Boss Tweed had spent $250,000 before the law caught up with him; it was completed by other men who added a bridal suite which duplicated the splendor of Marie Antoinette's boudoir in the Trianon Palace.

But it was Rector's restaurant, housed in a two-story yellow-facaded building on the east side of Broadway between Forty-third and Forty-fourth streets that was the centerpiece of this world, the extravaganza of the lobster-palace style, the top-drawer place for the conspicuous consumption of rich food, where a staff of sixty waiters, eight captains, and a score of busboys maintained a "service nonpareil." (For the mass, as opposed to the quality, dishing-out of food it could not compare with the Café de la Opera, on Forty-Second and Broadway across from the Knickerbocker, where more than 2,000 waiters served 20,000 dinners and suppers nightly.) Charles Rector, the founder, had worked as a conductor on the Second Avenue horsecars, managed the first Pullman dining car to cross the continent, and operated a restaurant in Chicago before opening the Broadway place. It took all his Chicago profits to put him in business on Broadway: The bill for the furnishings was said to have been $200,000. The decor was in green and gold, a soothing color scheme for his money-centered patrons, with an amiable mixture of Louis XIV and Byzantine styles. The red carpeting caressed your ankles. A Russian string orchestra played George M. Cohan airs with only an occasional lapse into the folk music of the Ukrainian steppes. The food was international and regularly included Egyptian quail, Scotch woodcock, English pheasant, African peaches, and French snails. Here Diamond Jim Brady was the reigning patron, Gustator Rex, "the best 25 customers we ever had," as Rector's son George flippantly expressed it.

After dinner you proceeded to one of the theaters, where the entertainment generally was of the sort not likely to tax the intellectual capacity of an audience whose collective belly rumbled with liquor, many-course dinners, and assorted wines. From the theater you went to supper and downed a rarebit or cold collation to keep your dinner tamped down. A trifle wobbly, perhaps, but doggedly determined to keep up with the pleasure-loving throng, you were swept along to one or more of the hundreds of cabarets, music halls, and deadfalls which blared on through the night from the Bowery to the Tenderloin or to one of the wide-open gambling houses which operated full blast until the killjoys voted in a reform administration. If you were still on your feet and had not been packed off to bed by fellow rounders, who stuffed you into a hansom cab and gave the cabbie your address, you would properly greet the dawn by breakfasting off Irish bacon and eggs at Jack Dunstan's near the Hippodrome on Sixth Avenue, now pompously restyled the Avenue of the Americas.

It was a time for full-blooded enjoyment, for uninhibited appreciation of the fleshly pleasures. There were no pricklings of social conscience over the sampling of the available pleasures at a time when millions of other Americans were struggling to keep body and soul together during the aftershocks of the panic of 1893.

As the late Lucius Beebe looked back on that vanished world of the high rollers and big spenders with a fond but undeceived eye:

> The lobster-palace set entered into the historic record. So did the places they frequented and the attitudes they assumed. Bet-a-Million Gates, Diamond Jim Brady, Stanford White, James R. Keene, Lillian Russell . . . are assured of a fragrant

immortality in the folklore of the land. . . . That the people who comprised the lobster-palace set were largely vulgarians of the first chop, often barbarians with the manners and attire of Texas and Oklahoma and the accents of Ohio well upholstered in diamonds and claw-hammer coats, has faded from their collective recollection. They have become an enviable era, like the never-never land of San Francisco "Before the Fire." They radiated good times and good humor and they spent money, always the ultimate American attribute of status, like crazy. . . .

It was generally believed by more sober-minded Americans that the lobster-palace world was one of the galleries of inferno. It became a part of American legend that the most beautiful girls of a generation sold their souls, or at least their virtue, for a warm bird (pheasant under glass) and a cold bottle (vintage champagne). The playwright Eugene Walter summed it all up in two lines of dialogue which brought down the curtain on his betrayed heroine, who with ringing defiance orders her maid: "Dress up my body and paint my face. I'm going to Rector's to make a hit—and to hell with the rest!"

By journalistic acclaim, at least, and with the general concurrence of their contemporaries, the uncrowned heads of that freewheeling world of pleasure were Jim Brady and Lillian Russell. They outspent, outate, and outlasted all pretenders to their unique supremacy. Watch them, in a flashback constructed from the dazzled recollections of their contemporaries, as they make an entrance at Rector's after the theater. Brady, with his diamonds winking like a showboat, almost distracting one from his small, shrewd eyes, his triple chin, his bulldog jaw, his moonlike red face, and a belly that seemed to sweep in an opulent curve from his sternum to his massive thighs. Russell with her imposing figure and her stately carriage, with a jiggle of flesh that caught every male eye. The entrance of Rector's was designed to serve as a showcase for the entrance of a Lillian Russell (or one of her rivals), with a play of lights to make certain she was noticed and a band of Hungarian gypsies with their violins weeping in the background. There is a low bow, almost a salaam, from the headwaiter as he convoys the majestic pair to their table. Jim acknowledges greetings from his peers. Miss Russell has her striking blue eyes fixed on the middle distance. No real queen ever walked more proudly. She moves down the center aisle under her plumed hat, with the long train of her evening dress trailing behind her, the layers of silk whispering, a gypsy fiddler sawing away in her wake, until she reaches her table. She seats herself without looking around, knowing that a waiter will be placing a chair under her celebrated bottom. Only then, slowly, tantalizingly removing her long gloves, does she look around and bow to acquaintances. The hush that attends the regal entrance ends, the diners return to their food and drink, and the waiters start converging on the Brady-Russell table.

It was all a production number, of course, as carefully staged as a scene in one of Lillian's theatrical appearances. Yet it was impressive enough to turn men's heads; her magnetism could transfix any male with normal eyesight at a hundred paces. Striking testimony to her sexual attraction was offered by a young Swiss immigrant named Oscar Tschirky, later the celebrated "Oscar of the Waldorf," but then a humble busboy at the Hoffman House. One evening when he left work and walked across Madison Square, he approached the main entrance of Delmonico's just as an important party of diners was leaving. "As I passed the doorman hurried forward and motioned a cab. I remember his exact words: 'Miss Russell's carriage, please!' At that moment the door was opened and Miss Russell came out with the party of friends. I was captivated by this fleeting glimpse. I remember the smooth flow of her blue gown, the exotic effect of her golden hair, but most of all the banked-down fire that smoldered in her beautiful face. She was the loveliest woman I had ever seen, lovelier than the picture on the poster I had stared at those first days I spent in New York. I could hear but a few snatched words, uttered in a clear, musical voice. Then her friends closed around her as she stepped into the carriage. . . ." That one glimpse was enough to send Oscar Tschirky over to Delmonico's the next morning to apply for a waiter's job, which he obtained, and the privilege of helping to feed that strikingly nonethereal love goddess of the nineties.

It occurred to a number of people that Lillian might have deliberately chosen the gross and unrefined Jim Brady, whom not even his most ferevent admirer would nominate for any male beauty awards, as her constant escort to point up and lend definition to her own opulent charms. No doubt she was unoffended by captions under photographs showing them together which usually read BEAUTY AND THE BEAST. No doubt she would have preferred that her escort was capable of a more polished address than that which he grunted as he hauled his 250-pound frame closer to the dining table: "Whenever I sit down to a meal, I always make a point to leave just four inches between my stummick and the edge of the table. And then, when I can feel 'em rubbin' together pretty hard, I *know* I've had enough."

Her own style was daintier than that, though she could match him steak for steak, lobster for lobster. Her own background was indelibly middle-class while his was indubitably that of the proletariat. But she valued him for his generosity, for the boyish smile that could light up his porcine features, for a delicacy of feeling no one else suspected the existence of beneath those layers of lard. She didn't need his gifts of jewelry, but she knew that he was more flattered by her acceptance of the diamonds he brought back from every road trip than she was by receiving them. She could trust Jim—not only his personal honesty, but the integrity which would not allow him to take advantage of her when she was lonely or depressed by emotional failures with other men. They were friends, and that was good enough for both of them. Most Broadway palships lasted about as long as a Mazda bulb, but this one, like the diamonds with which they decked themselves, was forever.

The friendship which burgeoned during the year following their meeting at the exposition was interrupted when they went their separate ways to England and the Continent in 1894. Lillian's journey was a flight from yet another outbreak of managerial troubles. She had been lured from the producing firm of Lederer and Canary by that of Abbey, Schoeffel, and Grau, the latter partnership promising her that they would groom her for and eventually present her in grand opera. The transition to the great classical roles was something she had been studying, practicing, and yearning for through the years.

Naturally Lederer and Canary objected to having their star box office attraction snatched away from them and obtained an injunction to prevent her from appearing under the new management. A squad of private detectives assigned to serving her with Lederer and Canary's writ laid siege to her house on West Seventy-seventh Street.

Lillian, however, was becoming adept at outwitting and outdistancing former employers, a necessary art for an actress in those pre-Equity days. Somehow she slipped through the cordon around her house without being tagged by the process servers. During her English sabbatical her new managers settled the contractual dispute with Lederer and Canary for a reported $30,000. Such wrangles were seldom likely to reach the courtroom because invariably both parties—despite the canons of the New York Bar—were represented by the same firm, Abe Hummel and William Howe, which at least saved a lot of judicial headaches.

In London her new producers established her at the Irving Theater, in Ellen Terry's dressing room, and presented her in *The Queen of Brilliants*, a trifling operetta of which only two acts had been completed when rehearsals began. Despite its helter-skelter presentation, London found the operetta satisfactory and its star more than charming. The social establishment, even royalty, lionized her, and she was presented to the Prince of Wales at a dinner party at Lord Rothschild's house, where she was to receive a $2,500 fee for singing a few songs.

"They appeared to enjoy the songs," she wrote later, "and

the Prince told me that he had enjoyed listening to my voice, and thanked me for singing the songs of his favorite composer, Tosti. He repeated again the wish that I would not leave England. When the ladies retired to the drawing room, I found myself among numerous Princesses and Duchesses, but I found them not at all antagonistic or patronizing. It was amusing to me to discover that they were exactly like all other women I had met all over the world. They wanted to know what kind of powder I used, whether my hair was naturally golden, how I kept my face free from wrinkles. They wanted beauty recipes and charm recipes."

If they were hoping for magic ointments and secret potions, the royal ladies instead heard a lecture on keeping regular hours and avoiding excesses in food and drink. Before she left England, Lillian was lectured in turn by Sir Henry Irving for leaving her jewels in the dressing room at his theater overnight. Sir Henry was amazed to learn what she used for a jewel case. "You were wrong to be so careless as to leave such valuable jewelry behind you in the dressing room, but you were mighty right to leave it in a soap box!"

Lillian returned home more or less triumphantly to appear in a New York production of her London success, but Broadway refused to be dazzled by *The Queen of Brilliants*. Abbey, Schoeffel, and Grau saved themselves from bankruptcy by reviving her old standby *The Grand Duchess* and followed it up with the equally durable *La Perichole*. Meanwhile, they were waiting for Reginald De Koven and Harry B. Smith to finish writing an operetta, *The Tzigane*, especially for Lillian.

Smith, the librettist, had attended public school in Chicago with Lillian and her sisters and was pleased to find that success had not spoiled her. "She was a woman of great charm and amiability, wholly without affectation," he would write in his autobiography. "She had a great sense of humor, too, which perhaps accounted for some of her marriages." Artistically, Smith would have to admit the reunion was not a success. "We wrote *The Tzigane,* the scene of which was laid in Russia in 1812. The idea was suggested to me by Tschaikovsky's '1812 Overture,' which was arranged for the finale of the second act and sung in connection with an original spectacular effect. On the first night in New York this finale was a sensation; but the opera was one of the things that seem born to bad luck. Few people could pronounce the title and still fewer had any idea of what it meant [It meant gypsy]. . . . Miss Russell did not like her part. Flora Finlayson, a brilliant contralto, had an effective role, and Miss Russell, 'the Queen of Comic Opera,' was not starring to exploit a member of her company. . . ."

Aside from all that, Lillian was clamoring for her managers to keep their promises and make her a grand opera star. Didn't everyone say she had a lyric soprano of extraordinary range and bell-like quality? Well, not quite everyone. The highbrow critic James Giddons Huneker had risked lynching by comparing her voice to the whistle of a tea kettle, and Reginald De Koven, then a critic with equally lofty standards, had delivered the opinion that her role in *La Perichole* just about stretched the limits of her pleasing but not quite world-shaking talent and warned that "hard and reckless work will ere long spoil her brilliant and powerful voice."

Word got around the musical world in 1895 that her managers were planning to present Lillian in *Lohengrin, Faust,* and other operatic vehicles, and Lillian did not deny the rumors. She had never lost her sense of proportion, however, and she listened carefully to her true friends when they argued that few singers had ever made the leap from light to heavy opera. Nellie Melba, it was said, delivered the clinching argument when she told Lillian: "You're the queen of light opera, with no serious rivals. If you take up grand opera, you will risk comparison with Nordica, Calvé, Sembrich and me. It means beginning all over for you. You will have to face internal rivalries and bitter enemies who will resent your intrusion on the classical stage. Right now all of us love you, because you do not compete with us. But I warn you as your friend that if you become a competitor we shall hate you. And I don't want that to happen for your sake and mine."

That insight into the dark and stormy world backstage at the opera apparently convinced Lillian that she should be content with the laurels of popular success, the adoration of the peanut gallery rather than the cultivated braying of the dress circle. Besides, did Nellie Melba have *her* profile decorating the band of a popular five-cent cigar? Had Emma Calvé ever been the unwitting cause of a six-shooter homicide out in the wilds of Nevada? Was the great Madame Nordica's talent and presence so overwhelming that she had been the cause of one of the most spectacular suicides ever devised?

The shooting had occurred in a dispute over whether Lillian Russell was more beautiful than Lola Montez, the pseudo-Spanish dancer who had turned royal heads earlier in the century and temporarily disrupted the government of Bavaria. A cowpuncher named Dave Colfax carried Lillian's picture in his saddle roll. He frequently took it out and displayed it in saloons, turning nasty if anyone disagreed with his pronouncement that Lillian was the most beautiful woman God ever made. Unfortunately, he made a saloon friendship with another cowhand named José Madero. A rift subsequently developed when Colfax learned that Madero passionately believed that the world beauty title belonged to Lola Montez, whom he mistakenly considered to have been Spanish (actually she was born in Limerick, Ireland). They decided to compare pictures of the two women. Colfax brought out his tattered oleograph of Lillian Russell; Madero found a picture of Lola Montez in his own saddlebag.

An aesthetic dispute arose, which Madero terminated by whipping out his revolver and shooting Lillian's image through the nose. Colfax defended the honor of Anglo-Saxon womanhood by shooting Madero dead. Colfax was brought to trial. The pictures of Lillian and Lola were offered in evidence. When the jury was shown the dastardly injury done Lillian

Russell's profile, Nevada chivalry was tested and found durable. Its verdict: justifiable homicide.

Perhaps even more striking testimony to Lillian's fascination was provided by one Hippolyte Schneider, a machinist who lived in Niagara Falls, New York, and all but impoverished himself and his wife and daughter by making trips to New York City to moon over his idol across the footlights. He repeatedly sent Lillian letters pleading with her to marry him but was tactfully turned down. Finally, in despair, Hippolyte Schneider stood on the ledge at Goat Island one morning and shot himself, then plunged over Niagara Falls to his death.

Happily, most of Lillian's faceless admirers were able to reconcile themselves to the fact they would never be able to claim her in the flesh.

If there was any sort of subconscious competition between Brady and Russell over who could attract the most publicity, Diamond Jim was managing to hold up his end. On his own semigrand tour overseas, he was greeted with almost as much newspaper attention as Lillian at her West End theater. Jim, however, didn't have much time for hobnobbing with royalty or the Rothschilds. He headed straight for Leeds, where he spent most of his time in England as the guest of Sampson Fox and trotting around the expanding shops of the Leeds Forge Company. He even managed to endear himself to the English workingmen, who at first were inclined to sneer at him as a Yank blowhard swanking around like a circus elephant in all his diamond gewgaws. They came to respect him for his technical knowledge; it was a rare sight for the English craftsmen to watch a nabob getting his hands dirty in the shops and asking questions that made sense. And he won all the hearts of oak by hosting a mammoth beer bust before leaving Leeds.

He found Paris less stimulating, though he may have been gratified by the Parisians' astonishment at the way he spent money and scattered tips. Apparently he was surprised in turn by the fact that the French spoke a language of their own, which he referred to as "damn foreign gabble." The Eiffel Tower was a structure to command a steelman's respect, and French cuisine was something he could wholeheartedly approve of, but he cut his European tour short and hastened back to the United States.

His excuse was a cable from Chicago stating that the horseless carriage he had ordered from its manufacturer was ready for delivery. His most pressing ambition of the moment, in keeping with his determination to maintain a coequal celebrity status with Lillian Russell, was to be the first man to display himself on the streets of New York in a horseless carriage.

The vehicle which figured in Brady's claim to fame as an automotive pioneer of sorts was an electric brougham hand-crafted in the shops of the A. H. Woods carriage factory in Chicago. He hurried from the New York docks to Chicago to inspect the vehicle. It was powered by storage batteries and had a cruising range of thirty-six miles. In appearance it was something like an ambulatory phone booth, and there was room only for the driver and one passenger. Because of its awkward proportions, being taller than it was long, it could not be maneuvered into an ordinary freight car but had to be shipped to New York lashed to a flat car.

Brady himself would not drive the devilish new contraption, which could attain a top speed of eleven miles an hour. Instead he hired as chauffeur a black mechanic at the Woods factory, William Johnson, at the then princely salary of $35 a week.

The electric car was kept in a livery stable on West Fifty-seventh Street, where Thomas A. Edison's company had installed battery-charging equipment. Brady was determined not to make a fool of himself when he exhibited his new toy and ordered Johnson to make trial runs on the New York streets every morning between three and four o'clock.

To get the maximum publicity value out of what he was certain would be regarded as a historic event, he decided to stage his exhibition on a Saturday morning on Fifth Avenue between Fifty-seventh Street and Madison Square, when the thoroughfare would be thronged with shoppers. Aside from an advance tipping of various city desks to make sure reporters and photographers were on hand, there was no announcement that Diamond Jim Brady would drive the first horseless carriage on the streets of New York; he wanted it to be a surprise for his fellow citizens. And it was. It was damn near a panic. People took the event calmly enough, but horses, as though sensing the machine spelled the end of their utility, objected violently to the debut of Brady's new vehicle.

The journey started out smoothly enough as Johnson, attired crisply in a bottle-green uniform that would not have shamed a Hungarian admiral, and Brady, in silk hat and diamonds, tooled out of the livery stable and headed eastward on Fifty-seventh Street. They reached the turn into Fifth Avenue without mishap, perhaps because there was little carriage traffic on the crosstown street that early in the morning. The electric machine purred along while people on the sidewalks gaped. It was known, of course, that such vehicles had been developed and had been tried out on country roads, but no one expected to see one on a New York street before the end of the century, when all sorts of miracles were promised.

With a yapping escort of mongrels in their wake, Brady and his chauffeur moved down Fifth Avenue at a ten-mile-an-hour clip. The first sign of trouble came when a team drawing a victoria with a dignified old lady as its passenger reared, snorted, and bolted down Fifth Avenue. Before they reached Thirty-sixth Street, according to the newspaper accounts, five horse-drawn vehicles suffered likewise. The machine, however, functioned perfectly. It appeared that the motorcar was ready to take up its burden but that the world that spring day in 1895 wasn't quite ready for it. Seventy-five years later it would appear that horses had more sense than people when they revolted at the sight of a horseless carriage.

Significantly enough, the first appearance of an automobile caused the first traffic jam. As Jim and his electric brougham approached Madison Square, the traffic was much heavier. His progress was halted while mounted police reserves were brought to the scene and tried to sort out the tangle of horse-drawn carriages and drays and hansom cabs, along with thousands of people who pressed around Brady's vehicle for a closer look at the new marvel. There was jeering from some members of the throng, and the first mocking cry of "Get a horse!" which would bedevil so many motorists bogged down by the wayside in the coming years, was heard in Madison Square.

Jim, who had not counted on quite that much public attention, got out of his conveyance and with some annoyance strode over to the bar of the Hoffman House while the police went to work on the problem he had brought them.

He sipped a lemon soda and accepted the congratulations of his friends until Chauffeur Johnson appeared with the word that the police had the situation under control. They drove back to the livery stable without causing much more commotion. Next morning he opened the Sunday papers to find they had given him front-page treatment under such headlines as:

JAMES B. BRADY DRIVES FIRST
HORSELESS CARRIAGE SEEN
IN NEW YORK CITY
Startling Happenings in Madison
Square as Traffic Is Tied
Up for Two Hours

He was gratified not only by the two- and three-column stories lavished on his escapade on the front pages of all the New York Sunday papers but by the reference to him as a "gentleman sportsman." What an accolade for a jumped-up traveling salesman. What a country in which you could become a gentleman in four decades. Less pleasing was a gently phrased communiqué from police headquarters that henceforth he would be allowed to use his frightening machine within the city limits only in the late-night hours when most of the horses were off the streets.

That regulation was soon abated as so many other well-heeled citizens, following Brady as a leader of fashion, began buying electric cars and the more powerful, more terrifying machines powered by gasoline or steam. An automobile in those early years sounded like a condensed version of a Chinatown New Year's celebration. A year after Brady's history-making run down Fifth Avenue there were quite a few Duryea and Benz automobiles disrupting traffic in New York, and on Memorial Day, 1896, there was a race from the City Hall to the suburban Ardsley Country Club. Alfred G. Vanderbilt turned into a speed demon and outraged the police by going eighteen miles an hour, eight over the limit. A cop on a bicycle patrol chased him up to Harlem and made the collar when Vanderbilt's big red touring car bogged down in a mudhole. J. Pierpont Morgan's coupe knocked down a woman pedestrian on Park Row and didn't bother to stop; he may well have been the country's first hit-and-run driver. The Duke of Manchester, visiting New York with his American-born wife, was indignant when he was refused a driver's license because of his reckless behavior behind the wheel, complaining that "a duke who is fit to be trusted with an American wife" ought to be trusted with an American automobile. No wonder the president of Princeton, Woodrow Wilson, warned that "nothing has spread socialistic feeling in this country more than the use of the automobile . . . they are a picture of the arrogance of wealth."

Obviously Brady had started something with his dash down Fifth Avenue. Automobiling in those early days was an exclusive sport, something like tiger hunting, and that was why it attracted him. Neither he nor his contemporaries considered the automobile to be a future means of mass transportation any more than it seemed possible the airplane tested by the Wright brothers in 1903 would one day wreck the railroad industry. Brady, however, did not participate in such sporting events as the Vanderbilt Cup races. He preferred to be driven by a chauffeur, with a footman in attendance, because it had more class, and he retired from automobiling competition with his much-prized designation of "millionaire sportsman." Journalistic recognition was enough for him. He knew he would never be accepted by Mrs. Astor or the mincing cotillion leaders, who regarded him as a cut below a parvenu.

Yet there was a sector where finance, sport, organized lechery, and the moneyed aristocracy converged and where his pedigree was of less importance than his wealth and his commercial aptitudes.

The locus of Brady's New York life for many years was America's newest and most elegant pleasure dome, the Waldorf-Astoria, which had just been constructed at the corner of Fifth Avenue and Thirty-fourth Street on the site of *the* Mrs. Astor's old mansion. Its public rooms—Peacock Alley, the Palm Garden, the Rose and Empire rooms—were the velvet jungle in which the leading predators of the city prowled. To enhance his position as a man of affairs, Jim had persuaded his mother to give up her boarding house and install her in a house on Lexington Avenue, at which he also resided when not on the road. She was a difficult old lady who had discovered a taste for fine old brandy, but Jim knew that a good Irishman's first duty was to his mother, one of the rare subjects on which Mrs. Brady agreed with him.

His real home, however, was the Waldorf-Astoria, where he could rub elbows with such personages as J. P. Morgan, John W. "Bet-a-Million" Gates, James R. Keene, Judge William H. Moore, and Judge Elbert H. Gary—all magnates of the top drawer in industry, business, banking, and Wall Street speculation. The Men's Café in the late afternoon was the gathering place of those moguls, who could sit under its high, ornately carved ceiling, brood over the day's missteps or triumphs downtown, and plot more capitalistic mischief with their equals. Banknotes in large denominations were the only entry requirements. Jim therefore was qualified and became the drinking companion (nothing stronger than orange juice or lemon soda for him) of the most powerful men in America. He was invited to attend the high-rolling baccarat and poker games over which Bet-a-Million Gates presided upstairs in a

$20,000-a-year suite. And Jim plunged in, even when the stakes became too high for the more cautious members of the Men's Café clique. During one all-night baccarat session more than one million dollars changed hands.*

High-rollers, men who not only had the liquid assets but the willingness to hazard them with the unflinching manner of real sports anywhere, were the only ones Gates would admit to his games. Cautious types who kept nervously counting their chips were shunned like plague-carriers. Once Judge Elbert H. Gary, the artificer of the United States Steel trust, went up to the door, with a waiter posted outside to keep cheapskates away, while Gates, Brady, and several others were playing poker with a $1,000 limit. Judge Gary was the number-one legal expert on how to maneuver around the provisions of the Sherman Act, but that didn't give him any standing as a big-time poker player. Gary told the waiter to go in and tell Gates that he wanted to sit in on the game. Gates heard the petition, rolled his cigar from one corner of his mouth to the other, then said, "Tell Judge Gary the game is going to be so high it would be over his head." The board chairman of U.S. Steel bowed his head and slunk down the corridor.

Jim Brady's portly figure was also on display several hours daily along Peacock Alley, a wide, first-floor corridor finished in amber marble which extended for 300 feet along the Thirty-fourth Street side of the hotel from the carriage entrance to the foyer, and later in the crystalline Palm Garden where full evening dress was required.

During National Horse Show Week every nabob and society queen in America seemed to have converged on the Waldorf. The horses pranced around the tanbark of Madison Square

---

* On this occasion, according to a historian of the period, "One of the crowd sitting in was a man who started off drinking highballs, and he kept it up throughout. He won. The more he drank, the higher his stacks grew. The lowest chip was for $100. At the end, the winner of the biggest pile was so inebriated he could not count. . . . He half-rose and, exclaiming, 'Oh, hell I've won a million!' he caught up the great stacks of chips in his arms, swept them to the floor and fell sprawling over them. . . ."

Garden while their owners and admirers preened themselves along Peacock Alley. People came from all over the United States to stand or sit along the marble walls of Peacock Alley and look upon the wealthiest, the most glamorous and notorious of their fellow citizens close up and in the flesh. No other tourist attraction, with the possible exception of a guided tour of fake opium pads in Chinatown, could rival it.

A sense of the pageantry offered by the Waldorf was conveyed in the awed dispatch of a Midwestern newspaperman:

> The great gilt clock in the main hall of the big hotel chimed midnight. All around, in the vast, outstretching corridors, there swarmed and swirled in a bewildering maze an endless, shifting crowd of men and women, the men all attired in formal evening dress, the women resplendent in gorgeous creations of the dressmaker's and milliner's arts. . . . From the big music gallery came the strains of a Strauss waltz, scarcely audible with the chatter of 5,000 voices, filling every nook and corner of the corridors. For a full hour after the show was over at the Garden, the revolving doors of the ten entrances to the hotel sang a steady song of whirring monotony, and there swept in a wonderful gathering. The country folks who had come to see and be dazzled feasted their eyes on the stream of men and women who had come to be seen. . . . The real horse show was there in the stretches of the dining room. . . . Until two in the morning there was no let-up in the music, the popping of corks, the incessant chatter and babble of voices. . . .

The Waldorf's public rooms were not only what one social historian called "a rallying point for big business"—the place from which the movers and shakers of Wall Street operated, with the big board downtown at the stock exchange merely serving as a seismic record of deals made at the Waldorf—but the capital of the American Dream. If you were accepted there by Oscar Tschirky and his ducal-mannered headwaiters, you had it made, you were one of the elect. The Men's Café alone, it was said, was appointed, designed, and conducted to provide a close approximation of the atmosphere of one of the more exclusive London clubs on St. James Street or Pall Mall.

Oscar's approval may not have been the equivalent of being listed in society's studbook, but it certified you as a 24-carat member of the conspicuous consumption club. Oscar's bows were even lower and his Swiss diplomatist's manner even more obsequious—naturally enough—when Jim Brady appeared in the Palm Garden with Lillian Russell on his arm.

One night they accidentally inscribed their benchmark on the gustatory history of their time. When they reached the dessert course in the Palm Garden, Miss Russell was indulging in one of her infrequent spoiled-darling moods to Brady's amusement. First she ordered ice cream, but that wasn't quite what she wanted. Then she decided on cantaloupe. "Why not have both?" Jim suggested, unaware that he would be adding an item to the American menu for all time. The waiter returned with half a cantaloupe in which a scoop of vanilla ice cream was imbedded. On the spot the dessert was christened Cantaloupe à la Lillian Russell, which placed her alongside Nellie Melba (Peach Melba) in the annals of inspired confectionery.

5

ON A BICYCLE BUILT FOR THREE

DURING the latter part of the nineties there were unwelcome hints in the press and from the public that America might prefer its love goddess to present a somewhat less voluptuous silhouette. There were ominous signs that corpulence was beginning to go out of fashion, that the hourglass figure for women and the aldermanic belly for men were becoming passé; perhaps the lingering depression of '93 had something to do with the trend. The most popular illustrator for the magazines was Charles Dana Gibson, who specialized in square-shouldered, flat-bellied young men and whose famous "Gibson girl" wore mannish shirtwaists and trimly tailored skirts which looked good only on slender figures. And there was the theatrical sensation caused by Frankie Bailey, with her racehorse legs, and Anna Held, with her elfin face and body, to indicate a change in popular tastes.

Lillian had always been proud of her country-girl appetite, but now she was beginning to regard it as a handicap. There was an ominous new word on everyone's lips: "slenderizing." How worrisome it was to hear that Anna Held tipped the scales at ninety-five pounds. How irritating it was to read in *Town Topics*, which had always been so fervent in its admiration of her, that a girl just elevated from the chorus ranks named Edna May posed a threat to her supremacy on the musical stage. ("Edna May is now what Lillian Russell was," the treacherous and fickle Colonel Mann wrote, "when I first saw her at Tony Pastor's on Lower Broadway in *Pinafore*. . . . Will the Casino managers allow her to remain as she is, or will she be subject to the same experience as Lillian Russell . . . and to be taught that champagne is cheaper than lager beer if somebody else pays for it . . . ?"

An unkindly and uncalled-for remark. What had she done to merit the displeasure of raffish old Colonel Mann?

And if she was still queen of the musical stage, why did another critic write so condescendingly of her performance in *The Goddess of Truth*, which opened on Broadway early in 1896: "Lillian Russell is an affable, kindly creature. She shows her audiences all they can expect for their money. She is as filling as a plum pudding. . . . When you go to Abbey's, you'll see not only her diamonds, but some ultra-gorgeous gowns, and as much pectoral flesh as she can reasonably be expected to exhibit."*

The grim prospects of diet and exercise loomed before her. She had been a star too long to yield her place on the marquee to younger and slimmer women simply because she could not resist ten-course dinners and because practicing her scales daily had been all the exercise she felt like taking.

Thus began a long and arduous struggle to contain those billowing curves regarded as so admirable only a few years before. It was an on-again-off-again campaign until she finally retired from the theater. In 1899 a New York newspaper reported on the success of her effort to eliminate all that excessive weight. At the start it was evident she was literally a

---

* There was also considerable journalistic criticism of Lillian when her father died on October 11, 1896, and she did not attend the funeral in Detroit. To do so, as she explained, she would have had to close down her current show, *An American Beauty*, and her fellow performers would have lost a week's pay. She also explained in a magazine article that her father was such a thorough-going professional that he would have understood her absence from his funeral.

heavyweight by prize-ring standards. She weighed 186 pounds, with a 42-inch bust and a 27-inch waist.

After eight weeks of dieting she had managed to reduce herself to a welterweight, bringing herself down to 156 pounds, with a 38-inch bust and a 22-inch waist.

Her friend Jim Brady was even quicker to sense that blubber was going out of style, perhaps because he had a lot more to worry about than Lillian. He was constitutionally fat, but there was no reason he couldn't tackle the problem in a businesslike way and look a little less like a beached whale.

Just then, according to the recollections of Oscar of the Waldorf, Brady began putting a damper on his appetite. "He would start off his supper with a dozen raw oysters. Then he would usually have a small filet mignon with one green vegetable. For dessert there would be either a slice of apple pie or a portion of watermelon, if it were in season. His only beverage was a glass of orange juice." (All of that, of course, was what he regarded as a "light supper," and had followed breakfast, lunch, and dinner of possibly heroic proportions. It still represented a considerable comedown from his usual feeding habits.) Lillian, not having succumbed at the time to the slenderizing craze, and his other guests had oysters, soup, fish, roast, two vegetables, sherbet, salad, ice cream, and cake, as Oscar recalled. No doubt it was an understatement when he added, "I had the surprise and disillusionment of my lifetime that night. Lillian Russell ate more than 'Diamond Jim.'" Shock waves must have emanated that night from the Waldorf to the rest of the restaurant world: Diamond Jim Brady on a diet. What was the world coming to? Only a few months before he had given a dinner for a party of fifty at the Waldorf; the price was $250 a head, and the feasting went on from four o'clock one afternoon to nine o'clock the next morning.

Jim, in fact, had just been advised by his physician—the first of many such advisories from the medical world—that he was packing too much weight for a man just past forty. He hadn't taken any more serious exercise than pushing himself away from the table since his stickball days down on the lower West Side, but now he was urged to consider it. At first he bought a couple of saddle horses and went riding on the Central Park bridle paths every morning before breakfast, but that didn't seem to have much effect. The horse, after all, got most of the exercise.

Just then a new fad was taking hold, which seemed to be the answer to Jim's and Lillian's yearning for less poundage. With the automobile only a smudge of smog on the horizon—"motoring" for many years would be the sport of the kind of dashing fellows who went tiger hunting in India or swam the Hellespont—America had fallen violently in love with the bicycle.

This was largely the result of a technological breakthrough. The first bicycles were tricky affairs with a huge front wheel and a tiny rear one, which only an acrobat could handle with ease. In the past decade, however, manufacturers had developed a bicycle with two equal-sized wheels and a chain-and-sprocket mechanism and other features which made cycling simpler, easier, and safer. Soon half the population of New York seemed to have taken up cycling; the streets, park pathways, and suburban roads streamed with the traffic, and at night it was said that Manhattan streets looked as though they were "filled with fireflies" from the flitting of bicycle lamps.

At first the clergy and other professional alarmists inveighed against the sport as, somehow, conducive to a breakdown in public morality, though just what a mixed twosome on a bicycle could to to invite temptation was not explained. The Reverend Asa D. Blackburn thundered from the pulpit of the Church of the Strangers that "You cannot serve God and skylark on a bicycle." The New York papers published editorials decrying what was called "blazing"—that is, pedaling along at madly reckless speeds.

Soon enough the tide turned in favor of the bicycle among public opinion leaders. Those like Cynthia Leonard and Susan B. Anthony, who labored in the vineyard of women's emancipation, declared that cycling, somehow, was doing more to lib-

Poster of Lillian Russell's appearance in *An American Beauty*
(New York Public Library)

Lillian Russell in *Brigands*

(The Bettmann Archive)

Lillian Russell in one of her celebrated roles as a Grand Duchess

(The Bettmann Archive)

Diamond Jim Brady being presented with a silver cup at Delmonico's

(Museum of the City of New York)

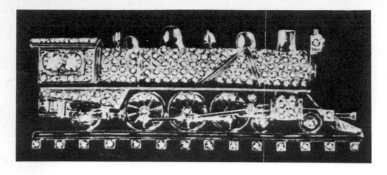

Eyeglass case in the form of a locomotive studded with 210 diamonds, which was part of Diamond Jim's $100,000 "Transportation Set"

(New York Public Library)

Lillian Russell and her husband Edward Solomon, 1883

(The Bettmann Archive)

Lillian Russell with one of her "winning bets" at Saratoga Springs

(Brown Brothers)

Edna McCauley, who
eloped with . . .

Jessie Lewisohn, who was
long Lillian Russell's companion

(both photos
Culver Pictures, Inc.)

Diamond Jim Brady with friends at the races

(Brown Brothers)

Old friends reunite for benefit performance at Globe Theater, May 23, 1920. *Front row, left to right:* Joe Weber, Lillian Russell, Lew Fields. *Back row:* J. J. Corbett and Sam Bernard

(*Brown Brothers*)

erate their sex than any number of street demonstrations. On wheels, at least, men and women were equal. The sedate Frances Willard, as president of the Women's Christian Temperance Union, announced that she too had been converted to the sport. High society was quick to succumb to the craze and even quicker to institutionalize it, a proper pecking order being established through the Michaux Club, near Columbus Circle, where the bluebloods set out on their wheels for the pathways of Central Park. Really sporty types from the Broadway sector took to the tandem bike so they could show off their girlfriends. Young couples, properly chaperoned, of course, would ride up through Central Park on a Sunday afternoon, then along Riverside Drive past Grant's Tomb to the Claremont Inn for dinner in a garden strung with Japanese lanterns. Tin Pan Alley quickly provided background music with "On a Bicycle Built for Two."

Lillian Russell and a short time later Jim Brady seized upon cycling as a solution to their weight problems. She appeared on the paths of Central Park in a costume of white serge with leg-of-mutton sleeves, usually with the pug-faced Marie Dressler puffing along behind her. Her enthusiasm for cycling grew as the weight began to drop off. "Every morning, rain or shine," as Miss Dressler recalled in her autobiography, "we would climb on our wheels and, bending low over the handlebars, give an imitation of two plump girls going somewhere in a hurry. Our route was nearly always the same. Into Central Park for a turn or two around the Reservoir. Afterwards, if we weren't panting too painfully, we would wheel over to Judge Smith's impressive house for a pre-luncheon call." Judge Smith was a sporty, well-heeled old gentleman with advanced ideas, who gave Lillian and Marie perfumed cigarettes to puff after making sure the draperies were drawn. Later they would wheel down Lexington Avenue to pay a call on Jim Brady.

Brady was infected by their enthusiasm for the sport and decided to take it up himself. Naturally his career as a cyclist had to be gaudier and more expensive than anyone else's; a career he mapped as carefully as any sales campaign. First he had a bicycle specially manufactured for him to withstand the rigors of carrying his weight. Then, as his personal mahout, he engaged one Dick Barton, who had ridden a trick cycle in the circus. Barton was his instructor and aide-de-camp when he ventured on the paths of Central Park.

Then Jim, his enthusiasm for the sport growing, ordered a dozen bicycles on which he and his friends could take Sunday excursions. He decided that he and his friends could hardly afford to be seen in public on wheels just like everyone else's. They must be gold-plated! "And while we're at it," he told Dick Barton, "maybe we'll have a few diamonds sprinkled on the handlebars to give 'em a touch of class." According to the story that soon circulated among those who regarded him as an overblown vulgarian, he loaded his dozen bicycles into an express wagon and hauled them down to Tiffany's. The purveyors of gold dinner plate to the Astors and Whitneys would have nothing to do with such an outlandish project as goldplating bicycles. Now his blood was up. He and his agents scoured the city until they found an electroplating shop on John Street operated by one William Mock, who was willing to take on the assignment. At Brady's orders Mock built a special tank for the job, electroplated the dozen cycles with gold, except for the spokes of the wheels, which were plated with silver. Every few weeks the whole batch was taken down to John Street for a fresh plating, so Jim and his friends always wheeled around on machines that looked as though they had just been issued by the United States Mint.

For Lillian, of course, a special job had to be turned out. It was not only gold-plated and silver-spoked but had her monogram in diamonds and emeralds imbedded on the handlebars. It was kept in a huge leather envelope lined with plush and was always taken with her on her theatrical tours.

Jim and Lillian, and sometimes a covey of their friends, made a suitably spectacular apppearance on the Central Park pathways. Traffic came to a halt as the golden procession whizzed by. Jim and his friends also undertook Sunday excursions to the Jersey shore. Their bicycles would be loaded into a wagon under the supervision of Dick Barton and conveyed to the Forty-second Street ferry. The party would mount up over on the Jersey side and pedal along to a German beer garden in Guttenberg, where the brass band struck up his favorite tunes as soon as Brady, in his plaid cycling suit with white gaiters and sometimes a deerstalker hat, appeared at the head of his party. They also stopped at a beer garden in Elizabethport and similar resorts every few miles along the route while Jim stoked his metabolism with pig's knuckles and sauerkraut and his friends sank seidels of Würzburger. Since they usually ended their tour with a large dinner in Bayonne, it would appear that Jim's weight-losing program was not greatly benefited by his Sundays on wheels.

Eventually, when tandem bicycles became popular, Jim felt compelled to maintain his reputation for excess by having fabricated a triple-seater. On this contraption, which caused collisions between gawkers cycling in Central Park, he would ride on the first seat, one of his lady friends (often Lillian Russell) on the second. Riding postern would be his cycling adviser, Dick Barton, who not only had to do the heavy-duty pumping on the hills but carried a gallon container of orange juice strapped to his back. Invariably when Brady's bicycle-built-for-three reached a certain hillock near the Eighty-sixth Street entrance of the park, he and his fellow riders halted for refreshment.

Disregarding KEEP OFF THE GRASS signs, blandly overlooking the fact that the Duke of Marlborough himself had recently been arrested on this same spot for lolling on the greensward, they climbed off their bicycle, sprawled on the grass, and drank orange juice. Often Lillian rested her back against a keep-off sign. The constabulary, instead of hauling them off in a paddy wagon, formed a ring to keep the crowd of celebrity-watchers which quickly gathered from pressing too close. The reason for the police protection became obvious when Jim and company finally pedaled away: He always gave each cop a five-dollar bill for services rendered.

Jim lost interest in the sport eventually when the Germania Cycle Club of Brooklyn, practicing what he regarded as a typically Teutonic form of one-upmanship, came tooling out with a six-man bicycle.

The late nineties were not all carefree self-indulgence for either Jim or Lillian. Jim had personal problems which soured his life, and Lillian was beginning to find it difficult to maintain her status as the queen of the musical theater, what with the competition growing younger and prettier every season.

Jim's troubles stemmed principally from his mother. Mrs. Brady was determined to keep her younger son firmly attached to her apron strings, especially since his brother, Dan, had recently married a young woman from a wealthy family. Nominally, while in New York Jim maintained his residence at the house he bought for his mother on Lexington Avenue.

Now that he had turned forty it seemed to him that he deserved a roost of his own, where he could entertain in the full-blooded style which suited him but offended Mrs. Brady, who did not take kindly to supper parties attended by actresses and chorus girls. What was the use of being a wealthy bachelor if you had old Mother Machree lurking in the background and quoting the Seventh Commandment?

Leaving Mother Brady with her place well staffed by servants and the liquor cabinet well stocked with brandy decanters, Jim moved out of the house on Lexington Avenue and into new and more sumptuous quarters at the Rutland, an apartment hotel at Broadway and Fifty-seventh Street, where he rented two six-room suites. It was lavishly furnished in the pseudo-Oriental style believed to have an aphrodisiac effect on impressionable young women. There is no record of Jim's conquests—a decent discretion was maintained about such matters except in the columns of *Town Topics*—but there is no reason to believe that his life was any more celibate than that of his fellow rounders and men about town. He was one up on most of them because he didn't drink. Eating was probably his overriding passion, and building a legend around himself was a consuming avocation, but he had plenty of time and energy to spare for womanizing.

His mother was outraged by his brazen decision to abandon himself to the life of a voluptuary, and his brother, long his worst enemy, encouraged her in her determination to bring Jim back under the Lexington Avenue roof. Dan Brady, according to Jim's friends, told their mother that Jim had abandoned her because he was keeping a mistress and also operating a harem for the benefit of visiting railroad tycoons. Mrs. Brady, wild-eyed and not entirely sober, began haunting the lobby of the building where Jim had his New York headquarters, at 26 Cortlandt Street, and telling everyone who would stop to listen to her complaints that James Buchanan Brady was an ingrate who had abandoned his mother in her old age. She also stopped his employees and business associates to demand whether they knew Jim was a thoroughly rotten human being. For several weeks she was virtually a one-woman picket line. Jim finally decided he had to do something about his mother's condition. The family physician, Dr. Paul Otterbridge, recommended that she be placed in a sanitarium until her nervous and mental condition improved. Jim started commitment proceedings but found himself blocked in the courts by his brother. A long and bitter court battle followed, one which the newspapers played up for all it was worth to the considerable damage of the Brady legend. Dan Brady even testified that Jim was trying to have their mother committed because he was trying to get control of her money (largely contributed by Jim himself). The court finally decided to place Mrs. Brady in the care and custody of a board it appointed. Jim then broke off all relations, permanently, with his mother and brother; theirs would be one Irish-American family history, beginning in the rooms over a saloon on the Hudson waterfront and ending in the city's glossiest precincts, which sentimentalists would find little to moon over.

Aside from his personal life, Diamond Jim Brady was prospering as never before. The railroad industry, like the rest of the economy, was recovering from the depression. He won $180,000 betting on William McKinley to win the Presidential election of 1896. Acting on inside information supplied by his friends at the Waldorf Men's Café bar, he plunged on the stock of the Philadelphia & Reading Railroad, which suddenly rose from 26 to 68 points on the stock market, and profited by $1,250,000.

About this time, a millionaire-plus, he established his custom of lavish Christmas-giving. Partly to counteract all the bad publicity from the court battle over his mother, even more because of an open-handed nature, he made himself a Manhattan version of Maecenas. One hundred and seventeen of his best friends were placed on the list for a Christmas basket; among them were section hands, chief clerks, purchasing agents, even locomotive engineers and firemen whose goodwill had made him the top salesman in the country. The cornucopia included twenty-pound turkeys, which Brady picked out himself down at the Washington Market, near the old Brady saloon, along with cranberries, celery, jellies, dried fruits, and nuts.

Nobody, he often vowed, would ever call Diamond Jim Brady a cheapskate.

Another gift list comprised what his friends called the Brady Beneficent Society and included three hundred friends outside the railroad industry. The persons on that list received a five-pound box of chocolates one week, a huge basket of fruit the next, another box of candy the third week, and flowers the fourth week. The fifth week the routine started all over again.

Undoubtedly there was something compulsive about this giving, as though, somehow, a fat, frog-faced man had to pay higher dues than anyone else. Often he pressed money or jewelry on girls who went dancing with him, even though they would have been content with a magnificent dinner and though they were expected to render no other favors than their company.

One of his friends once complained about getting all those gifts with metronomic regularity. Greatly offended, Brady roared in reply, "God damn it, if it gives me pleasure to send you presents, I'm gonna go right on sending 'em whether you like it or not!"

Another friend who was unwilling to accept one of Brady's gold-plated bicycles was threatened with having it "wrapped around your God damn neck."

Some of his gestures along those lines attained proportions more often associated with Roman emperors and Armenian oil magnates; how he must have envied the Baku oilman who had his mansion plated with platinum. However, Brady partisans could always cite his commandeering the output of a candy factory as evidence of his prodigality.

He went up to Boston one weekend to prepare his campaign to sell the Boston & Maine Railroad a million dollars' worth of the new steel passenger cars, and as the finishing touch to dinner at the Parker House he munched his way through a five-pound box of Page & Shaw chocolates. "Best God damn chocolates I ever ate," he commented. Then he neglected the Boston & Maine to ensure himself a corner on the bonbon market. First he went to S. S. Pierce, the eminent grocer's, and ordered their entire supply of Page & Shaw products, announcing that he intended to send a box weekly to members of the Brady Beneficent Society. S. S. Pierce regretfully informed him that other customers were devoted to the Page & Shaw product, that the factory was small and had a limited output, and Brady would have to stand in line like everyone else. That wasn't Brady's way of doing business. He hurried out to the Page & Shaw factory, inspected the production facilities, and handed its management a check for $150,000, as a loan against his future consumption of their goodies, to expand their plant and guarantee him an unlimited supply of chocolate creams, French bonbons, and glazed walnuts. He often consumed a five-pound box as a final dessert.

In the late nineties Lillian Russell, though still known as the American Beauty, though her profile on cigarette cards was still that decade's prototype of the pinup girl and the *Playboy* centerfold, was having problems with her career. Despite hundreds of miles of pedaling on her bicycles, and occasional attempts at strenuous dieting, her figure remained, well, statuesque. Her voice sometimes showed signs of strain, and it wouldn't be too long before she reached the age of forty, the most alarming of female milestones. Theatrical managers passed the word that Lillian, for all her high-handedness when it came to negotiating contracts, had lost her magnetism at the box office. Abbey, Schoeffel, and Grau were unchivalrous enough to let it be known that they had lost $200,000 in the past two seasons largely because of her $1,500-a-week salary.

Just then the musical stage in America was evolving from the light opera to the musical comedy stage, and Lillian's talents were suited to the former more than the latter. Operetta, comic opera, *opéra bouffe*, whatever the precise form, were of European origin while musical comedy was developed in the American idiom, brisker, less sentimental, somewhat mechanized. "The European flavor of light opera was, no doubt, one of its weaknesses in America and an explanation of why it had been all but driven from our stage by musical comedy fifteen years later," as De Wolf Hopper, who had started out as a light opera star, analyzed it. "The former was purely romantic and far removed from American life. Musical comedy was of our own soil, its wit native, its book topical, its music generally livelier, if cheaper, and it bore down heavily on the comedy. . . ."

The leading developer of the musical comedy form, ironically, was George W. Lederer, with whom Lillian had engaged in a lengthy contract dispute some years before. It was not a case of revenge, but the popularity of musical comedy was bad news for Lillian's career. In a few years the Floradora Sextette would heavily outdraw her. When she signed up with a new management to appear in *The Wedding Day* in the spring of 1897 at the Casino—still her lucky showhouse—the production turned out to be a financial success, but she had to share top billing with Jefferson de Angelis and Della Fox.

The following year she undertook a lucrative tour of Germany, beginning with six weeks at the Winter Garden in Berlin, for which she successfully demanded $3,000 a week plus all expenses, thus drawing the reproof of a New York daily that "On account of her diamonds, gowns and general methods of advertising, they call her 'Lillian Rustle.'" She sailed on the *Teutonic*, with her sister Susie as her companion. The enthusiasm of her reception by audiences in Berlin and elsewhere exceeded that of American audiences, but later she indicated that the circumstances of the tour made her earn every penny of her salary. She didn't like Germany or most Germans. She was especially irked by the "overbearing manner" of the German steel barons and the heel-clicking, hand-kissing general staff officers who swanned around her dressing room and laid siege to her hotel suite. She was even more outraged when a German female claimed to be her daughter, and she was appalled at the kaiser's taste in diamonds.

One of her few "amusing" but equally irksome admirers was Prince Henry of Pless, who surveyed her through his monocle from the royal box at her opening performance in the Winter Garden. Next day she received a seven-foot purple-and-white floral piece with a note curtly signed, "Admiration. Prince Henry of Pless."

That was the beginning of a dogged, peremptory, then pleading courtship on the part of Prince Henry. The next two nights he sent a huge bouquet of white violets and a large basket of red roses. Lillian ignored the offerings. The third night Prince Henry upped the ante and dispatched a bejeweled dragonfly sprinkled with rubies and diamonds. Lillian asked her German lawyer to return the trinket, but he was "too German" to risk offending the nobility.

On the fifth day after her opening Prince Henry stepped up what Lillian later called his "delicate advances." She and Susie, both in negligees, were having breakfast in their hotel suite when two Prussian grenadiers stomped in, followed by Count Hohnlau, the Prince's factotum, in full morning dress. Count Hohnlau clicked his heels, bowed low, and inquired, "Is this the celebrated, most high-born and beautiful Miss Lillian Russell?"

When Lillian owned up to the fact, Count Hohnlau bowed again and declared: "Prince Henry of Pless presents his esteemed compliments to Miss Lillian Russell and desires her company in Parlor L at twelve o'clock this evening to take supper with him."

She had never been propositioned with such punctilio, such Prussian precision, but declined the offer. "Tell the gentleman that I do not know him, and I never take supper with anyone whom I do not know."

Prince Henry, however, persisted. The next morning Count Hohnlau appeared again at her hotel suite with his guard of honor and presented Lillian with a note written by the prince himself. It read: "Miss Russell should take her golden bicycle. She should ride out to the Grunewald at eight o'clock tomorrow morning. She should ride the North Drive and she will see an officer in a green uniform on a white horse, who, if she descends from her bicycle when she sees him, will dismount from his horse and speak to her. Henry."

Lillian was amused by the military precision of the invitation and his descent from aristocratic formality to plain "Henry," but she told Count Hohnlau, "I would not get up at eight o'clock in the morning to watch George Washington cross the Delaware. You can also tell Prince Henry that I am an American and not obliged to obey his royal commands. And give him this." She dropped the ruby and diamond dragonfly in Count Hohnlau's hand, and he withdrew in dismay.*

The highlight of her Berlin engagement was her meeting with forty American girls who were studying at Berlin schools at a *kaffee-klatsch* in the Tiergarten at Lillian's invitation. This was followed by an all-American luncheon arranged by Lillian at the Hotel Bristol, with sweet corn imported from Budapest and pork and beans from London. Lillian and the young American students hit it off so well that they lunched together twice more before she left Germany.

The lowlight of her tour undoubtedly was the suit filed by a Hamburg woman who claimed that Lillian was her mother. The woman was two years older than Lillian, and as Lillian later wrote, "No wild imagination could picture me as a German frau with a big, fat and forty-year-old daughter," but Lillian was forced to obtain affidavits showing there could be no possible relationship with the Hamburg claimant. And she was only slightly less outraged when she was forced to pay $5 to both the "Empress' manicure" and the "Hairdresser to the Empress" for trifling services. Nor was she pleased by the fact that the imperial treasury was levying a 10-percent income tax on her German earnings.

Somewhat grudgingly, therefore, she responded to an imperial summons to appear at the Potsdam Palace and sing for Kaiser Wilhelm II, his family, and the court. The kaiser insisted on looking over her repertoire himself and selecting the five songs she was to sing. She made a hit at the drearily military royal palace in Potsdam. The royal reward, however, she deemed inferior to tokens from less lordly sources elsewhere.

The kaiser's master of ceremonies told her to go to the court jeweler's on the Unter den Linden and pick out anything she liked from a collection of gifts assembled for the kaiser's coming tour of Egypt. Lillian looked over the array of snuffboxes,

---

* Years later she told the story of Prince Henry's courtship to Theodore Roosevelt on a visit to Sagamore Hill. Roosevelt, who knew the prince, "enjoyed the story so much that he asked me to repeat it."

cigarette boxes, brooches, bracelets, lockets, and rings, all of them badly enameled and surmounted by a miniature of the kaiser surrounded by "the most terrible looking diamonds I ever saw. The diamonds were so filled with flaws that they looked like dirty cracked ice. I was obliged to choose something so I diplomatically made an arrangement with the jeweler to reset the bracelet I selected." With American bluntness, she asked the jeweler why the kaiser would permit such "awful" souvenirs to be selected and given in his name. The jeweler replied that he supposed the kaiser believed that "just to have a souvenir from the hand of His Highness was sufficient." Not for Lillian.

After fulfilling her German engagements, she lingered for a week to take a Zeppelin ride over Berlin and attend a performance of *Tristan and Isolde* in Munich. Then, thankfully, she returned home with her sister.

The German tour had left her with the feeling that she had been slightly bruised all over by contact with an alien culture. The psychic wounds were hardly soothed a few months after her return to New York when she appeared in Offenbach's *La Belle Helene*. She was particularly offended by journalistic comparisons of her appearance with that of Edna Wallace Hopper, a younger and slimmer member of the supporting cast.

"Lillian," wrote Alan Dale, the New York *Journal* critic, "has no beauty beneath the chin. She could not possibly wear three-quarters of a yard of silk and corset lace with the confident effrontery of Edna Wallace Hopper, and she moved with the soft heaviness of a nice white elephant." In an elephantine rage, highly unusual for her, she agreed to go on tour with *La Belle Helene* only because the producer threatened her with a lawsuit if she backed out.

In Philadelphia, Edna Wallace Hopper only caused more friction with the prima donna when she kept appearing in scantier and flimsier costumes. The cheers from the balcony, packed with college students who thought Lillian looked like their favorite aunt, kept growing louder and more raucous. Finally Lillian quit the company and returned to New York in a shower of suits and countersuits which eventually, as usual, were dropped. She did not, apparently, recall the earlier stages of her career when she stole attention from senior actresses by appearing in purple tights.

Before the old century was shuffled into the discard both Brady and Russell were in love and had formed liaisons of some permanence. Considering how those affairs turned out, they might have done better to fall in love with each other. As it was, the old twosome was expanded to a foursome also including Jesse Lewisohn and Edna McCauley.

Brady's romance might have served as the scenario for an O. Henry short story. Both the beginning and the ending provided twists that O. Henry, in his hectic production of stories about shopgirls and millionaire roués, might have borrowed but could hardly have improved on.

Edna McCauley was the daughter of a Brooklyn policeman, in her early twenties when she met Brady, who crossed the river, like all ambitious Brooklynites, and sought her fortune in Manhattan. She worked as an eight-dollar-a-week salesgirl in a department store and kept a weather eye for Mr. Right. Her contemporaries recalled her as a great beauty, but the surviving photographic evidence does not bear out the claim. Bright red hair and a lovely complexion were her chief assets. She was also intelligent, adaptable, and had a sense of humor.

There is a question as to how the eight-dollar-a-week shopgirl met one of the city's wealthiest men. In an O. Henry story, the Brady character, wolfishly prowling the aisles of the department store, would have spotted her at the perfume counter and then taken dead aim on her virtue. For once, at least, fact was more interesting than fiction. An admirer took Edna to dine in the Palm Garden of the Waldorf-Astoria, where she caught a glimpse of Brady in all his splendor. Learning something of his habits, she tracked him down in Peacock Alley at the Waldorf the following afternoon. A dropped handkerchief—cliché though it was—did the trick. Brady invited Edna over to his apartment for tea. As it turned out, Edna came for "tea" and stayed for breakfast. Stayed for more than a decade, in fact. Jim had fancied her for a one-night stand but found himself madly, instantly in love. He took her to Atlantic City for the weekend and then installed her at the Rutland as his mistress.

Jim, according to his friends, wanted to marry Edna Mc-Cauley but she always refused. As an Irish Catholic, whose mother's admonitions had echoed around him until his fortieth year, he did not take "living in sin" lightly. Somehow the transitory affairs of a traveling salesman and of a man-about-Manhattan did not seem to weigh as heavily on the moral scale as a full-time affair with one woman. But Edna refused all his pleas; it seems plain enough that she fancied the life he could provide for her, starting with a gorgeous new wardrobe, jewelry, and a personal maid, more than she did her provider. He gave her an allowance of $1,000 a month plus charge accounts anywhere she wanted them and a tiara with an eleven-carat diamond glowing like a miner's lamp. She was introduced to all his more or less glamorous friends. Lillian Russell practically adopted her, taught her to smoke the jasmine-scented cigarettes Lillian imported from Havana and smoked in private, and offered to obtain the job of understudy to Ada Rehan for Edna until Jim strenuously objected. Edna, in any case, felt no great ambition to go on the stage. Essentially indolent, she would stay with Diamond Jim Brady as long as the arrangement was satisfactory to both parties.

When she accompanied him to such more or less respectable events as a railroad convention in Newport, he introduced her as his niece. Eyebrows arched, of course, but a lot of rich men traveled with shapely young nieces to whom they bore little or no family resemblance. The main thing was that you observed the code, you didn't brazenly identify your traveling companion as your mistress.

Traveling abroad with your niece was likely to be a bit more complicated, as Brady learned. He took her to Paris in the summer of 1898, and there was a *contretemps* just after they checked into a seven-room suite at the Continental. Edna, of course, was registered as his niece. A member of the Sûreté, checking their passports, which had to be surrendered at the reception desk, came up to investigate. The name on Edna's passport and her status on the hotel register were incompatible, no? "What the hell," Brady snorted, peeling off thousand-franc notes. "I thought you Frenchies could understand a thing like this!"

This time Jim made a breakthrough in Parisian society with the golden-haired, doll-like little fop Count Boni de Castellane as his sponsor. Several years before, when his family's fortunes had gone down the drain at various casinos and watering places, Count Boni had undertaken the conventional trek to America to find a suitable heiress. His prize was swarthy little Anna Gould, the daughter of the late Jay Gould. During his wife-hunting expedition to New York, he had been royally entertained by Jim Brady. Now Count Boni wanted to return the favor and invite Brady to be the guest of honor at his rococo mansion on the Avenue du Bois de Boulogne. Five hundred servants and an equal number of representatives of the more raffish sectors of Paris society were assembled to pay their respects to Diamond Jim Brady and his alleged niece.

At the start of the festivities Count Boni commanded silence while he delivered a brief tribute to the guest of honor. "As the greatest party-giver in all of France I salute you, Monsieur Brady, as my most worthy American rival."

Brady's usual composure under social pressure broke under the barracuda-eyed inspection of the French aristocracy.

"Why, Count," he finally blurted out, "it's God damn nice of you to say that!"

Another damper on the occasion was the unexplained absence of Anna Gould, the person who paid the bills for the entertainment but who could not bring herself to act as hostess for Diamond Jim Brady, a vastly vulgar nobody of the sort the countess was bent on escaping, though the foundation of the Gould fortune was her father's talent for embezzlement, thimblerigging, and corporate piracy. No doubt Jim was more amused than offended by her absence.

On their return from a modicum of social triumphs in Europe, Jim and Edna moved into a large and expensively furnished house on East Eighty-sixth Street. Jim would live there for many years, even after it was no longer a love nest and was more of a one-patient hospital. Every year he would install new furniture and furnishings; spring cleaning meant all the old stuff went out on the street. Every room was furnished in the heavy contemporary style. The living room, entirely Louis XIV with spindly chairs which sometimes splintered under Brady's weight, was the exception. The walls were lined with shelves holding an astonishing collection of bric-a-brac, small statues, figurines—objects of questionable art, which appealed to the lace-curtain Irish element in him. Jim, in fact, considered that he had advanced from lace-curtain to cut-glass Irish; the lavish display of all these bits and pieces testified to his status as a patron of the arts. Among all the artistic detritus were also three Rodin statues. One of the more magnificent rooms was in the basement. The game room included a specially made pool table encrusted with lapis lazuli, onyx, chrysoprase, and other semiprecious stones. Resting on a massive card table was a solid-gold croupier's rake.

Jim's new home may not have attained any Astorbilt standard of elegance, but as he often pointed out, it cost a hell of a lot of money.

At the same time that Jim's romantic life was assuming a settled aspect, Lillian Russell had become involved in her long affair with Jesse Lewisohn. If Jim always introduced Edna as his niece when they traveled outside the orbit of their understanding New York friends, Lillian regally, for many years, introduced *her* inveterate companion as her fiancé.

At least, as her friends assured each other, Lewisohn was not another of those damned leeching musicians. The only music that appealed to Jesse Lewisohn, aside from Lillian's trilling, was the rattle of poker chips and the whirring of the roulette wheel. He also was able to pay his own way, and Lillian's too, if necessary, as one of the heirs to the Lewisohn copper fortune. Like her three former husbands—in vivid contrast to her own buxom blond physique—Jesse was small, dark, and rather fragile in appearance.

From acceptance as a member of her poker-playing circle, he had progressed to admirer, escort, and finally protector. It was always a matter of controversy on Lillian Russell opening nights whether the largest bouquets and most expensive diamonds came from Jim Brady or Jesse Lewisohn. But it was an amiable contest. Soon Jim and Edna, Lillian and Jesse made up the most glamorous foursome in the lobster-palace world. Jim and Jesse were Damon and Pythias; Lillian and Edna loved each other like sisters. But it would not always be so.

6

A SUMMER IN THE SERAGLIO

JAMES GORDON BENNETT, Jr., had not been regarded as a social arbiter since the New Year's Day he urinated in his fiancee's fireplace, but he still held himself, as one of the ruling caste of Newport, to be an authority on what was done and how it was done in America's instant aristocracy. He was the son of a printer who happened to invent modern journalism, but his hauteur matched that of a Hapsburg. In contrast to Newport, he declared Saratoga in upstate New York was the "seraglio of the prurient aristocracy." Another socialite put it more delicately: "Liaisons are accepted in Saratoga."

In Saratoga, during the August race meet, late-Victorian morality was outflanked in various ways. At the stately old Grand Union or the States with its "millionaires' piazza" all entrances except one, which was guarded by a house detective, were locked at 11 P.M. and the grounds were patrolled by night watchmen to prevent anyone from smuggling in unregistered females. Yet the sinner who was both well heeled and determined to have his licentious way was also accommodated, because the hotels were surrounded by cottages which were rented out with no questions asked and no surveillance from the management: America's first motel in embryo. One season

an oil magnate, lending the color of reality to Bennett's definition of Saratoga as a Topkapi transplanted to the north woods,
appeared with no less than five pretty secretaries to adorn his
cottage, not one of whom was accomplished in any of the secre-
tarial crafts. Sex was made respectable by confining it to Saratoga's cottages. The late Hugh Bradley, as the resort's chief
historian, remarked that "In accordance with the still-preva-
lent American belief than sin becomes somehow sanctified if a
sitting room is attached to the bedchamber, the cottages solved
the problems of numerous Wall Street tycoons and Western
copper kings."

Saratoga in August could boast a rich assortment of personages, such as White Hat McCarty, who had made a fortune in
breeding and racing horses but was barely literate. Once he
checked in at the United States and watched while the man
ahead of him registered as so-and-so "and Valet." McCarty
seized the pen and signed in as "White Hat McCarty and
valise." Other summer visitors included Squire Abingdon
Baird, the English sportsman who wore a $5,000 sable coat
(though not in August); Berry Wall, the "King of the Dudes,"
who changed his costume one day, by actual count, forty times;
Peter Lorillard, the tobacco heir, for whom the *Police Gazette*'s society reporter suggested a coat of arms with "a cuspi-
dor couchant, with two cigars and a plug of tobacco rampant";
Jay Gould and family; and an even more notorious pillager,
Frank James of the James brothers.

Saratoga was a proving ground for exhibitionists, and inevitably it attracted Brady, Russell, and their entourages. The
opportunity to outexhibit the flashiest personalities on the
American scene undoubtedly was a challenge. But Saratoga
had something else: the best summertime grazing available
outside heat-stricken New York City for two notable gour-
mandizers. Many of New York's best chefs, in fact, sojourned in
cooler Saratoga and manned the kitchens of the hotels and
casinos. One dinner menu at the United States Hotel included:

A Summer in the Seraglio

Oysters on Half Shell
Sauterne
Green turtle soup   Olives
Boiled salmon   Lobster sauce   Potato balls
Sweetbread cutlets   Peas
Claret
Filet of beef   Mushroom sauce
Lima beans   Mashed potatoes
Champagne
Roman Punch
Supreme of Chicken   Truffle sauce
Terrapin   Saratoga Chips
Partridges on toast   Salted almonds
Lettuce   Cheese   Crackers
Roquefort and Neufchâtel
Ices   Meringues   Fruits
Coffee   Cigars   Benedictine

Newport and Tuxedo Park were too high-toned for Jim Brady and too censorious for Lillian Russell, her liaison with Jesse Lewisohn being so widely known. Even in *laissez-faire* Saratoga she was usually referred to as "that woman" by the senior lionesses of the resort. But Saratoga, with supposedly health-giving waters to purge organs abused by rich food, with the horse-racing Jim and Lillian and their consorts were passionately devoted to, with all the gay and fine-feathered and uninhibited folk who gathered for the August frolic, seemed to be just right for the summer days they spent on leave from business and the theater.

As just about the most famous personages on the scene—though Berry Wall with his hourly costume changes and his nineteen-year-old bride, and Miss Giulia Morosini, a banker's daughter who drove three spirited horses in tandem harnessed to her black-and-yellow Brewster coach, provided a certain specious competition—they helped to bring about a mini-revolution in American society. They encouraged a confluence of the old society (two generations or more of money) and celebrities of the more interesting kind.

This may seem barely credible, an actress and a salesman, both teetering on the knife-edge boundary between celebrity and notoriety, breaking through the encrusted traditions of the upper class. They were, however, the symbols of a great expansion of the national wealth and its wide distribution during the decades just before and just after the turn of the century.

The preeminent social historian Cleveland Amory has defined the Brady-Russell influence on the leavening of society through their joint appearance in Saratoga:

> The importance of the hotel cottages . . . cannot be over-estimated in its future effect on Saratoga society. The cottage colonies of Newport and Bar Harbor and other great resorts were soon entirely free of their hotel beginnings—at Newport the hotels all but disappeared completely—but at Saratoga, where the grand hotels still flourished, the cottage colony still retained the gay, early-day spirit. One manifestation of this gaiety was in the mixing of Society with stage celebrities. Up until the First World War there was at other resorts a great gulf between Society and the stage; even Newport's Mrs. Fish failed to break it down completely. "You must remember," said Berry Wall, who spoke for the Newport-Tuxedo circuit, "that Broadway only cuts across Fifth Avenue; it never parallels it." What Harry Lehr and Mrs. Fish were to Newport, Diamond Jim Brady and Lillian Russell were, in their way, to Saratoga, and while neither that well-traveled salesman nor "that woman," as old-time Saratogians still recall her, would have attempted to set up cottage-keeping at Newport, they were, at Saratoga, the uncrowned rulers of the spa.

For almost a century Saratoga had been a spa, but not one on the European model, not a Marienbad or Baden-Baden, where bilious Frenchmen drank German water to pacify their livers. Originally it was the favorite summer resort of the plantation aristocrats of the Deep South, who came North to escape the malaria and yellow fever epidemics. After a winterlong diet of quinine, the planters could sluice out their systems with water from Saratoga's 175 mineral springs. The Civil War, of course, ended the summer invasion from Dixieland. The planters were replaced by the magnates of the Flash Age who had enriched themselves on war contracts, the railroads, and the New York City treasury. Boss Tweed and his followers evacuated Tammany Hall every summer for the pilgrimage to Saratoga. A. T. Stewart, the New York merchant, built the Grand Union to satisfy the tastes of Flash Age magnificoes, who felt downright elegant when they squirted tobacco juice into china cuspidors with hand-painted flowers. In the past two decades, however, a more genteel patronage had taken over the Grand Union, the States and other hostelries, and the cottages surrounding them, New York society people who wanted a more relaxing atmosphere than they could find among the marble palaces and baroque villas of Newport and Bar Harbor. At least one President, Chester A. Arthur, came up for his vacation and incidentally epitomized what he and others considered the particular ambience of Saratoga. A hostess asked him for his views on alcohol, and President Arthur snappishly replied, "Madam, I may be the President of the United States, but my private life is nobody's damn business."

The social/financial arbiter of the spa was a cold-eyed gambler named Richard A. Canfield. He had established a Saratoga branch of his Manhattan gambling place early in the nineties so his best customers could lose their money to him on a year-round basis. No matter what your pedigree, no matter what your rating in Dun & Bradstreet, you counted for very little in Saratoga if Dick Canfield refused to allow you into Canfield's Club House; he was death on tinhorns, poor losers, and the more vulgar type of crap shooters, and the absolute social cachet of the time was to lose your money gracefully enough over Canfield's green baize tables and receive a kind word from the proprietor. Needless to say, Jim Brady's rating with Canfield was AAA, likewise that of Jesse Lewisohn, whose passion for roulette and baccarat sometimes seemed to exceed his feelings for Lillian Russell.

What a splash Jim Brady made his first season at Saratoga. His first appearance was largely dictated by commercial considerations, but thereafter he spent every August in Saratoga without a thought for business. In 1896, the Master Car Builders nominated Saratoga as the site for their annual convention. Jim had recently become a greater power in the car-building industry. The Schoen Pressed Steel Company had broken the monopoly of Fox Pressed Steel, Jim's company, in manufacturing all-steel railroad undercarriages; subsequently Jim arranged a merger of the rivals and was asked to assume one of the executive posts but declared himself satisfied with having Brady men on the board of directors.

But that merger was still a year in the future, and Jim was determined to impress on the Master Car Builders that Fox Pressed Steel was still number one. A saturnalia must be provided. His move to Saratoga that summer was more of a logistics masterpiece than a vacation jaunt; it took almost as much planning as getting the Sells-Floto Circus on the road or the movement of an infantry division. Up the tracks went tons of food, everything from imported paté and caviar to corned beef and cabbage, and case lots of beer, ale, wine, whiskey, brandy, and about everything else that was potable and potent.

Brady himself was accompanied by twenty-seven Japanese servants to staff the three cottages he had rented to accommodate his best customers. Hundreds of boxes of Havana cigars also went up with him, fifty-cent claros. One of the Japanese houseboys, with the sort of stuff in him that Jim could admire, sequestered so many boxes of Havanas that when he returned to New York that fall he was able to open his own cigar store.

Saratoga suited him fine, and he came up every summer thereafter, he and Edna in one cottage and Lillian and her entourage in another. Saratoga had "class," and he had come to appreciate classiness. By then he had given up hope of rising any higher on the social scale. That ambition had fermented briefly a year or two before, when he plotted to arrange an introduction to Harry Lehr, who had taken Ward McAllister's place as adviser to the Fifth Avenue dowagers on who might safely be admitted to their drawing rooms. He had played up to a certain man about town who claimed friendship with Lehr until he realized that he was being used. Jim didn't mind being a sucker for the girls, but it griped to be conned by a man. "To hell with him," he said of his ex-friend. "I buy his wine and give him tips on the stock market and then he always remembers an important engagement when I start talking to him about society."

Classiness, in his opinion, was being a good sport and spending your money with flair; it had nothing to do with fish-faced old dowagers and their fagoty cotillion leaders and "old" money tied up in perpetual trusts. Lillian Russell had class in everything she did; so did Jesse Lewisohn when he dropped thousands at Canfield's tables without wincing, and Edna Mc-Cauley because she could wear furs and jewelry as though they were her birthright.

So he urged Lillian to spend August in Saratoga, and they were the joint leaders of their own uninhibited social set. She always spent part of June and all of July at her country house, Cedar Hill, on Long Island, the fourteen guest rooms of which were usually occupied, many of them by what she called her "farm flirts," a group of young actresses including the soon-to-be-famous Blanche Bates, Margaret Robinson, Isadora Perry, and others whose beauty provided distraction for her male guests.

The territory around Great Neck had recently been claimed by the more prosperous members of show business. It was only a half hour from Broadway on the Long Island Express, to which Jesse Lewisohn's private car was often attached for Lillian's convenience. Near Cedar Hill were the mansions occupied during the summer months by various celebrities, including George M. Cohan and Florenz Ziegfeld. A showy extravagance of the sort that would soon be transplanted to Beverly Hills and other environs of Hollywood was the approved style. When Ziegfeld's chief assistant, Gene Buck, built himself a showplace in the Great Neck colony, it caused little astonishment when he had it decorated by the stage manager for Ziegfeld's productions. When the sardonic humorist Ring Lardner got a look at Buck's mansion he pronounced its living room "the Yale Bowl, with lamps." Some years later the colony acquired a somewhat more restrained literary flavor, with many of the more affluent writers moving in beside the Broadway magnificoes, among them F. Scott Fitzgerald. It was, in fact, the setting of Fitzgerald's greatest novel, *The Great Gatsby*, which conveyed its atmosphere, its empty illusions, its hollow pretensions with a pitiless employment of the literary scalpel.

Six weeks of reenacting Marie Antoinette at play with her milkmaids became irksome for the restless Lillian. At the end of July she gathered up her "farm flirts" and whatever house guests were still loitering on the premises of Cedar Hill and moved in state, aboard Lewisohn's private car, to a cottage in Saratoga.

She also brought with her "Mooksie," her Japanese spaniel with his $1,800 diamond-studded, gold-plated collar, and her gold-plated bicycle in its leather pod, and a carriage complete with silver-mounted harness and white doeskin reins.

Lillian demanded only one thing of her guests: that they join her for a daily hour of exercise either at her outdoor gymnasium or on the cycling paths. The battle with her waistline went on. Little wonder, since she wasted that hour's exercise by appearing nightly in the dining room of Canfield's casino, where chef Columbin prepared mounds of sweet corn and crepes suzette for her.

Her preparations for the nightly descent on Canfield's or one of the hotel dining rooms provided young male Saratogians with an early-evening interlude of spectator sport. This was made possible by the fact that her maid neglected to draw the blinds in her bedroom. While the young bloods watched and snickered outside in the darkness, Lillian would clutch the bedpost and her maid would struggle to tighten the strings on her corset, which helped to preserve the hourglass illusion. Often there was betting on how long it would take to contain the Russell midriff in its whalebone cage. Still, aside from irreverent youth, Lillian managed to maintain the fiction of ageless glamor even as she reached the shady side of forty. No one watching her in a crisp shirtwaist with the sun on her shining blond hair, handling the white reins of her dashing bays and gleaming carriage as they trotted along a Saratoga roadway, could have denied her that.

Occasionally there were foreshadowings of the day when men would no longer gasp and grow stalks on their eyes on catching sight of her.

One day she posed prettily on the steps of the United States Hotel, hoping someone would give her a ride out to the track. Tom Williams, a wealthy Western sportsman whose name would live long in infamy so far as the Russell fan club was concerned, came driving up in his carriage with a blonde at his side. One of Williams' superstitions was that he must be accompanied by one blonde and one brunette if he hoped to win at the races. Lillian asked him for a lift out to the track. Sorry, replied Williams; his carriage already had filled its blonde quota. Off he drove while Lillian bit her lips. There had been a time when Williams would have booted the other blonde out of his equipage and hastened to help Lillian aboard.

Occasionally, too, she had to fight off challenges by bold young women, more lissome of figure, who challenged her right to the title of queen of the spa. One of the more determined challengers was Miss Louise Montague, who had just won the first nationwide beauty contest. The brunette Miss Montague had the edge in youth and shapeliness, Miss Russell in fame and experience. Their rivalry took on a rather curious aspect. The queenship, it seemed, would be decided by which was most successful at picking winners at the racetrack. The whole race-following element chose sides, with stable owners, trainers, jockeys, and bookmakers wearing either the Russell or the Montague colors. Her supporters vied with her rival's to provide Lillian with the best handicapping expertise.

Lillian, however, usually relied on her own methods of picking winners, which was to close her eyes and stab at the racing program with her hatpin. The Russell technique of handicapping proved to be slightly more successful than Miss Montague's reliance on information straight from the paddock and the feedbox.

At the end of the season, with Lillian clearly ahead as a picker of winners and with her admirers claiming she had also maintained her supremacy as the most glamorous female on the scene, Louise Montague was determined to have the ultimate feminine solace of the last word. Lillian was giving her cottage-closing party, and Louise visited the branch of Tiffany's located in the Grand Union Hotel. There she bought a beautifully engraved fish fork.

The next day, unbidden, Louise appeared at Lillian's party and handed the hostess the gift-wrapped package. Lillian smiled graciously and opened it. Out tumbled the fish fork.

"What's this for?" she asked Louise.

"You see the three prongs on this fork?" Louise replied. "Now you can pick place and show as well as the winner."

Both in the material and emotional sense the several years following the turn of the century were happy ones for Jim and Lillian and their loved ones. For Jim the money rolled in as the country experienced another upsurge of industrial expansion. For Lillian her career once again took on momentum just about the time most theatrical managers were affixing the "box office poison" label to her name. You needed luck as well as talent to keep ahead of the Broadway wolf pack, and Lillian had both. Sometimes the luck seemed to be as essential as the talent.

She was not exactly a prospect for oblivion, but before the end of the century it was apparent her career needed a booster shot of some kind. Theatergoers simply weren't buying those Graustarkian extravaganzas built around Lillian, her costumes, and her cadenzas and were demanding something more indigenous, something closer to the center of American life than the intrigues of a Ruritanian court.

Indigenous, certainly, was the word for Weber and Fields, who had come up from burlesque as "Dutch" (meaning German) comics. It was the heyday of ethnic comedy, which boisterously but without undue malice pictured the various minorities in the broadest stereotypes. The German was always a stupid and belligerent lout, the Irishman was a stupid and drunken lout, the Negro was a stupid and lazy lout, the Italian was a feckless fellow with a monkey and a portable organ, the Jew was a cunning knave.

By the last decade of the century Joe Weber and Lew Fields, who were born on the Lower East Side of Manhattan, had greatly prospered as outrageously Teutonic buffoons. They had incorporated themselves as the Weberfields Company and established themselves in their own theater, with a supporting company which from time to time included such luminaries as Fay Templeton, Sam Bernard, John T. Kelly, Truly Shattuck, Pete Dailey, Mabel Fenton, David Warfield, and Frankie Bailey. From 1896 on they held forth at the Weber and Fields Music Hall on Twenty-ninth Street.

The Weberfields school of comedy was based on mangled English and knockabout action; the dialogue composed for their sketches could hardly have been studied with profit by young George Bernard Shaw. They invented the who-was-that-lady? gag and concocted the most violent insult ever hurled across the comedy stage: "Your family got t'rown out on the street so many times that your mother had to buy curtains vot matched the sidevalk." A Weber and Fields skit usually ended with the elongated Fields setting upon the smaller Weber, with his padded stomach, batting him with a pool cue, kicking him in the stomach, and choking him; then Weber would turn the tables, hook his cane around Fields' neck, and drag him off stage. Tumult in the galleries. A typical Weberfields encounter with the English language:

> WEBER: I am delightfulness to meet you.
> FIELDS: Der disgust is all mine.
> *A violent argument then ensued.*
> WEBER: Don't poosh me, Myer.
> FIELDS: Didn't I telling you, watch your etiquette?
> WEBER: Who says I et a cat?

Could the regal, the stately and statuesque Lillian Russell, whose comedic essays had always been of the most refined sort, possibly fit herself into this Weberfields world of exploding slapsticks, violent pratfalls, and crossfire of simpleminded gags?

The question, as momentous to some as the fate of Dewey's squadron in Manila Bay, would be answered in 1899.

Weber and Fields were then bemused by the necessity of finding a glamorous name to decorate the marquee of their music hall, Fay Templeton having defected from their company. Weber nominated Fields to scout the possibilities of replacing Templeton with Russell, since Fields often saw her (at a respectful distance) at the Sheepshead Bay racetrack. Fields trembled at the thought of approaching Miss Russell, the highest paid actress in America, with the suggestion that she join their knockabout troupe; he shook even more violently at the prospect of paying her salary.

Fields struck up an acquaintance with Jesse Lewisohn, and the latter agreed to take Fields over to Lillian's box. As Fields approached, Lillian, as usual, was picking winners by sticking her hatpin into the racing program.

She laughed heartily when Fields suggested that she join the Weberfields company as their leading lady.

"I'm too expensive for you," she explained.

"How much would you ask?"

Lillian briskly replied: "Twelve hundred and fifty dollars a week. A guaranteed season of thirty-five weeks a year. All costumes to be bought and paid for by you."

A Summer in the Seraglio

Offstage Lew Fields was a man of few words. "We'll expect you at rehearsal late in August," he told her.

The agreement was sealed with a handshake. She never signed a contract with Weber and Fields; their word was good enough for her. It was the beginning of a half dozen happy years as the foil (much like Margaret Dumont under constant assault from Groucho in the Marx Brothers films) for Weber and Fields and their associate madcaps. Her reputation for being difficult with other producers was not sustained at the Weber and Fields Music Hall. Thereafter Weber and Fields always held her up as a model of how a real star should behave. She put up with David Warfield's scene-stealing. She was undisturbed by the eccentricities of Pete Dailey, a genius at impromptu and often alcoholically inspired comedy. Dailey rarely showed up on time for rehearsals and was often severely hungover when he did appear. He always kept a quart of whiskey on his makeup table, along with a quart of champagne for chasers. Once his wife, Mary, protested that she saw so little of him because he stayed out all night and slept all day. "Come along with me then, my dear," Dailey replied. After three nights of helping him close up the Broadway saloons and cafés, Mrs. Dailey gave up the role of drinking companion and waited at home for him without further complaint. Dailey's performances were almost entirely ad-lib, and neither Lillian nor any of his other colleagues ever knew exactly what he was going to say or do when he made his fragrant appearance, more or less on cue, from the wings.

Working with Pete Dailey and other nimble, spontaneous talents at the Music Hall sharpened and redefined Lillian's talent for comedy and would serve to bolster her career when she could no longer depend on a smashing figure and a bell-like voice to attract the customers. For their part, Weber and Fields were more than delighted with Lillian. "This was no mortal woman, or so it seemed to us," as Felix Isman, the stage manager of the Music Hall, would remember her joining the troupe. "She was the queen to all the company within the first month. . . . First at rehearsals, last to leave, asking no privilege or indulgence; as unassuming as a new chorus girl; the most beautiful and the highest salaried woman on the stage, and as gracious and merry as beautiful."

For the opening night of the new Weber and Fields revue in the autumn of 1899, the Music Hall went to considerable pains to let everyone know that Lillian was making her debut with the company. The show was built around a burlesque of the current Broadway success, *The Girl from Maxim's*, a naughty import from the French stage. There was much excitement generated over the "new" turn her career had taken, though older heads could remember that she had started out at Tony Pastor's in similar burlesques. Lillian's salary was a staggering burden for a company with only 605 seats to sell each performance, so a week before the opening the more expensive seats were sold at an auction from the Music Hall stage. Jesse Lewisohn gallantly bid $1,000 for two boxes in what Weber and Fields called the Horseshoe Circle (in mockery of the Metropolitan Opera's diamond-studded dress circle), and Diamond Jim Brady, Stanford White, Abe Hummel, Louis Sherry, Richard Croker, William Randolph Hearst, Mrs. Herman Oelrichs, and James R. Keene paid as much as $750 for single boxes and $100 for orchestra seats. Young Mr. Hearst, a fervent admirer of Lillian's, though too bashful to present his compliments in person, was a frequent patron of the Music Hall from then on.

Lillian's debut attracted such crowds in and around the tiny theater that many of the ticket-holders had to be ushered through the stage door on Twenty-ninth Street. They found the house newly decorated in pink and buff—the former motif was turkey red and gold—to complement Lillian's Nordic charms. The critic Alan Dale remarked that the interior was like a salmon mayonnaise.

Lillian provided something of a shocker when the curtain went up: She was lying in bed in what appeared to be a nightgown, with a plug hat on her mass of golden hair. When she threw off the covers, she revealed herself to be clad in a low-cut evening gown which provided a generous exposure of the breasts which were one of the glories of her era. (Complaints from patrons of the Music Hall, presumably penned by envious females, caused Weber and Fields to tone down that opening scene.) Some of the feeling she aroused in her male contemporaries was conveyed in John Heywood's newspaper poem on the occasion:

> Give place, you ladies, and begone!
> Boast not yourselves at all!
> For here at hand approacheth one
> Whose face will stain you all.
>
> I think Nature hath lost the mold
> Where she her shape did take,
> Or else I doubt if Nature could
> So fair a creature make.
>
> Truly she did so far exceed
> Our women nowadays
> As doth the gillyflower a weed;
> And more a thousand ways.

Equally acclaimed in the 1899 Weberfields revue was a newcomer named David Warfield, whose talent for striking an artistic balance between comedy and tragedy has been matched only by Charlie Chaplin. He appeared as a Jewish millionaire vacationing in Paris with his daughter Uneeda. One exchange which brought roars of laughter:

UNEEDA: The captain is my idea of a hero.

COHENSKI: A hero! Is dot a business? A tailor is a business, a shoemaker is a business, but a hero? Better you should marry a bookkeeper!

UNEEDA: A bookkeeper? I suppose you think the pen is mightier than the sword.

COHENSKI: You bet my life! Could you sign checks with a sword?

Theatergoers of the period would always treasure another of the skits in which Lillian appeared as a classy Parisian, War-field (as the parvenu) occupied an adjoining table at Maxim's, and Lew Fields came on as a waiter. Lillian summoned Fields and set up a classic two-liner.

LILLIAN: Waiter, bring me a demi-tasse.
WARFIELD: Bring me the same, waiter, and I'll also have a cup of coffee.

In a subsequent scene Lillian caroled the joys of her life in the demimonde and also learned the dastardly distracting powers of a great comedian. While she trilled away, Warfield stood in the background, absolutely still but with tears pouring down his cheeks. The laughter drowned out the voice which, under more dignified auspices, had always been received in a hushed silence. Lillian didn't object; she had no false sense of importance and was trouper enough to realize that in the Music Hall a laugh took precedence over everything else. If the audience chose to guffaw while she sang, she could always enjoy a private chuckle when the management delivered her nightly paycheck.

Anyway, she was given her innings in subsequent Weber and Fields revues. The 1900 edition, *Fiddle-dee-dee*, was built around the socially significant concept of the resemblance of the industrial trusts to bands of thieves, and William Randolph Hearst, then a trust-buster himself, was in the audience vigorously applauding both the satiric assault and Miss Russell's thrusting bosom. In the opening scene she and De Wolf Hopper, a new addition to the company, were discovered sitting in the branches of a tree. Just as they were about to descend, Lillian clutched Hopper's arm and urgently whispered, "Have you got a safety pin? My bloomers are coming down." Hopper didn't, and the audience was delighted by a glimpse of the Russell backside.

In the 1901 edition, *Hoity-Toity*, she was fittingly cast as a member of the larcenous poker-game skit with Sam Bernard,

Weber, and Fields, which was played with huge cards visible to the audience. On the first hand Fields would ask Bernard if he had stacked the cards. "Sure," Bernard replied. "I was trained by a gambler." To which Fields growled: "You must have been overtrained. I've got five aces of spades!" The game invariably ended with Lillian fleecing her three fellow sharpers.

But the set piece of the revues was the song which was written especially for her, the song which became as much the signature of her career as Madame Schumann-Heink singing "Silent Night, Holy Night." The Music Hall's brilliant young composer, John Stromberg, wrote "Come Down My Evenin' Star," with lyrics by Robert Smith, which owed much of its inspiration to the Negro spiritual, just before he ended a pain-racked life by committing suicide. Ever afterward Lillian could command the transfixed attention of an audience simply by pausing dramatically for a few seconds, lifting her large blue eyes, and swinging into her theme song:

> . . . Search de sky from east to west
> She's de brightest and de best,
> But she's so far above me,
> I knows she cannot love me,
> Still I loves her, an' more dan all de rest.
>
> Ma evenin' star,
> I wonder who you are,
> Set up so high like a diamond in de sky.
> No matter what I do,
> I can't go up to you.
> So come down from dar, ma evenin' star.
> Come down! Come down!
> Come down from dar, ma evenin' star.

Her collaborator in high living did not lift his eyes wistfully for a "diamond in de sky." Brady's were all on his person or in the drawers of his huge mahogany dresser on Eighty-sixth Street—an incredible collection of personal jewelry.

He had spent hundreds of thousands of dollars, in the much firmer currency of the 1890's, in collecting thirty different sets of jewelry for each day of the week. The most expensive was what he called the Number-one Diamond Set, the ring of which was set with a diamond weighing 25½ carats. Each set included a watch, watch chain, ring, scarf pin, necktie pin, pen, pencil, cuff links, belt buckle, eyeglass case, shirt studs, collar buttons, and even underwear buttons. When Jim and his valet prepared him for a night on the town, it must have been roughly comparable to a knight being buckled into his armor. And in full panoply, glittering with refracted light from stem to stern, he looked like a Mississippi riverboat at night coming around the bend with all its illumination turned on.

Included in his collection were rubies, pearls, sapphires, star sapphires, black opals, turquoise, garnets, amethysts, abalone pearl, coral, moonstones, sardonyx, amatrice, thompsonite, and imperial jade. The most ornate was his Transportation Set, which included large diamonds and rubies mounted on platinum in the shape of Pullman cars, tank cars, a bicycle, a motorcar, and a locomotive sparkling with 210 diamonds. In all there were 2,548 diamonds and assorted rubies included in the Transportation Set. Its value in today's inflated dollars would be hard to estimate, but certainly it would be more than a million dollars.

The most valuable gemstone in his collection was a cabochon emerald weighing 23 carats, which was set in a ring and was the size of a ping-pong ball. It was almost matched in opulence by the emerald weighing 17 carats set in his scarf pin. The watch chain in this set contained emeralds weighing in at 83 carats. His emeralds were probably as valuable as any collection outside the Topkapi Palace in Constantinople, but he never aspired to be called Emerald Jim Brady. The watch compartment of his dresser contained thirty-odd timepieces, including many of the costliest workmanship, one diamond-studded evening watch being valued at $17,500.

To most of his fellow citizens he may have resembled a

bedizened circus elephant, but Jim regarded himself as a stand-ard-bearer of good taste and something of a sartorial arbiter. Either the reporter who interviewed him or Jim himself must have been joshing, however, when the latter was quoted as saying:

> The trouble with our American men is that they overdress. They do not understand that beauty unadorned is adorned the most. Now, I take it that I am considered a handsome man and one who would be called well dressed. Never by any chance do I permit more than seventeen colors to creep into the pattern of my waistcoat. Moreover, I consider that twenty-eight rings are enough for any man to wear at one time. The others may be carried in the pocket and exhibited as occasion requires. A similar rule applies to the cuff buttons and shirt studs. . . . Three of them may be worn without entirely covering the shirt bosom. Diamonds larger than door knobs should never be worn except in the evening. . . .

He could afford all that personal adornment, and bear up under journalistic hyperbole, with his fortune then estimated at roughly twelve million dollars.

Not a cent was paid, pre-1913, in income taxes. Much of his fortune was accumulated through speculation, which usually came about through his close friendship with the high-rolling John F. Gates, whose manners were so uncouth they made Brady seem a French diplomat by comparison.

A barbed-wire salesman from Illinois, Bet-a-Million Gates had accumulated a sizable fortune through various piratical maneuvers on Wall Street. He had the sleek hair, blazing eyes, and feral face of a panther, and a pantherish instinct for ambushing and eliminating his enemies. The latter included most of the Ivy League-educated, pious-mannered gentlemen who unofficially managed the nation's money supply and called the turn on stock market speculation, for whom Gates did not demonstrate the proper respect. "He called them by their first name and they resented it," as one of his biographers, Robert I. Warshow, wrote. "They hated him because they could not control him. But Gates only smiled, as he planned new schemes to prove his keenness and dismay the imperial house. He had only his degree from the 'Drummers' University,' his honorary titles as the King of Salesmen and Prince of Good Fellows, but that was to prove able to cope with the galaxy of Eastern bankers massed in fervent hatred against this colorful intruder." Gates' worst sin against the financial establishment was to consider Wall Street a big crap game and to strip away the sacerdotal mysteries and long-established ritual which cloaked speculation on the big board.

Some of his more spectacular power plays were motivated by a seething hatred for J. P. Morgan, whose nose resembled a purple squash. Gates called him Old Liver Nose. If Morgan was the mogul of what was called high finance, with a quick genuflection toward the Subtreasury building, Gates was a master of low finance, a compulsive gambler who could not stay away from the horses, the dice, and the cards during the hours the stock market was closed.

In one of his more spectacular coups, Gates had forced Morgan to pay him roughly fifty million more than the stock was worth when Morgan acquired the American Steel and Wire Company for his United States Steel trust. That deal gave Gates an insight into Morgan's character: Old Liver Nose couldn't bear to leave one chip on the table for someone else. The enmity between the two was deepened when Gates asked Morgan for a seat on the board of U.S. Steel and the latter frigidly replied, "That would be impossible. You have made your own reputation, and we are not responsible for it. Good day, sir." It turned out to be a most costly snub.

Morgan and other quality folk simply were not equipped to understand a fellow like Gates, a maverick, a mucker, a semi-literate ruffian from the Midwest. How they rolled their eyes at the story of Gates acquiring an art collection. He went to a gallery at which an exhibition was being held, bringing with him Victor, his valet, social mentor, and cultural adviser. After a brisk inspection of the pictures hanging on the walls, Gates turned to Victor and asked his opinion of their artistic merits. Victor signified approval. "Right," Gates snapped. "Tell the feller who runs this place to pack up the lot and send 'em to my house."

The acquisition of an art collection did not turn Gates into a limp and sated aesthete, however, and he brooded for several years over the way Morgan and his friends had treated him. Early in 1902 he saw an opportunity to get revenge, the chosen sector being the railroad industry, which had always been susceptible to financial skulduggery. Morgan and his associates, having engulfed the steel industry, had decided to gain control of the Southern railroad system. They already controlled the Southern Railway Company, a combination of a number of bankrupt railroads, and through pooling arrangements they dominated the Louisville & Nashville and several other supposedly independent carriers.

Gates, with the financial assistance of Jim Brady, Jesse Lewisohn, and several other plungers with whom he was on friendly terms, decided to capture control of the Louisville & Nashville's stock in the belief that Morgan would then be forced to buy him out at Gates' inflated price. Gates secretly began buying large blocks of L. & N. stock at bargain prices on what was then a declining market. By April he had rounded up more than 300,000 shares before Morgan realized that Gates, through various blinds and fronts, had surreptitiously obtained a corner on the company's stock. Morgan's Southern railroad monopoly was seriously threatened. Gates' education at the poker table proved more useful than Morgan's more formal schooling; he had sized up Morgan as the type who makes a reckless move when the chips are down. Morgan's pride simply could not allow him to be outwitted and outfaced by such a rude specimen as Bet-a-Million Gates.

The conventional riposte to an attempt to corner a stock was to flood the market and make your opponent buy more than he could afford. Morgan, going by the book, seized upon the idea of throwing on the market 50,000 shares of treasury stock kept in the L. & N. offices. This stock had never been registered with the New York Stock Exchange, and it was highly irregular, illegal in fact, to dispose of it without registration.

With the help of Jim Brady's coffers, Gates was able to buy up the new offering. He now had an absolute corner on L. & N. stock, and Morgan and his friends were sweating blood. The Gates syndicate was jubilant and determined to squeeze Morgan for all he was worth. After a few days of rueful consideration, the contemporary Titan of American finance was forced to send an emissary under a flag of truce to the Gates syndicate's headquarters in the Waldorf-Astoria. Prolonged haggling followed, but Morgan was forced to buy out Gates at an average profit to Gates and his partners of $25 per share.

Brady's share of the plunder, for the use of his money and his moral support, was $1,250,000. It was easy to make money, he observed, if you knew the right people. He increased that nest egg by gambling on the commodity market and participating in pool operations which usually turned out to be lucrative.

Many of the tips which led to successful speculation came to him as a bonus for his lavish hospitality in the house on Eighty-sixth Street. Magnificoes like Thomas Fortune Ryan, who was piling up an immense fortune in streetcar franchises, tobacco, and the exploitation of the Belgian Congo, the Western railroad magnate James J. Hill, James R. Keane, and other predators from the financial jungle accepted his invitations because they knew he would always have plenty of female talent of the most toothsome variety from Broadway to help keep everyone's spirits high and soothe away executive cares. He kept the wine and whiskey flowing and listened attentively, and soberly, while his overserved guests committed indiscretions, talked too freely, and unwittingly helped him build up his own fortune.

The Brady method of entertaining, then trimming out-of-town wassailers was observed with amused appreciation by Albert Stevens Crockett as a star reporter for the New York *Herald*:

A Summer in the Seraglio

In strictly private life, Diamond Jim acted as a getter-up of parties where the Big Fellows, aided by a lavish application of liquors and by pleasant attentions from light but passably pretty ladies, might coax gentlemen from The Sticks into business commitments from which daylight and sober sense might have made them revolt. Jim had a wide acquaintance along Broadway, and his particular blonde [Edna McCauley] knew others. Besides, if the preference of the gentlemen was for brunettes, his address book was filled with telephone numbers, each indicating a young woman . . . willing to "go as far as you like," provided assurance was given that a hundred-dollar bill would be found under her plate at table, or would be deposited in what was called her "national bank" in a method acceptable to the donor. Tales used to persist of one such party where the twenty girls who acted as "hostesses" each received a thousand-dollar bill for their presence—and performances. . . . More than once the male guests corralled by Jim for the Big Fellows consisted largely of legislators whose good opinion— or otherwise—of certain measures then under consideration, was desirable.

Brady even put his "illuminated shirtfront," as the wits called his constant display of jewelry, to work for him. "If he wanted to sell a man a big order of machinery," according to Crockett, "his method was to work through the other's wife, particularly if the customer was the head of some big company.

He would invite the intended victim to dinner and insist upon his "bringing the wife." The dinner would always prove to be elaborate, and the wine abundant. But the lady, once she spied the jewels which sparkled on her host, would almost invariably go into envious spasms, and could see nothing else. She would express admiration for Jim's emeralds, or his diamonds, or what not, and if he thought it would help a sale, Jim would then not hesitate to present the lady with a diamond or a ruby or a sapphire, sure that he would recover far more than its cost in the commission he was bound to make on the deal with her husband. . . .

Through most of his career Brady was content with being a supersalesman testing the tensile strength of expense accounts provided by other men. It was more fun making deals in the raffish atmosphere of the Broadway night spots than presiding over board meetings and brooding over balance sheets. Simple observation was enough to convince him that the executives had all the headaches and the salesmen all the fun.

He was finally, and reluctantly, persuaded to shoulder an executive burden himself when he discovered that the Pressed Steel Car Company, in which he had acquired a large portion of the stock after arranging the Schoen-Fox merger several years before, was being mismanaged. Jim suddenly dumped his stock on the market and retired from its affairs. Then with John M. Hansen, the chief engineer of Pressed Steel and the man who tipped him off on how the company was going down the drain, he organized his own company, the Standard Steel Car, with the help of a loan obtained from Andrew Mellon. That Mellon, a cautious Pittsburgh banker who would become Secretary of the Treasury under Harding, Coolidge, and Hoover and whose family interests encompassed the Gulf Oil Company and the aluminum trust, would loan him money on little more than his reputation testified to the respect the flashy Brady had won from the staider sector of the financial community.

Reluctant though he ordinarily was to approve large loans without substantial collateral, Mellon coughed up three million dollars to back Brady and Hansen in their venture. Hansen was named president, Brady vice-president, with Mellon appointees filling the rest of the offices and most of the board of directors. Brady was even cagier than Mellon when it came to backing his own play. He insisted on being allowed to acquire a large block of Standard Steel Car stock but to pay for it out of future commissions as the company's salesman-in-chief. Still the drummer at heart, he had more confidence in commissions than in dividends.

Standard Steel turned out to be a flourishing enterprise, and it must have seemed to less fortunate entrepreneurs that his luck improved as his balloonlike waistline expanded.

He even avoided coming a cropper when he was tempted into the ownership of a racing stable, the sort of venture capitalism which had been the downfall of better men. The hugger-mugger of racing in those days (and perhaps in ours) made it less a sport than a battle of wits. For many years Brady had been an enthusiastic follower of the racetrack. His excursions on a Saturday afternoon to Sheepshead Bay, Gravesend, or Belmont were planned and undertaken with all the Brady panache and showiness. Accompanied by Edna McCauley, Lillian Russell, and Jesse Lewisohn, he would drive to the track in one of his carriages, with both the occupants and the horses splendidly caparisoned, Ascot style, and two midgets in scarlet-and-gold livery riding on the box and pretending to be footmen. He finally had to discharge the midgets because they kept falling off the box when the carriage hit any sizable bump in the road.

Brady became an active participant in the sport in the spring of 1901 when a Brooklyn sportsman named Phil Dwyer, hard up for cash, persuaded him to buy two of his horses for $10,-000. One was Gold Heels, a particularly promising three-year-old. This was the start of the Brady stable, though its entries would not be registered in his name.

For some reason Brady did not want to operate on the turf under his own name. The reason he gave was that many of his Western railroad clients were men of conservative tastes and might be offended if he took up such a questionable avocation; there was so much hanky-panky in American racing, before the Jockey Club asserted a tighter control over its membership, that anyone who participated was slightly tarnished (guilt by association). Jim's announced reason didn't quite stand up. In the first place, his reputation was so raffish that a fling on the turf could hardly have made much difference. And there were plenty of respectable citizens, including railroad magnates (A. J. Cassatt, president of the Pennsylvania, for instance), who owned racing stables. Whatever his motive, he placed the nominal ownership of his stable under one F. C. McLewee, who also managed it.

Gold Heels, a beautiful specimen of horseflesh, did his sub-rosa owner proud from the beginning. Late in the summer of 1901 he was entered for his first race under the Brady false colors, the Woodlawn Cup, which he won in track-record time. Brady bought ten other colts and began operating on a large scale. Gold Heels and his stablemate, Major Daingerfield, won every race during the first month of the 1902 season. Together they compiled a phenomenal and, given the naughtiness of racing circles, a rather suspiciously flawless record. Gold Heels won the Suburban Handicap, the Brighton Cup, the Brighton Handicap, and the Advance Stakes; Major Daingerfield nosed out the field in the Tidal Stakes, the Brighton Derby, and the Realization Stakes. Track followers were beginning to mutter that Brady's horses seemed incapable of losing a race.

The Jockey Club decided to investigate the seeming invincibility of the Brady stable. Whatever their findings, which were not made public, they came up with a new regulation: Henceforth the owner of a stable could not operate clandestinely. Brady then sold his stable at auction.

A magnificent gesture topped his retirement as the uncrowned, and indeed anonymous, King of the Turf. He celebrated the occasion with what was possibly the costliest party of the decade. It was a beefsteak dinner on the roof of the Holland House, such an orgy of beef-eating that the guests wore smocks, like surgeons, over their evening dress. The rout lasted for seventeen hours, from four o'clock of a November Sunday afternoon to nine o'clock Monday morning. How many steers fell under the steak knives was not calculated, but a bottle count was kept: 500 bottles of Mumm's champagne, or about ten for each of Jim's fifty guests. They sat around a horseshoe-shaped table dominated by a life-size statue of Gold Heels garlanded with roses. When the steaks ran out around midnight, Jim ordered the Holland House kitchen to stay open and keep producing other dishes under forced draft. About the time that belts and corsets were snapping under the pressure of that marathon gourmandizing, Jim signaled a corps of waiters to enter, each bearing a cushion on which nestled favors for each of the guests, diamond brooches for the women, diamond-encrusted stopwatches for the men. The souvenirs alone cost Jim $60,000, the whole affair more than $100,000. Thus he wiped out the $82,230 he had won in stakes on Gold Heels and Major Daingerfield.

There were other memorable parties, some which the participants would later have preferred to forget, particularly after the June night in 1906 when the Pittsburgh playboy Harry K. Thaw shot and killed the wealthy architect Stanford White in the theater on the Madison Square Garden roof. The killjoys were hunting in packs by then. They had elected William Travers Jerome as district attorney on his pledge to clean up the town. The public, in fact, was experiencing a revulsion against the commercial vice centered in the Tenderloin and the careless morals of so many of the top-dog class. The demand for higher moral standards became feverish when the motive for the murder of Stanford White was published in eight-column streamers. Thaw claimed that he slew the architect, a prominent member of the lobster-palace world with a ruinous penchant for young actresses and models whom he seduced after introducing them to a pink velvet swing in his apartment, because White had tampered with the morals (to use the polite phrase of the time) of Thaw's young bride, Evelyn Nesbit.

Most of White's friends ran for cover after the slaying. Not Jim Brady. He at least had the courage to show up at White's funeral, from which so many of the architect's friends were discreetly absent out of fear of being identified as one of his fellow sybarites.

Jim, in fact, had every reason to remember White with affection. How could he forget the Jack Horner party White had given for him in White's notorious mirrored apartment? On that occasion White, Brady, and a dozen of their friends sat down to supper, the *pièce de résistance* of which was a huge cardboard pie carried into the dining room by three waiters. As the birthday boy, Jim Brady was given a red ribbon, the other guests white ribbons to pull at White's command. When Brady pulled his red ribbon, he found a beautiful and naked girl at the other end; she sat on his lap and spooned dessert under his walrus mustache. The other guests, having found their own ribbons unattached to similar favors, groaned in protest. Eleven other naked nymphs then pranced into the room. What happened after that is unhappily veiled in conjecture, a fabric which is seldom diaphanous.

Jim, though he was still in love with the elusive Edna McCauley and wanted to make an honest woman of her, attended a number of such saturnalias given by Stanford White. He could ease his conscience by reflecting that the parties were good for business, and anything good for business, by the standards of the early 1900's, could hardly be immoral. After one of White's Roman-style banquets, at which nude females fed the guests while perched on velvet swings, Jim always showed up the next morning with his order book to talk business with the hungover survivors of the night before. He found that a customer with the collywobbles is the best kind.

By this time, the middle of the first decade of the new century, both Diamond Jim and Lillian Russell had given up the battle against their waistlines. Heft was back in fashion; the Edwardians were, if anything, heartier in their appetites and less abashed in their lusts than the Victorians. Edward VII, as the style-setter of his brief era, was a fat boy with appetites and proclivities greatly resembling those of the American commoner Jim Brady.

Once again the dining-out accomplishments of Brady and Russell were a matter of astonishment. They seemed determined to outguzzle each other for the eating championship of the world. Invariably their companions, or seconds, on such occasions were Jesse Lewisohn and Edna McCauley, and often Flo Ziegfeld and his present wife, the tiny French-born singer Anna Held. Jim and Lillian had been witnesses when the Ziegfelds were married, more or less, in a Manhattan hotel suite simply by announcing that they intended to live together as man and wife, without any clerical sanction.

Many years later Jacques Bustanoby would recall for a newspaper interviewer how his restaurant would come alive when the sextet walked in and Lillian sang "Come Down My Evenin' Star" and Anna sang her famous "I Cannot Make My Eyes Behave" in competition for the loudest applause from their fellow diners.

One night, Bustanoby recalled in 1931, when his restaurant was only a nostalgic memory, Brady bet Lillian a diamond ring that he could eat more than she could. Before the contest began, Lillian adjourned to the ladies' room and returned with a sizable bundle which, in a whispered aside, she asked Bustanoby to keep for her until the next day. Then she "went back to the table," Bustanoby recalled, "and ate plate for plate with Brady, and beat him fair and square." Perhaps, but it seems more likely that Brady was merely being gallant. Next day Lillian collected her bundle; it contained the corsets she removed before engaging in the set-to with Brady.

Even solo, without dining companions to encourage his appetite and marvel at his capacity, Brady's feats as a trencherman awed his contemporaries. Among his admirers was Irvin S. Cobb, then a reporter for the New York *World* but later a celebrated humorist. The rotund Cobb himself was a gastronome of considerable attainment, but he was willing to concede the world championship to Brady after watching him in action.

Cobb and three colleagues, Samuel Blythe, Charley Hand, and Carl von Guttenberg, met at the Café Martin on lower Madison Avenue for a Sunday breakfast. Blythe nudged Cobb, directed his attention to a man being seated at an adjoining table, and told him, "You think you're some eater, eh? And you think William Jennings Bryan is pretty good, too? Well, you are and he is. But yonder comes the champion of the ages. Watch him, Cobb, watch him and weep."

Cobb surveyed the man at the next table, whose physical proportions alone indicated that his life was dedicated to the pleasures of the table. As Cobb later wrote:

His gross displacement was awe-inspiring. He had a huge frame to start with and fat was draped upon it in creases and folds. He had three distinct chins and the nethermost one ran all the way around his neck as though, being fearful of punctures, he was carrying an extra spare on behind. His coat was of a shrieking checked pattern, needing only the name of the stable across the rear to be a blanket for some racing filly—and about the right dimensions, too. It being the Sabbath day he was content to wear his comparatively inobtrusive star sapphire set: matched stones, the size of plover eggs in his cuff links, on his watch fob, upon two of his dropsical-looking fingers, down his shirt front, in his vest buttons and, if rumor had it right, mounted also in his front and rear collar studs, his suspender buckles, his gold penknife and his sock supporters.

Tip-hungry waiters converged on Brady's table, Cobb said, "like gulls following a Turnverein excursion barge." A quart of orange juice served to wake up Jim's taste buds. With only a touch or two of hyperbole, Cobb then described the manful way Brady tackled his breakfast.

Next, arriving on a silver platter suitable for a roast turkey's accommodation, there appeared a quadruple portion of corned-beef hash, mounded like an igloo and shingled over with at least eight poached eggs. Maybe there were more than eight—anyhow, practically a setting of eggs. With this order came a towering edifice of hot cakes. Like a fast workman double-tiling a bathroom, he tessellated that mighty dome of hash with two layers of hot cakes, fitting them on top of the poached eggs. He then sluiced the ensemble with large quantities of melted butter and maple syrup, and using a carving knife and fork—no ordinary table tools would have served—he chopped the whole thing into chaos. And then, by Saint Appetitious I swear it, then with a dessert spoon he ate it to the last bite and the last lick. Sam discounted the suggestion that Mr. Brady might be putting on airs for our benefit. This was just average for him, he said. I figured he must have a waiting list of at least eight tapeworms. . . .

Cobb, as a journalist and an envious rival trencherman, later had occasion to observe Brady as a guest at banquets and other public functions. Brady always had two places reserved for himself at the table, not only to accommodate his bulky figure but to make sure of double helpings of everything. "Then he would wallow pensively down to the grill room," Cobb noted, "and for a savory, as the English say, would have a tenderloin steak measuring about fourteen inches from tip to tip, with mushrooms and the fixings; also a tall tankard of orange juice. He never drank anything stronger."

One wonders—unfortunately for them, Jim and Lillian apparently did not—whether the dainty, birdlike Edna McCauley and the thin, dyspeptic Jesse Lewisohn ever gazed at each other, with a glint of speculation, across the lobster shells, the corncobs, and the melting Baked Alaska which represented the jousting grounds of their two well-fleshed companions—gazed and wondered whether two delicate appetites might not be more complementary than the present arrangement.

7

A FAMOUS FOURSOME BREAKS UP

THE relationship between Jim Brady and Edna McCauley, Lillian Russell and Jesse Lewisohn had settled into a serene domestic routine. All they lacked was the formality of marriage. Edna was Jim's mistress, but she seemed to be content with her life. Jesse accompanied Lillian everywhere, on the road and on her summer layoffs at the Long Island retreat and the Saratoga cottage.

Jim had bought a gentleman-farmer's hideaway, Ellendale Manor, near South Branch, New Jersey. Here he entertained royally in July and provided surcease for the married men of his wide and uninhibited social circle. Their wives were out of town for the summer, and they brought their temporary consorts down to Ellendale Manor, knowing their host was an understanding fellow who was not, in fact, married to their hostess. The goings-on there did not meet with the approval of the neighbors, but to Jim and Edna they were only distant, bewhiskered yokels whose opinions were of small account. Edna liked the farm life so much that she stayed at Ellendale for months at a time and told Jim that she was tired of the hectic pace of Manhattan night life. To Jim this seemed a hopeful sign that she might one day complete the process of domestication and agree to marry him.

In Lillian's life, because of the uncertainties and hazards of a theatrical career, there was perhaps a little less serenity. It had seemed that she would be the permanent resident star of the Weber and Fields Music Hall and would round off her career there, but it didn't turn out that way.

During her fourth season at the Music Hall, a rift developed between Weber and Fields, the exact cause of which was unknown even to their stage manager and subsequent biographer, Felix Isman. For business reasons, however, they decided to maintain the partnership. "They continued as they had for a quarter of a century to use the same dressing room," Isman noted, "and not a whisper came to the ears of the company. Such was the business acumen of the two that when a vague rumor did get loose, Joe and Lew killed it quickly and cunningly by sitting for three hours on a shoe-shine stand at Twenty-ninth Street and Broadway and eating peanuts from the same bag while all the Rialto passed. . . ."

The Music Hall, if not the partnership, was doomed in any case after 575 persons lost their lives in the Iroquois Theater fire in Chicago on December 30, 1903. After that catastrophe, every American city revised its theater-building code. The Music Hall would have to be rebuilt or abandoned, and Weber and Fields chose the latter course.

On the night of January 30, 1904, the Weberfields company gave its last performance in the Music Hall, and two days later it set out on a transcontinental tour. The company was augmented by Miss Frankie Bailey, whose legs were so symmetrical that they had been copyrighted, somehow, with the Library of Congress. The current edition of the revue, *Whoop-dee-doo*, was a great success in San Francisco, but a squabble over bookings left the company temporarily stranded there until it was arranged to break the jump back East by giving a performance in Albuquerque, New Mexico. It was unheard of for a major theatrical enterprise to appear in what was then a cow town of 6,238 population.

The certified appearance, in the flesh, of Lillian Russell and Frankie Bailey caused the greatest commotion since Pat Garrett shot Billy the Kid. When the Weberfields special train arrived, it was greeted by a brass band and most of the population of the territory, including hundreds of cowpunchers who had galloped in from the range to determine whether Lillian Russell and Frankie Bailey, in her geranium tights, looked like the cigarette cards tacked on the walls of every bunkhouse in the West. The governor and the entire territorial government were part of the reception committee. Lillian and her colleagues had to make do with dressing rooms recently tenanted by the hounds of an *Uncle Tom's Cabin* troupe which had preceded them, but the enthusiasm of their yippeeing audience more than made up for the discomforts of the Albuquerque Opera House.

Late in April the company returned to New York, and a few days later Broadway was astounded by the announcement that Weber and Fields were breaking up their partnership, though not before offering *Whoop-dee-doo* for a month's run at the New Amsterdam Theater. On May 29, 1904, they gave their final performance. An orgy of sentiment attended the fall of the final curtain. "A Broadway audience," reported the New York *Herald* the next morning, "is not particularly sentimental, but the tears that streaked the painted and powdered faces of the stage were multiplied many times in the audience as 'Auld Lang Syne' became the final musical number." The *Herald* society reporter listed among the weepers such gilded names as James Hazen Hyde, Mr. and Mrs. Howard Gould, Frank Crowninshield, Mr. and Mrs. Ernest G. Stedman, Jesse Lewisohn, and most of the New York State Supreme Court bench. The New York *Sun* account was characteristically laced with a touch of alum: "The chorus girls wept . . . Lillian Russell shed real tears, and it was twelve o'clock before the obsequies ended and the mourners departed."

From the backstage side of the proscenium, despite the Park Row cynicism, the sentimentality of the occasion was as real as anything can be in the theater. The Weberfields company had been known along Broadway as the Happy Family; everyone loved the bosses and each other. Lillian Russell in her autobiography would recall her years at the Music Hall as the longest and happiest of her professional life. It was a matter of atmosphere, of the personalities of Joe Weber and Lew Fields, of an equalitarian tradition which encompassed the stars, the chorus girls, and the stage crew. De Wolf Hopper, looking back on his years as a Weberfields comic, said he could not remember a single unpleasant word or incident, "yet there was never another stage so cluttered up with the high explosives of temperament. Half a dozen stars managed by two other stars! There was no parallel for it in my knowledge of the theater. I don't know how it was done." (Presumably it was the self-effacing quality of Weber and Fields themselves, their unselfishness and consideration, which still comprise one of the untarnished legends of show business.) "I do not say there was no jealousy; that would be absurd. Had there been no jealousy, there would have been nothing remarkable in the harmony. The astonishing thing was that everyone kept a tight rein on his or her envy. If anyone had a gag or a bit of business he could not use at the moment, it was nothing for him to pass it along. With six or seven exceptions—my wives—those were the happiest moments of my life."

Lillian Russell found the atmosphere of the Weberfields company so congenial that she could even take a certain amount of ribbing on one of the few subjects she was sensitive about. Enormously easygoing, with a low threshold of risibility, she misplaced her sense of humor only on one issue: that of actresses wearing tights. That she had worn purple tights in at least one stage appearance, during her first engagement in San Francisco, was undeniable. Russell nevertheless loudly and firmly denied that she had ever bared her limbs from tip to toe; either she had developed a convenient lapse of memory, or anything that happened west of the Rockies didn't count. One of the resident comedians, Sam Bernard, heard her protestations with a sly smile. For the next few weeks his offstage hours were filled with scurrying around the Broadway photographers' shops in search of documentary proof to the contrary. Finally at the Albert Davis Studios he found what he was looking for: Lillian posing, one arm akimbo, in revealing but not entirely flattering tights. He hurried back to the theater to show it to her.

"I never sat for that picture!" she angrily protested.

"No," Bernard replied, "you had to stand for it."

Lillian, despite such put-downs, was as saddened as any of the chorus girls by the disbanding of the Weberfields company. About the same time she was worrying over Jesse Lewisohn's troubles with District Attorney William Travers Jerome. The ax-wielding Jerome had raided Richard Canfield's Manhattan establishment and the gambler's patrons were being badgered into testifying against him. One was Lewisohn, who was unflatteringly described in the subpoena as "a known frequenter of a common gambling den." Jerome got him on the witness stand, but Lewisohn refused to testify on grounds that he might be forced to incriminate himself. The State Legislature then passed a bill designed to outflank the Fifth Amendment and, in effect, required that Lewisohn testify under guarantees of immunity. The copper heir had to admit that he had gambled at Canfield's tables, which was sufficient for Jerome to obtain a conviction, but at least he was off the district attorney's hook.

Lillian's career obviously had been rejuvenated by her service as a Weber and Fields comedienne. The newspaper critics remarked on her sharper timing and improved delivery of her speaking lines when she opened in the title role of *Lady Teazle*, a musical adaptation of *The School for Scandal*, on December 24, 1904. It was a resounding success and its star was showered with almost unanimously enthusiastic notices, though there was one picayune comment from an evening newspaper: "Miss Russell has the arts preservative at her fingers' ends.

The house sat up when it first saw her in the golden wig, the bluish-gray hat and the blue brocades of the period. Somehow, she had summoned the freshness and charm of youth to melt the ripeness of maturity." The same critic rightly added that "Weber and Fields was a better school of acting than it was of singing."

Lillian confided to reporters after the opening of *Lady Teazle* that she had been so despondent over the closing of the Weber and Fields Music Hall that she had considered retirement. She particularly missed David Warfield, underhanded scene-stealer though he was. Every night, she recalled, she and Warfield would play a private scene at her dressing room door. " 'Nellie,' he would say (he always called me Nellie), 'are you going out tonight?' 'Yes, Father,' I'd answer. 'You know I must go get some cigarettes for breakfast.' Then the tears would trickle down his face. I never saw anyone who could shed false tears as easily as Warfield does."

During the next two years she also achieved financial if not critical success in such lightweight offerings as *Barbara's Millions* and *The Butterfly*. She was in her middle forties and had survived the difficult passage from transitory stardom to national institution. Professionally and emotionally her life seemed to be secure.

Then in the spring of 1906 Jesse Lewisohn was stricken by a mysterious, wasting malady. Weight dropped away from his slender frame at an alarming rate. His complexion was waxen, and he trembled constantly. Lewisohn visited a number of specialists, who suggested various therapies ranging from electricity to an extended stay at a European spa. One, without offering a diagnosis, advocated immediate surgery.

Finally he consulted a plain-spoken practitioner who told him he was dissipating his life away. "You will have to stay away from women," Lewisohn was bluntly told. "You'll have to give up theater-going, drinking, gambling, staying up to all hours. No more wine, women, or song."

That advice was almost as shocking to Lewisohn as if he had

been given a month to live. How did a dedicated rounder reform himself overnight? Besides, he had promised to accompany Lillian on her tour with the *Barbara's Millions* company.

Naturally he turned to his best friend, Jim Brady, for advice and comfort. "God damn it," Brady said (he would never be the patron saint of the Holy Name Society), "you're going to follow the doctor's orders."

Jesse pointed out that Lillian would never be able to manage without him.

"She's old enough to take care of herself," Brady retorted, unaware that his dictum would be turned against him not too long from then. "She was looking after herself for thirty years before you came along. This is what you're going to do: pack up and go to my farm at South Branch. Edna," he added, "will take care of you, nurse you back to health."

Lewisohn finally agreed to submit to a summer on the farm under Edna's ministrations.

That summer of 1906, as it happened, both Jim and Lillian were unable to spend any time at their usual pursuits. Lillian was on the road with *Barbara's Millions*, and business affairs kept Jim away from the farm and from New York all summer. Both received occasional bulletins from Ellendale Manor that Jesse Lewisohn was coming along fine, that he was recovering his health almost as quickly as he had lost it.

It wasn't until mid-September that Jim managed to break away from his business affairs and make a trip to South Branch with his old friend Jules Weiss. Jim may not have been the most sensitive man, but the tension his arrival created was palpable and unmistakable.

They were playing cards after dinner the night of his arrival when Brady was unable to contain himself any longer. "What the hell is the matter around here?" he blurted out.

Lewisohn mustered his courage and told his former best friend, "Edna and I are in love, Jim. We're going to be married."

Brady raged at Edna for being unfaithful to him, at Lewisohn for "double-crossing a woman who's never looked at another man all these years," but his tirade did not sway them. Brady was so mad he stomped out of the farmhouse and with Jules Weiss returned to New York that night. The next day, Weiss later recalled, he tried to convince Jim he should return to South Branch and talk Edna out of her decision to marry Lewisohn. But Jim refused, saying, "There ain't a woman in the world who'd marry an ugly-looking guy like me."

About a week later Jim was waiting at Grand Central for Lillian's return with the *Barbara's Millions* company and broke the news about Jesse and Edna to her with a tact and sympathy she would always remember. He didn't tell her that just before he left Jesse and Edna at the New Jersey farmhouse Lewisohn had reminded him of his own statement when Brady was persuading him to take the farm cure: "She's old enough to take care of herself."

Lillian was an old hand at surviving unhappy endings to her love affairs. Philosophically she had cushioned herself against a blow like Jesse Lewisohn's defection almost as though she'd foreseen it. While traveling with *Barbara's Millions*, she had revealed to reporters that she was studying the works of the Roman Stoic Marcus Aurelius and never went anywhere without them. She was fond of quoting the Roman's belief that whatever happens to an individual is an enriching experience: "Accept the gifts of fortune without pride and part with them without reluctance."

While Jim underwent a period of black depression, from which not even the glazed splendor of a suckling pig could rouse him, Lillian with her more flexible nature, and with Marcus Aurelius as her new bedside companion, carried on as though nothing had happened. Edna and Jesse were married, but Lillian got in the last word—and it was a better line than any of her playwrights had supplied her with. When they sailed for Europe on their honeymoon, Lillian sent a telegram to the *Deutschland* reading: DON'T BE IN SUCH A HURRY.

Hard work was Lillian's consolation, just as Brady's was sitting around the Broadway cafés, sunk in misery and gloom, and being lavishly pitied by his friends. Work was also a necessity in her case, since the sudden collapse of a Manhattan bank in which most of her fluid assets were deposited left her with a severe case of the shorts. To remedy her financial situation, she sold her house and put up most of its furnishings for auction at the Fifth Avenue Art Galleries. The auction cleared almost $75,000. A good part of that went into leasing and extravagantly furnishing a private Pullman car, the *Iolanthe*, in which she launched herself on a coast-to-coast tour with several of her recent successes. The *Iolanthe* contained three bedrooms, a drawing room, a library (including the collected works of Marcus Aurelius), a kitchen, a dining room, two servants' rooms, and a small conservatory.

Lillian was a part owner of the road company, taking a salary plus a percentage of the receipts, which brought in close to $2,000 a week. The girls in the company would always remember her maternal solicitude, her generosity and camaraderie. One of them, Sally Winwood, would recall how Lillian always divided the flowers and other presents she received with the chorus girls and stagehands. Her sole demonstrations of temperament were reserved for managers; among her fellow players she never demanded the prerogatives of stardom or indicated that she lived on a superior level. "Wherever she went," Sally Winwood related, "she always carried her little Japanese spaniel in her muff. When we would have only ten minutes for lunch, she would pull up at the counter with the rest of us. . . . She loved custard pie, and if train time was called too soon, she would grab a piece and run along to the train while eating it. . . . She used to call us girls into her dressing room between matinee and evening performances and tell us the most complimentary things about our work. . . ."

It was a time for reappraisal and reassessment. She knew that her voice had lost its timbre, that her figure was less lissome, that she couldn't get away with playing youthful roles in musical comedy for much longer. Furthermore, the operetta was losing its following in America. From now on she would have to concentrate on whatever acting ability she could develop—glimmerings of which the drama critics had noted following her training with the Weber and Fields troupe, which may not have been the Royal Academy of Dramatic Art but which did teach her how to get the most out of a line, the economy of movement and gesture for maximum effect, the art of riveting an audience's attention. When she was young, shapely, and in full voice, it was enough simply to make a swanlike entrance and burst into song. Now she had to compete, she had to project her personality with sufficient force to claim her share of attention against younger and more beautiful women—in a word, she had to grow up.

Lillian Russell rarely took herself seriously, but her career was something else, it was 90 percent of her life. She was determined to make her mark as an actress, if not in heavyweight drama, at least in comedy. A splendid sense of humor was a good base on which to build, though not all comediennes have that quality. Furthermore, when she returned to New York from her transcontinental tour, she began studying daily with Mrs. Scott Siddons, who was reputed to be the best dramatic coach in the country.

In furtherance of her new program, she had tried out on the road a new comedy titled *Wildfire*, written by George Broadhurst and George V. Hobart as a Russell vehicle. The subject was horse racing, which Lillian felt an affinity for. Her role was that of a widow left with an estate consisting of little more than a racing stable; the plot involved her attempts to bring home a few winners and her courtship by an automobile fancier (modern touch) and a fellow admirer of horseflesh whose campaign to win the fair widow is thwarted by a villainous bookmaker. These were the standard ingredients of a well-made commercial play of the time, but Lillian's vibrant personality and compelling presence gave it an undeserved luster and even distracted the audience from wondering how an impoverished widow could be dressed in the latest Parisian imports.

The effort of a middle-aged woman, inevitably spoiled by more than two decades of stardom and easy acclaim, to school herself in new techniques, paid off where it counted—at the ticket window. *Wildfire* opened September 7, 1908, in New York and became the greatest success of her postmusical career. The critic of the often-quibbling New York *Sun* threw his hat in the air and proclaimed that Lillian "made the biggest killing of her career. . . . She acted so well that you only remembered she hadn't sung when you got home. If she had stepped upon the stage for the first time last night, she would have won in a walk."

Wildfire ran for 566 performances on Broadway, and during the run, enthused by the new turn in her career, Lillian trained like an athlete with several hours of gymnastics every morning. She could hardly have lived a more disciplined life outside a nunnery. It was thus a matter of grinding outrage, which even a neo-Stoic found hard to bear, when a violent controversy broke out over plans to hang her portrait in the Iowa Hall of Fame. Most people considered her Iowa's most famous daughter, an opinion in which the State Historical Department concurred. Yet there was a backlash from cornbelt Puritans who believed that any woman connected with the theater was wildly immoral. They were not even appeased when that most eminent of Baptists, that primmest of plutocrats, John D. Rockefeller, Sr., bestowed his approval on her. He had given a $500 check to the Ossining Hospital on the understanding that Lillian would appear in person and sing "Come Down My Evenin' Star," to which Lillian agreed.

Even so, the more Gothic types of Iowa Christianity continued to protest against the hanging of Lillian's portrait in their rather understocked Hall of Fame. They were roused to more passionate outcries when one Rev. Hubert D. Knickerbocker of Fort Worth, Texas—a state which seemed to be oversupplied with reverend Pecksniffs eager to be outraged—

horned in on the controversy by declaring all actresses were wantons. "They spend their time after the play," he added, without supplying the source of his information on this recondite subject, "in low-down resorts, drinking, gambling, singing, carousing and carrying on in an indecent way. . . . Sarah Bernhardt, Lily Langtry and Lillian Russell are but leaders in the vast army of fallen women."

Lillian made a spirited reply, starting out by calling the Reverend Knickerbocker a fanatic, arguing that actresses had to work harder than any housewife and that they were always ready to appear at benefits and other charitable functions. Her defense was unnecessary, for the state placed her portrait in the Hall of Fame with the announcement: "France gave Sarah Bernhardt the Cross of the Legion of Honor, and the State of Iowa has officially decided to hang the portrait of Lillian Russell in the State Historical Society Building as a representative daughter of the Commonwealth."

Meanwhile Diamond Jim Brady was setting new gastronomic records, evidently turning to food as solace for his bitter disappointment over losing Edna McCauley. Night after night he devastated the menus of the lobster-palace world. The number-one tourist attraction of New York in the early 1900's was Diamond Jim, ablaze with diamonds, tucking in a meal that would have foundered one of the jungle's larger carnivores.

Not that he would eat anything that was set before him. His palate, according to the experts, had attained the quality of a gourmand if not a gourmet. That expert on the Edwardian epicure, the late Lucius Beebe, in one of his magisterial surveys noted that Brady was:

> A gourmand rather than a gourmet, but so heroic were his skirmishes with the roasts, entrees and *pieces montees* as to elevate them to an actually epic dimension. Brady not only ate the full twelve-course dinner which was the conventional evening snack of the early decades of this century, he usually

consumed three or four helpings of the more substantial dishes, beginning his repast with a gallon of chilled orange juice and finishing with the greater part of a five-pound box of the richest available chocolates. In between he might well consume six dozen Lynnhaven oysters, a saddle of mutton, half a dozen venison chops, a roasting chicken with caper sauce, a brace or so of mallard or canvasback ducks, partridge or pheasant, and a twelve-egg souffle.

Mr. Beebe was not surprised that Broadway sports would "cheer him on his progress through the cutlets and make side bets on whether or not he'd fall dead before dessert."

George Rector, who was perhaps his favorite provider, recalled in his memoirs that Brady's appetite was not only heroic but, considering the amounts of food it took to stoke his metabolism, selective, thanks in part to the postgraduate course he had taken in the finer restaurants of Paris. As Rector would recall:

> We used to have our oysters shipped up to us from Baltimore daily, and every second or third shipment would include a barrel of extra large Lynnhavens with the words "For Mr. Brady" painted on the side of it. Even down in Maryland, the seafood dealers knew about Diamond Jim and saved all the giant oysters for him.
>
> He used to come into our place every evening about seven-thirty, and the first thing he would call for would be his orange juice. "I always want my orange juice fresh, George," he said to me once. "I'm willing to pay more, and I'm willing to wait, but I want the oranges squeezed fresh." There was no sense in trying to fool him with stale orange juice—he could tell it the first sip he took. Then, after he'd drained a gallon pitcher of this, I knew it was time to send the oysters out to him.
>
> I used to watch him eat those giant Lynnhavens. Nearly all of them had extra large oyster crabs in them, and Diamond Jim considered these a great delicacy—as they really are. Of course as soon as the oysters were opened and served the crabs took a new interest in life, and started exploring.

Among true connoisseurs, it seems, the ultimate delight was to spear the live crabs on the run, as it were, and crunch them down. Presumably this was not the pursuit for a man with a delicate stomach, or even a dedicated member of the Humane Society.

Jim [as Rector remembered] would be busy talking to the pretty lady who happened to be with him at the moment and the crabs would slip out of the shells and start crawling about the table. Then, without even stopping his conversation, Jim would strike out with his fork and impale those crabs so fast that the eye couldn't follow his hand. And he'd pop them into his mouth one by one, still talking all the while.

When he'd eaten about four portions of the oysters—some nights it varied a portion or two either way—it would be time for his *Lobster Americain*. I always made it myself, in the largest chafing dish we had in the place. And where the recipe called for one lobster, for Diamond Jim I used two—always two of everything.

After the lobster he'd have a dozen or so hard-shelled crabs, and when he had finished with those, he was ready to settle down to the regular dinner.

And the regular dinner was usually twelve courses. The monstrous guzzling would have been disgusting, perhaps, except that Jim Brady was as generous with everyone else as he was with himself. Rector often sat with Brady when the latter did not bring guests of his own, and during the evening a dozen or more petitioners would appear at his table. Their plaints were unimaginative: "I had a bad day at the track, Jim; can you let me have a hundred or two for a day? . . . Mr. Brady, my show closed last night and I'm out of a job. Can you let me have enough money to get home to my folks? . . . Jim, my wife has to go to the hospital for an operation and I haven't got enough money to pay the doctor. Can you tide me over for a little while?"

Naturally Rector was appalled that his magnificent restaurant should be turned into a branch of the Society for the Preservation of Decayed Gentlefolk or some such eleemosynary institution, equally that so many of his fine-feathered customers, who put up such an elegant front, else they wouldn't have been admitted beyond the velvet rope, were in the habit of panhandling. Once he told Brady that people were taking advantage of him, which was hardly news to Brady. "As long as I live," Rector would recall, "I'll never forget the way he looked at me, closed one eye in a wink and said, 'George I know they're all pullin' my leg; but did you ever stop to think it's fun to be a sucker, if you can afford it?' " No doubt there was a dark side to his open-handedness; it confirmed his more cynical suspicions of human nature, particularly after Edna McCauley and Jesse Lewisohn let him down, and provided a perverse pleasure in observing the self-degradation of his species. Everybody was "on the take." After his death it was estimated that he had given more than $1,500,000 in jewelry to various women; some, no doubt, for favors rendered. No doubt this contributed to his feeling that female virtue was not the most precious commodity in the world. On the other hand, suspect though his generosity with poor working girls would have been to an O. Henry, he did impersonally and with the best intentions bestow a large part of his fortune on various charitable and medical institutions; nor did he forget to leave $2,500 to his favorite Pullman porter.

During the five-year period between the breakup of her lengthy "engagement" to Jesse Lewisohn and her fourth and final marriage, Lillian, though approaching the half-century mark, was courted by a number of gallants, but Diamond Jim was always on one arm, her current suitor on the other, when she went out in public. Some of her suitors, of course, resented having an elephantine chaperone who, at times, almost seemed a rival.

One fellow who for a time made up an odd trio with Lillian Russell and Jim Brady was Wilson Mizner. A razor-edged wit, Mizner would somewhat biliously remember that "Brady liked his oysters sprinkled with clams, and his steaks smothered in veal cutlets."

Lillian had acquired catholic tastes in men, once she got over her fixation on musical types, but surely Wilson Mizner—as amusing a misanthrope as ever walked down Broadway—was a scandalously unconventional choice. The black sheep of a respectable California family, he had prospected for gold in the Klondike (mostly as a gambler and badger-game operator), served as the manager of middleweight champion Stanley Ketchel, managed a Broadway hotel in the corridors of which the scent of opium was omnipresent, and was briefly the consort of the former wife of the traction magnate Charles Yerkes until she objected to his converting her Fifth Avenue mansion into training quarters for his pugilistic stable. Mizner was a huge man with a long white face and the manner of an archbishop; he looked more than a little like a larcenous Woodrow Wilson. His biting witticisms had made him the Voltaire of Broadway: "I never saw a mob rush across town to do a good deed. . . . I respect faith but doubt is what gets you an education. . . . He'd steal a hot stove and come back for the smoke. . . . I hate careless flattery, the kind that exhausts you in your effort to believe it. . . . Those who welcome death have only tried it from the ears up. . . . If you steal from one author it's plagiarism; if you steal from many it's research. . . ." Reflecting on the latter maxim, Mizner had recently turned to dramatic literature and collaborated on *The Deep Purple* with Paul Armstrong. It was one of the hits of the 1911 season, a realistic study of the underworld and what one Broadway historian has called "the first effective drama about city-bred criminals."

Lillian was briefly enthralled by the rush of sardonic quips which Mizner tossed off so effortlessly, but Jim Brady intensified his chaperonage during that period. Mizner, in his opinion, was a sharpshooter who could not benefit Lillian either in her emotional or professional life. Mizner made no secret of the fact that he regarded a few pipes of opium more relaxing than a Caribbean cruise, yet he was a man of formidable if careless charm. By then Jim had assumed an almost paternal protectiveness toward Lillian, though she had secretly celebrated, if that is the word, her fiftieth birthday and Jim himself was only five years older.

It was shortly after her whirl with Wilson Mizner that he made up his mind to personally bring a little more permanence and stability into Lillian's life. They had been close friends for eighteen years, had known each other casually long before that. Loyalty, affection, companionship, mutual interests—so many things they had in common ought to count for more than the sexual/romantic impulse with two mature persons.

One day, unusually solemn, he showed up at Lillian's house and entered the parlor where Lillian and her daughter, Dorothy, now a young woman in her twenties, were sitting.

As Dorothy Solomon later told the story, Jim informed Lillian, abruptly and with less preamble than he would devote to a business transaction, "Lillian, I want you to marry me. And this is going to be your wedding present."

"This," according to Dorothy Solomon's account, was one million dollars, which he laid in Lillian's lap. Just what form the proffered dowry took was not explained. A million dollars even in one-thousand-dollar bills would have made a sizable bale. Even in ten-thousand-dollar bills it would have made an awesome bundle. A mere check for a million, however, would have lacked the Brady panache on such occasions.

Lillian was unimpressed by the fortune literally dumped in her lap but greatly touched by Jim's proposal. She could not accept it, she explained to Jim as gently and tactfully as possible, because marriage might wreck a beautiful friendship, which she valued more than anything else in the world.

"Let me build a theater for you, then," he suggested. "The Lillian Russell Theater. Biggest and most expensive showplace on Broadway."

She shook her head. "You can find better uses for a million dollars, Jim. They can name a theater for me after I'm dead."

8

L'AFFAIRE SOLE MARGUERY:
A SPY STORY

LONG ago Jim Brady had discovered what Lillian's house philosopher and many others could stoically have informed him, if he had placed any value in book learning. Experience was a crueler but more impressive instructor. Beyond a certain but fortunately incalculable amount there wasn't much you could buy with money. It could buy him false friends and specious companionship on lonely nights, it could keep the girls buzzing around like bees at a honeypot, it could deck him with more diamonds than he could transport in a wheelbarrow. But it also left a hollowness which only food, for the moment, could fill. He had everything money could buy, but literally nothing of what it couldn't buy. Romantic love was unattainable on self-respecting terms; he had no family except in the formal sense, no more real friends than any junior clerk in his office. His life had all the cold glitter of the diamonds in their special drawers of his dresser; it had only the transitory warmth of the reflected envy of his contemporaries.

In the predawn hour when Diamond Jim Brady finally packed it in, and the lights on Longacre Square dimmed, and he went home alone to the house on Eighty-sixth Street—an hour for morbid introspection and unwelcome intimations of mortality—he could still comfort himself with the minor, material triumphs of his life. The money was still rolling in, and people were referring to him as the Croesus of Manhattan; it was an incoming tide he could no more have reversed than King Canute could; the cumulative power of money to increase itself, without effort from its owner, by geometric degrees was one of the wonders of the capitalistic society which had raised him up from bellboy to magnate. The progressive income tax, enacted in 1913, was still only an evil rumor. Business was still a game inhibited by only the flimsiest regulation from the government. Nothing foreseeable could prevent James Buchanan Brady from dying in his massive bed, attended by as many physicians as could be crowded into the room, with more millions than he could ever spend.

There were souring moments, of course, when various four-flushers tried to snatch away his crown as the king of the big spenders. One pretender was Pearl Jim Murray, who had struck it rich in the Montana copper mines and tried to outflash Brady by carrying around and displaying at the least provocation a chamois bag full of huge pearls, more than 200 of them; but Murray could no more outshine Brady than pearls could outsparkle diamonds. There was also a challenge from an oddity who called himself Death Valley Scotty, an amiable and grizzled fraud whose picturesque manners and free hand with hundred-dollar bills temporarily stole the journalistic limelight from Brady. It was the mystery of Death Valley Scotty that compelled attention. He lived in a castle—still standing—out on the California desert and claimed, during annual descents on Manhattan, that his income came from a hidden gold mine in Death Valley. Actually Death Valley Scotty was a legend made from whole cloth, the weaver being a Chicago millionaire with a sardonic sense of humor who supplied Scotty with the money to make his occasional splashes in New York; probably it was a Chicagoan's vengeful way of pointing up the gullibility of New Yorkers. And there was the hectic competition for the title of All-time Big Spender offered by an influx known as the Pittsburgh Millionaires. These were overnight millionaires created, without that purpose in mind, by Andrew Carnegie when he sold his steel combine to J. P. Morgan. Casting themselves in Brady's image, or inept approximations thereof, they coursed through mid-Manhattan from the Tenderloin to Columbus Circle for several delirious years.

None of those rivals could match Diamond Jim Brady's resources. More importantly, they lacked his panache and imagination, the lordly dimension, the expansive geniality of his ventures in high living.

Who but Diamond Jim could have engineered the gastronomic coup code-named *L'Affaire Sole Marguery*, an adventure in culinary espionage which (had the details not been kept top secret for many years) might have brought on World War I several years earlier and pitted France against the United States? One wonders whether there wasn't a double agent owing primary allegiance to Kaiser Wilhelm lurking in the background.

Brady's venture into international intrigue came about one convivial evening around a table at Rector's, then managed by the founder, Charles Rector, whose son and successor, George, was still a student at Cornell University.

Brady was dining with Lillian Russell, the Broadway producer Sam Shubert (with whom Lillian had recently been involved in a lawsuit, but theatrical litigation was always a trifle frivolous, and the matter had been forgotten), the composer Victor Herbert, and other theatrical luminaries. Charles Rector was sitting with them. Someone at the table mentioned that supreme delicacy of *fin de siècle* Paris, *filet de sole Marguery*. Brady, lovingly recalling having sampled the dish on his visits to Paris, demanded to know why Rector's never had it on the menu. Charles Rector explained that the secret of its preparation was known only to the fish chef of the Café Marguery in

Paris; and it was as closely guarded as the French general staff's plans for a counteroffensive across the Rhine if and when the Germans became obstreperous.

"God damn it, Charles," Brady expostulated, "I want sole Marguery and to hell with the Frenchies. No matter what it costs. I don't want to have to travel all the way to Paris just to have fish properly prepared."

The honor, or perhaps the dishonor, of Rector's was placed in hazard by Brady's challenge. Culinary espionage was not unheard of, of course, but it was a tricky business. Your spy had to be absolutely trustworthy, otherwise word would get around that your establishment was so desperate it had to steal secrets from the kitchens of your betters. He also had to be a man of iron nerves, a master of dissembling innocence, otherwise you risked having him carved up by an outraged chef.

Who could Charles Rector trust with such a delicate mission? Only his son George, who was in the third year of law school at Cornell. This matter was more important than learning the intricacies of torts. Charles Rector called Cornell that night and summoned George to New York. He was given a steamer ticket to Le Havre and told not to return to his homeland until he had learned the recipe for the fish sauce.

Three weeks later young George Rector, having assumed the cover of a stranded American desperate for employment, which was close enough to the truth of his circumstances, obtained a job washing pots and pans in the kitchen of the Café Marguery. This sort of undercover work was grueling. He worked fifteen hours a day as a pot-walloper, peering over the shoulder of the fish chef as often as was discreetly possible. It took him two months—or approximately 720 hours of pot-washing—to ferret out the exact ingredients and the method of combining them. Before leaving Paris young Rector, as he later recorded, tried out his own version of *filet de sole Marguery* on "a jury of seven master chefs" who "voted my sauce perfect."

George Rector hastened back to America. "When the boat arrived in New York," he related, "Mr. Brady and my father were at the dock to greet me. 'Have you got the sauce?' Diamond Jim shouted as I came down the gangplank. I assured him that I did have the recipe for it, and the three of us entered his big car and were quickly driven uptown to our restaurant, where I went into the kitchen and started making preparations for the dinner which was to be given that night."

Brady and a group including Sam Shubert, Victor Herbert, the Chicago department store owner Marshall Field, the St. Louis brewer Adolphus Busch, and the Broadway chronicler Alfred Henry Lewis of the *Morning Telegraph*, sat down to dinner at Rector's that night at eight o'clock. Anxiously hovering over the scene was Charles Rector, who wondered, not for the first time, whether it had been wise to send a young law student to investigate something as complex as a sauce, which was a more intricate matter than any United States Supreme Court decision. The senior Mr. Rector was reassured when the gastronomic jury deliberated for four hours, sending back to the kitchen for more helpings, until at midnight Brady summoned the junior Mr. Rector to offer his congratulations.

"George, that sole was marvelous," Brady told him. "I've had nine helpings, and even right now, if you poured some of the sauce over a Turkish towel, I believe I could eat all of it."

Young Rector was so inspired that he stayed in the restaurant business, thus assuring Diamond Jim of a steady supply of *filet de sole Marguery*. France never learned how the secret had been filched, and Franco-American relations were undisturbed until a man named De Gaulle began denouncing Anglo-American perfidy. He may have had *L'Affaire Sole Marguery* in mind.

For a time it looked as though 1912 would be a vintage year. Next to his gastronomic compulsion, Brady was most obsessed by his love of the theater; he once estimated that he had attended more than 2,500 opening nights, and his producer friend Flo Ziegfeld declared that Brady was the best nonwriting critic around, because "If Diamond Jim went to sleep before the first act was over managers knew it was a sure bet that the show would be a failure. If he stayed awake for two acts they knew the chances were the show would have a fair run. And if he stayed awake for all three acts, they knew that there was nothing to do but go out front and hang up the 'Seats Reserved for Six Weeks in Advance' sign."

Like all other inveterate first-nighters, Brady was exhilarated by a report that Weber and Fields had made up their differences and would revive the old Music Hall revues; better still, that Lillian Russell and other Weberfields stars would rejoin them. If Broadway had one hallowed memory, it was that of the old Weber and Fields Music Hall. The loyalty of a theatrical following like that is incredible today; perhaps it had something to do with the primacy of live entertainment in those days.

For once a Broadway rumor proved to be true. Early in January Lew Fields' father had died, and Joe Weber attended the funeral. On the way back from the cemetery, they rode through the Bowery and Lower East Side, the scenes of their boyhood and their start in the theater, and made up their differences. A short time later they decided to go back into partnership; their first mutual inspiration was to ask Lillian Russell to join up. An hour later they were standing in her parlor and telling her their plans. "Most certainly I want a part in the reunion," she told them. "Try to keep me out of it. And you can pay me what you like."

Lillian had been trouping diligently but had lost momentum in the past year or two. A tour with a drama titled *In Search of a Sinner* had not caused any stampedes to the box office; business was so bad in Pittsburgh that the house was partly "papered" with nonpaying customers. She had even tried a tour in vaudeville. It looked like a new lease on her professional life when Weber and Fields offered to pay her $2,000 a week to throw in with them again. The vehicle of their reunion would be *Hokey Pokey*, a revue largely composed of their most successful songs and skits from the past. (Really ancient New Yorkers will remember that the "hokey-pokey man" was a street peddler selling various delicacies.) Such Weberfields graduates as Fay Templeton, Frankie Bailey, Willie Collier, John T. Kelly, and Ada Lewis were also drawn back into the Happy Family.

The opening night, February 8, 1912, was a sentimental rout not to be duplicated until *No, No, Nanette* was revived almost sixty years later with a similar resurgence of nostalgia.

Lillian's dressing room was bowered with American Beauty roses, and carpeted with the same flowers, by Felix Isman, who now managed the Broadway Theater, in which *Hokey Pokey* began its run. Ten years before, as stage manager of the prankish troupe, Isman had substituted the name of a chorus girl for Lillian's on the card accompanying a huge floral piece handed over the footlights at the end of a performance. Lillian knew that she was designated as the recipient, and as she passed Isman in the wings she merely said, "You did that," and then let the matter drop. When Lillian walked into her rose-smothered dressing room the night of the *Hokey Pokey* opening, she knew that Isman was trying to make amends. "You got even," she whispered after throwing her arms around him.

No matter what happened onstage that night, *Hokey Pokey* would have been acclaimed by the audience, packed as it was by Weberfields' most enthusiastic followers. Jim Brady sat in a box, outshining the stage lighting with his Number-one Diamond Set, worn on only the most momentous occasions. Equally resplendent were such actresses as Grace George and Gertrude Vanderbilt, one box crowded with William Randolph Hearst and his family, another with his bitterest journalistic rivals, the Pulitzers.

Lillian wore $150,000 worth of jewelry, according to the theater's press agent, and certainly outdressed anyone in the audience. She was draped in a gown sequined with opals and diamond chips, wore a huge picture hat plumed with pink ostrich feathers, gold shoes with diamond buckles, and carried a shepherd's crook of ebony with a diamond-studded handle. Somebody said she tinkled like a crystal chandelier whenever she moved.

The audience was tear-drenched when she sang "Come Down My Evenin' Star," and it almost collapsed from emotion when David Warfield, still in makeup for his title role in *The Return of Peter Grimm* at another theater, shuffled across the stage in his old Jewish peddler's disguise.

Lillian and the rest of the company adjourned to the Friars Club after the performance to attend a dinner in their honor, at which the great tenor Enrico Caruso was the most quotable speaker. He had been a rival of Brady's and Hearst's as the most faithful attendant at the Music Hall, and his tangled syntax may have resulted partly from listening to Weber and Fields tormenting the English language in their violent dialogues. Caruso's words that night must have offered Lillian much consolation for not having pursued a grand opera career.

> At the Metropolitan Opera House [Caruso declared] we study so hard all our lives to learn to sing. Mr. Gatti-Casazza gives you an all-star cast. We sing like angels and you pay $10,000 [into the box office]. But Fields here, who sticks his finger in Weber's eye, plays to thirteen-fourteen thousand dollars. How is that?

After its successful New York run *Hokey Pokey* went on tour and was so enthusiastically greeted in the provinces that the theaters in various cities weren't large enough to handle the ticket requests and the Weberfields troupe had to perform in armories and convention halls.

But 1912 turned out to be a bad year, after all, and not only because Woodrow Wilson (foreshadowing the income tax and other liberal legislation) won the Democratic nomination for the Presidency over the more conservative candidates favored by Brady, Thomas Fortune Ryan, and other apprehensive Wall Street figures.

L'Affaire Sole Marguery: *A Spy Story*

For some months Brady had been troubled by various internal disturbances, the exact nature of which had not been defined by the specialists. Frequently in the past, of course, his medical advisers had warned him against the predictable result of his enormous eating habits. Rich food undoubtedly was causing him gastric disorders, but the trouble this time eventually was traced to his quaffing of orange juice in such great quantities. He would have been better off taking a few glasses of wine with a meal, but unfortunately he was a member of what was then known as the Cold Water Army.

In addition to a gallon or two of orange juice taken as an aperitif before dinner, he guzzled orangeade after retiring for the night. Every evening his valet would prepare several pitchers and leave them on Brady's night table.

During one illness early in the spring, his physician decided Brady was taking too much sugar—all that orangeade in addition to several desserts topped off by five-pound boxes of chocolates.

"What do you drink?" the doctor asked him.

"Only orangeade," Brady replied.

"You must use sugar in that."

"Not much," Brady insisted. He turned to his valet and asked, "How much sugar do you use a day in my orangeade?"

"Two pounds, sir."

One night late in May he was stricken again, this time by an agonizing abdominal pain. Various doctors were summoned to his bedside but were unable to determine the cause of his trouble. Before the night was out the news spread around the city that Diamond Jim Brady was dying, though he was only fifty-six years old.

Later it became known (with considerable joy in some quarters) that while he lay cursing and groaning on his massive mahogany bed in the house on Eighty-sixth Street, Jim had ordered his servants to empty a certain drawer in his safe and burn its contents. These included various letters which might be embarrassing to both their recipient and their senders. A sheaf of IOU's adding up to about $200,000 also went up in smoke. Though he believed that he was on his deathbed, Jim still could spare a thought for his friends, and that midnight incineration proved he was a sport—"dead loyal," as Broadway would put it, through and through.

His doctors decided that diagnosis and treatment would have to be done at Johns Hopkins Hospital in Baltimore, with all its specialists in internal medicine. An ambulance took him to Pennsylvania Station, where a special train had been laid on for the journey to Baltimore. Meanwhile at Johns Hopkins Hospital special equipment, including a reinforced operating table and bed, were being prepared for a patient weighing close to 300 pounds. Jim was fluoroscoped immediately on arrival. His insides were surveyed with scientific marveling by the specialists who discovered that Brady had a stomach six times larger than normal and that the source of his trouble was a kidney stone of spectacular dimensions.

A member of the Johns Hopkins staff, Dr. Hugh H. Young, an expert in internal surgery, had just perfected a new technique for the removal of kidney stones of awkward size and location. Dr. Young, however, was scheduled to leave in a few hours for a medical meeting in Europe. He objected to performing the operation because he always saw his patients through the first stages of recovery, and there wouldn't be time for that. Finally Dr. Young was prevailed upon to go ahead with the operation and leave the postoperative details to other members of the staff.

Dr. Young penetrated the layers of fat covering Brady's abdomen, cut into the tube in which the kidney stone was lodged, and removed an object about the size of one of Jim's larger diamonds. He then hurried to catch his train to New York and the liner for Europe. On reaching the liner's berth he learned that the princely Brady touch could reach out even from what could have been Jim's deathbed. "I found that all my reservations had been changed," Dr. Young said later. "I was transferred from the small stateroom I had engaged to the most luxurious suite on the boat. There were flowers and fruit and champagne, all I could want to eat and drink and read. Nothing had been overlooked. All was planned by Mr. Brady. All this thought and care and generosity were the work of a man whom the doctors had given twenty-four hours to live. He had thought of these little things for the comfort of someone else while he was on what he considered his deathbed."

The Brady constitution, though raddled by a lifetime of gluttony, was a marvel to his attendants. He recovered from the operation with amazing swiftness. He also succeeded in turning the hospital's discipline upside down, what with nurses and interns struggling for the privilege to attend him and enormous meals being wheeled over from the Hotel Belvedere, which he insisted must be shared by his various attendants. Once he was well on the road to recovery, he ordered his secretary to bring fifty two-carat diamond rings up from New York for distribution to the nurses. Inside a week, it was said, the administrators were muttering that the place should be renamed the James Buchanan Brady Hospital. His amazingly expansive personality, the geniality which seemed to break through walls and ceilings and radiate throughout the institution, made him the most remarkable patient in the hospital's annals. He did not object, he was actually delighted, when groups of medical students were brought to his bedside and senior staff members lectured on Dr. Young's surgical technique. The hospital room was turned into the court of King James in which, late every afternoon, there was a gathering of nurses, doctors, and visitors from New York and elsewhere consuming the food and drink Brady had brought in and listening to his stories.

One thing he learned during his convalescence at Johns Hopkins was that inordinate quantities of orange juice could be harmful. Jim had always considered his favorite beverage a health-giving element of his diet, but that was true only to a certain point. The doctors, demonstrating the litmus-paper test, showed how orange juice added to beakers of starchy food turned akaline. By this process, kidney stones were formed. "I'll be God damned," said Jim Brady. From then on, he would be chary of orange juice, but his gourmandizing would continue unabated for several years.

Before he was released from Johns Hopkins, his deliverer returned from Europe. Jim was so grateful to Dr. Young and the medical profession for saving his life that, he told the surgeon, "I've got everything I need and want, and since I've been down here I've begun to realize the best thing I can do is to help other people a bit." The result of their consultations was the James Buchanan Brady Urological Institute, the first specializing institution of its kind in America, which would be attached to Johns Hopkins Hospital. For this purpose he gave $220,000 for construction plus $15,000 a year for maintenance, and through the years there were thousands of people who could be thankful that Jim Brady had once suffered from an outsize kidney stone. The institute opened in the summer of 1915, about three years after Brady was released from the hospital.

Glad hearts and outstretched hands, not to mention an outbreak of false rumors, attended his return to New York. One rumor antedated medical progress by an untold number of years, alleging that Brady had been given a stomach transplant after paying a Baltimore widow $200,000 for her deceased husband's stomach. Another report, also published, was that he had been given the stomach of a pig in place of his own. A covey of reporters interviewed him as he lay convalescent in his huge mahogany bed in the house on Eighty-sixth Street, and judging from the usually accurate New York *World*'s account, he did not bother to inform the public that it was a kidney stone, not his stomach, that had caused the trouble.

HIS GOLD-LINED STOMACH MAKES LIFE A JOY AGAIN, the *World* headlined its front-page account. Its reporter quoted Brady as saying: "They certainly handed me back a newly lined, high-powered, pliant, and pleasantly dispositioned stomach—the kind I had when I was twelve years old and could eat a raw turnip with relish. Why, if you roasted a full-size bull moose and just put it down in front of me, I guess I could eat the whole thing, and you'd probably find me gnawing at the hoofs and antlers. And no pepsin powders, either!"

The newspaper revealed that for some time after his hospitalization Brady had been on a diet of the most dismal rigidity, including milk toast for breakfast, one potato and buttermilk for lunch, bacon and one egg, with lettuce and a half cup of tea for dinner. Each meal was chased with a dose of pepsin and bismuth.

That insipid and near-starvation regimen had now been expanded to something Brady could live with. Breakfast now included cantaloupe, oatmeal, bacon and eggs, and toast and marmalade. On the luncheon menu were clams, olives, broiled bass, asparagus, potatoes, and omelette soufflé, and for dinner turtle soup, broiled bluefish, potatoes, peas, spinach, sweetbreads, broiled guinea hen, salad, ice cream, fancy cakes, and cheese. He would stick to that diet only so long as his doctor's admonitions echoed and he was confined to bed.

"His eyes," the *World* man reported, "were shining as brightly as his seventy-four horsepower diamond stickpin, or his incandescent cuff buttons, or his glittering waistcoat buttons, or his gem encrusted fingers as he said: 'Two hundred and twenty thousand dollars isn't much to give for a new stomach when you need one as much as I did. I had to go through months of rigorous treatment to get it. That was no joke. But the reward is great stuff. I do not feel at liberty to go into details of the treatment through which I have come out of the hospital a fully restored man, though I went there a wreck. But I do know that I made up my mind to give persons less fortunate than myself, and afflicted as I was, a chance for treatment.' "

Every New York journalist of the time prided himself on his powers of hyperbole, and there was plenty of that in every account of the interview. None of them bothered, however, to straighten out the exact nature of Brady's illness. With Brady himself, as well as his admiring public, there was so intense a fixation with his stomach that lesser organs, perhaps, were discounted. Another oddity was that the newspapers quoted Brady as saying he felt as though "my sixty years were only sixteen," though indubitably he was only fifty-six. Such picayune details didn't matter, in any case, compared to the fact that his return to New York garnered more publicity than any similar event since Colonel Theodore Roosevelt came back from rampaging around Cuba.

If there was a flaw in Jim's rejoicing over his recovery, it was the fact that Lillian hadn't been among those who rushed to his bedside in Baltimore. Of course, she was on tour with Weber and Fields in *Hokey Pokey*, and she had not closed down her show even to attend her father's funeral. But while Jim lay struggling for his health, Lillian, without consulting him, had gone and got herself married for the fourth time. Her new husband was older than Jim, and worse yet, he was a Republican. "Even in my state," he growled when he heard the news, "she could have done a lot worse than to take me."

9

LILLIAN RUSSELL FOR
PRESIDENT—OR SOMETHING

A S the kind of star who played pinochle with the stagehands and did not mind being seen running down
station platforms with a wedge of custard pie in her hand,
Lillian Russell had rarely taken herself seriously except in
contract negotiations with theatrical producers. Her idea of
high society was taking off her corset and sitting in on an
all-night poker session. She enjoyed puncturing masculine self-
esteem, in a joking sort of way, but she had never agreed with
her mother that masculinity was an open conspiracy dedicated
to keeping women subordinate. Nor had she ever regarded love
or marriage as a sort of emotional shelter; if she had, she would
have accepted Jim Brady's proposal and the protection of his
millions.

When she reached her fiftieth birthday, however, her outlook underwent a definite change. Pomposity is not a feminine
attribute, and Lillian would never become a stuffed shirtwaist,
but she did start taking herself and her opinions more seriously. Perhaps it had all started with her discovery that the
writings of Marcus Aurelius were more interesting than the
racing charts of the *Morning Telegraph* and the further dis-

covery that she had a mind as well as a body that had become a national institution.

The last ten years of her life would see Lillian Russell cast herself in the role of a crusader. Perhaps as an actress she had always fancied the role of Joan of Arc (as tempting to an actress as Hamlet to an actor). The burning issue of the day, for most American women with any spark of independence, was winning the right to vote; an issue so calefactory that, when the *Titanic* went down in 1912, one women's suffrage leader declared that the women aboard the liner "should have insisted that the boats be filled with an equal number of men." The same year, to prove a similar point, a Texas schoolmarm went over Niagara Falls in a barrel; yet only a few years before a mounted cop had thundered up to a young woman trying to sneak a smoke in the rear seat of an automobile on Fifth Avenue and arrested her for smoking in public.

Oddly enough, ironically too, her career as a feminist and public figure was boosted along by the man she married on June 12, 1912.

The fourth Mr. Lillian Russell, as snide observers would put it, was a solid citizen—in contrast to his three predecessors—named Alexander P. Moore, publisher of the Pittsburgh *Leader*, prominent Republican, future confidant of President Harding, and ambassador to Spain. This time, it was evident, Lillian's head was ruling her heart; her new husband was some years older than she, white-haired and distinguished, one of Theodore Roosevelt's leading supporters in the Bull Moose faction of dissident Republicans. A year before he met Lillian he had been divorced from his first wife. In every way he promised to be the sort of husband she needed in middle age, one who guaranteed stability and security.

They were married at the Hotel Schenley in Pittsburgh, where the Weber and Fields company was just ending its tour with *Hokey Pokey*. Weber and Fields were among the witnesses. Immediately after the wedding the bridal couple split in separate directions; Moore had been summoned by ex-President Roosevelt to Chicago, and Lillian was returning to New York.

Journalistic rumor mongers had cast a temporary blight over the marriage by reporting, inaccurately, that Lillian had held out for a marriage settlement of $60,000 annually. Lillian vigorously denied the rumors, pointing out that she had all the money she needed and furthermore she would be independent in all respects. "Marriage," she said, "must be an equal partnership. There must be tolerance and understanding. I have told Mr. Moore that I would insist upon having all my own undisturbed privacy, as I have now." She did not explain why or how she had lopped four years off her age, listing her birth date as December 4, 1865, in applying for a marriage license. Feminine prerogative, presumably.

Lillian and her new husband temporarily established themselves in her New York apartment for the duration of the 1912 political campaign. Moore was one of Roosevelt's closest advisers in his calculated disruption of the Republican Party and in the campaign that pitted Roosevelt as a Progressive Republican against William Howard Taft, the regular Republicans' candidate, and Woodrow Wilson. Lillian joined the campaign, making speeches, handing out campaign buttons, and greatly enjoying her fling at politics. She made speeches arguing for Roosevelt's platform, which included the eight-hour working day, and declared that Roosevelt's election "means an advancement of one hundred years for women in this country and the world. It means there will be legislation for women."

Lillian had come around to her mother's way of thinking a year or two before her fourth marriage. In 1911 she told a newspaper interviewer that "Woman has forced herself into a position where she has to fight for her rights, and now that she is fighting in organized earnest, why not take the real step—the consummation—of suffrage for women and the abolishment of the male vote? Absolute suffrage for women and the withdrawal of the power and reins of government from men's hands will give men themselves a fuller opportunity to play the games in which they have been most successful. If they have women to fight for in business and on the battlefields—if that is necessary—they will be doing their full share. . . ." Even Cynthia Leonard hadn't gone quite so far as to suggest that men give up all political power, turn the government over to women, and satisfy themselves with the roles of breadwinner and soldier, the donkey work of civilization.

In time, of course, Lillian modified her approach to the problem of persuading men to share their power; her initial overenthusiasm for the project was that of the convert. But from then until the end of her life, she was to dedicate a large part of her life and energy to the cause. She would never be able to claim the moral courage it took for the real pioneers in the feminist movement, women like her mother, to assault the citadel of the Victorian male establishment. The cause of enfranchising women had now become a popular crusade, which had attracted the support of social and political reformers. Many males had seen the light, even the exuberantly masculine Theodore Roosevelt. Yet Lillian Russell's participation in the movement was a factor of considerable importance; she was still a star of the first magnitude, though her following now was influenced more by sentimental than sexual attraction, and if her name could sell cigars, it could help sell women's suffrage. It also certified that the movement was not solely peopled by Carrie Nation-type battle-axes and soured spinsters. "Suffrage became fashionable," as one social historian has deftly defined Lillian Russell's part in the movement. "Attractive society girls like Inez Milholland and Portia Willis entered the fold, adding a glamorous touch that was badly needed. And if there was still any doubt that the movement was feminine as well as feminist, it vanished the day Lillian Russell joined up."

After the Bull Moose movement foundered at the polls, despite the best efforts of Lillian Russell and Theodore Roosevelt, she and her new husband returned to Pittsburgh. There she assumed a queenly role in society, and the city would be her home base from then on. Jim Brady's steel interests were centered in Pittsburgh, and the old friendship was renewed and revived on his frequent business visits to the city.

Lillian did not go into retirement, however. One way or another she would be a public figure until her last breath. The theater was less alluring and less able to offer suitable roles for a mature star unwilling to descend gracefully into character roles; she would always be a star or she would be nothing, and let someone else play the sweet old ladies. However, she made several forays into the theater, comebacks more or less, whenever there was a demand for her services that included a star's salary and perquisites. The rest of the time she spent crusading, either on the lecture platform or as a demijournalist.

During a Chicago appearance two years earlier, the Chicago *Tribune* had suggested that she try her hand at writing a column that would be concentrated on various feminine concerns. Eventually she supplied the three samples requested by the *Tribune* editor; they were published and found wide acceptance. Now she and the *Tribune* came to terms on a two-year contract for a syndicated column "Care of Beauty of Face and Form," which would pay her twelve thousand dollars a year, about one-tenth the salary she demanded as an actress but still as much as any star reporter could hope to earn. She was assisted in her columning career by a woman reporter in Chicago but tended to stray from the agreed theme of beauty hints. It was her editors' opinion that the public wanted practical advice, not bits of philosophy or feminist propaganda, from Lillian Russell. One *Tribune* editor, exasperated at her tendency to stray from the point, wired her to "write less about soul and more about pimples."

In addition to the syndicated column, she wrote a long series of articles for her husband's newspaper based on interviews with various actors who appeared in Pittsburgh. Essentially, though, from then on she lived off the magic her name still held, particularly for the middle-aged generation, an afterglow that would linger long after her death. Later in 1912, after the Presidential election, she set forth on a lecture tour on the subject of health and beauty. The lecture was illustrated by a motion picture showing Lillian taking her exercise and practicing deep breathing. She had always been a near fanatic on the subject of health, had practiced "clean living" herself and rarely drank more than a glass or two of wine, and had indulged herself only with food. (In her youth, of course, a robust, even an inordinate appetite for food was regarded as a sign of good health. Cholesterol was unheard of. The suspicion that overweight could be the cause, rather than preventive of, physical breakdowns did not really take hold until after World War I, and even then the slender figure was largely propagated by the bosomless, hipless flapper ideal of the 1920's.)

Lillian summed up her credo for lecture audiences with brevity and good sense: "Keep the mind just as clean as the body and ventilate it as you would a room. Keep yourself from thinking thoughts that will make you worry and fret. Let your thoughts be young and joyous. Don't let your intellect become stagnant. Read and work and laugh and live."

Obviously Lillian was doing some of the spadework for the Dale Carnegies, the power-of-positive-thinking advocates, the life-begins-at-forty theorists, and other practitioners of various kinds of uplift who came along many years later. The trouble with Lillian, as with those who followed her into the field of self-improvement, was that she could tell people what to do, but not *how* to do it.

Her audiences were receptive and satisfactorily large, but she abandoned her lecture tour early in 1913, largely because the opportunity arose to combine her lecturing with show business. She had been a performer too long to be satisfied by the busywork of lecturing and columning. The possibility of a comeback was always too tempting to be ignored. So she signed a contract to headline a vaudeville tour, with part of her act to be a mini-lecture on the subject of "How to Live One Hundred Years." One segment of her act was to make a grand appearance, laden with all her jewelry, to demonstrate how too many brooches, necklaces, lavalieres, etc., could add years to a woman's appearance. No doubt that part of her act was a trifle unconvincing to housewives fingering a wedding band or an amethyst ring and not at all disgusted by the blaze of diamonds across the footlights.

During the fall of 1913 she embarked on a personal-appearance tour under the management of John Cort, who, to his subsequent distress, was required to pay her the standard $2,500 a week despite the failure of the public to line up at the box office. Her tour of Southern and Midwestern cities was something of a disaster, which was underlined by the blunt advice of newspaper critics that the time had come for Lillian Russell to retire with her scrapbooks.

Sick with disappointment, Lillian returned to Pittsburgh to seek consolation from Marcus Aurelius, a newly discovered fount of solace in the writings of Mary Baker Eddy and the teachings of Christian Science, and perhaps in her own musings for the Chicago *Tribune* syndicated column, such as one of those soulful flights to which her editors sometimes objected, "Let your air be cheerful; depend not upon external supports, nor beg your tranquility from another. The soul is tinged with the color and complexion of thought." The tactful and understanding Alexander Moore was also a great help during the period when she was learning to adjust to the evidence that the public no longer clamored to be enthralled by a fifty-three-year-old Lillian Russell.

Besides the doubts and regrets that assailed her regarding her theatrical decline, she continued to be confronted by the tribulations of motherhood. She had been a warmly protective mother all during Dorothy Solomon's childhood, but as she once confessed to a newspaper interviewer, "No actress can be a good mother." She made that statement in 1901 when Dorothy was nineteen, before the latter made the first of four marriages which equaled her mother's distressing matrimonial experience.

During Dorothy's infancy, mindful of what had happened to her first child, Lillian would not trust a governess alone with the child. She took Dorothy to the theater with her, making a bed out of a drawer of the steamer trunk in her dressing room. Later Dorothy was placed in a New Jersey convent, then sent to study abroad, but for all the advantages a doting mother could provide she apparently could not find emotional security in the inescapable shadow of her mother's fame. In August, 1903, when she was twenty-one years old, Dorothy eloped with a New York attorney named Abbot Louis Einstein. A year later she made her stage debut in the cast of *Olympe*, which also included one Gilbert Miller, the son of Henry Miller, appearing professionally for the first time. Gilbert Miller was later renowned as a New York and London theatrical producer.

Dorothy soon divorced Einstein, then married and divorced an ethnically diverse succession of husbands named Dunsmuir, O'Reilly, and Calvit. For all the discomfitures of having so famous and busy a mother, Dorothy would always be a staunch defender of Lillian Russell's reputation. Twenty years ago a spread on Lillian Russell appearing in a national magazine attracted Dorothy's indignant comment. She regarded as undignified the magazine's detailing how Lillian had worn a corset specially fabricated and costing $3,900, how Lillian "swore like a trooper," and how she had accepted costly gifts from Diamond Jim Brady. Despite all the evidence to the contrary, Dorothy Solomon denied that Brady's diamonds were part of her mother's collection. "Mr. Brady," she wrote the magazine, "held her in such awe that he would not dare offer her jewels no matter what the occasion. . . . You may think that these vicious tales cannot hurt Lillian Russell because she has passed on. But these tales do hurt her because she is very much alive in the hearts and minds of those who loved and admired her. She died in the service of her country, and was buried with military honors, as she was an honorary colonel in the United States Marine Corps."

After the debacle of her personal appearance tour, Lillian stayed away from show business for almost a year, keeping her-

self occupied by acting as her husband's hostess at political/
social gatherings designed to advance his influence and pres-
tige. Moore relied on her mental as well as her social capabili-
ties. "All the world talked of her beauty," he remarked shortly
after her death. "It is strange that I think only of her mind. I
have seldom met its equal in any walk of life."

Between such soirees there were always consoling visits from
Jim Brady to remind her of past glories; her following might
be shrinking to a rear guard of old-timers, but her number-one
fan was still loyal. She also threw some effort into another
burgeoning social movement, that of the vociferous advocates
of national prohibition of the manufacture and sale of alco-
holic beverages, and wrote an article titled "Drink and Be
Ugly" for her syndicate.

By late in 1914, however, her unquenchable theatrical ambitions sprang back to life. For an actress there is no satisfactory
substitute for the psychic need to display herself and her talents. Her revived hopes were nourished by what some people
derisively called "the flickers" and others hopefully nominated
as "the new art form." The motion picture was still suffering
from a sickly childhood but it was emerging from the nickelo-
deon phase and even gaining respectability. Until now stage
actors with any sort of reputation had appeared in films under
assumed names during low-water periods of their careers. The
movies were one- or two-reel affairs filmed in a barn over in
New Jersey or up in the Bronx. Their luminaries were people
Broadway had never heard of: Mary Pickford, Norma Tal-
madge, the Keystone Cops. But the "galloping tintypes" had
gathered a constituency which could no longer be ignored, the
same constituency—semiliterate recruits to the American dream
who had recently passed through Ellis Island—that made
the comic strip so popular and bought the mass-circulation
daily newspapers with their garish type and their emphasis on
photographic illustration. Between 1900 and 1910 almost nine
million immigrants, most of whom could not speak English,
had entered the United States. Correspondingly the number of

movie theaters had increased to 3,000 by 1907; the silent films erected no language barrier and their content was simplistic, their message was the medium of continuous action. Thus the wild popularity of Pearl White in her serial film adventures *The Perils of Pauline,* each episode of which was breathlessly followed as readers had once awaited the latest installment of a Charles Dickens novel. The plot summary for one two-reel episode ran: "Pauline flees to the shore, persuades the hydroplane pilot to take her to safety. As they soar aloft, he lights a cigaret, flicks away the match, which lights on one of the wings, and in a few minutes the machine is in flames. Coward that he is, he grabs the only parachute and leaves Pauline to her fate. . . ." The viewer was left hanging on the edge of the seat as the legend was flashing on the screen: CONTINUED NEXT WEEK.

Now, however, the films were attracting a more general and sophisticated mass audience, and their producers had to look to the legitimate theater for talent and dramatic material. Lillian Russell was no starlet; even the most skilled lighting and the most discreet choice of camera angles could not convert her image to the cameolike allure of young Mary Pickford or the elfin charm of Mabel Normand, but she was still a big name.

Particularly to one Lewis J. Selznick, who not many years before had gaped at her from the cheapest gallery seats at the Casino and the Weber and Fields Music Hall. Now Selznick, the founder of one of those typical two-generation Hollywood dynasties, was an embryonic film magnate. His firm, the World Film Corporation, had bought the rights to *Wildfire,* in which she had made her last great success. Selznick could see no one but Lillian in the lead, and she took little persuasion to accept. The film would not be shot in Hollywood, where Lillian would have run into Jim Brady, who was then making a great splash in the rudimentary society of the film colony, but in New York, where a finer cast could be assembled.

Lillian's leading man was the rising dramatic actor Lionel Barrymore, who unfortunately for the *Wildfire* budget was a prankster who delighted in breaking Lillian up while the camera was turning and money was going down the drain. It was difficult for the director to impress upon Lillian that in this new medium time, and exposed film, was precious. Often she started laughing midway through a scene; that meant the whole take was spoiled and had to be refilmed. In one scene Barrymore held her hand for a moment and ad-libbed some dialogue, which was meaningless for all but deaf-mutes, since the sense of a scene was conveyed not only by the actors' gestures and facial expressions but the subtitles. Barrymore, instead of dropping her hand as the script required, held it up closer and examined her rings. "What a beautiful piece of green glass," he declared, eyeing her emerald ring. "Was it made from a beer bottle?" Lillian burst into giggles, and more footage went into the trash can. There was such a merry, feckless spirit about moviemaking that she couldn't quite take it seriously. All the offscreen horseplay and the chummy atmosphere of the *Wildfire* company was not reflected in the finished product; audiences and critics found it laborious, and Selznick's company was almost ruined. Lionel Barrymore went on to finer things, but for Lillian it was her first and last motion picture.

Wildfire was, in fact, her next-to-last fling at show business. More and more deeply she became involved in the crusade for women's emancipation. At one meeting she addressed, to a waving of parasols which reminded one or two masculine observers of a barbaric tribe brandishing its weapons, she sounded very much like her late mother when she proclaimed, "If women ever get the vote, I would willingly run for mayor of New York City!" She paused, possibly recalling that Mrs. Cynthia Leonard had polled only eighty-odd votes in a similar venture. Then, possibly figuring she might as well go wholehog, she added that it was not unthinkable that she might one day be addressed as Madame President Lillian Russell.

The auto-intoxication of her new career as a social crusader was almost as compelling as her triumphs in the theater. More so, perhaps, because she was being taken seriously, she was being cheered for something more than a voluptuous figure, and the audiences were larger. She was, according to all reports, a spellbinding orator; more effective and believable as an advocate of women's rights than, say, as the Duchess of Gerolstein.

Certainly she did not hesitate to speak out on any subject pertaining to women's rights, though her formal education in such matters as politics and history had ended with her attendance at a Chicago finishing school. She toured the lecture circuit during 1915 to picture in glowing terms what would happen after women got their rights. It was an emphatically liberal program she outlined, in striking contrast to her political views a half dozen years later when she, unlike most of her sisters, finally got a taste of power. No more child labor. Free lunches and free medical care for underprivileged schoolchildren. Anyone too poor to buy food would be supplied at markets established for the purpose. Women judges would reform the judicial system, women members of prison boards would make imprisonment more humane.

She was so carried away by her crusading role that she insisted on converting her syndicated column into a political forum, immediately becoming embroiled with the stodgy, antifeminist editors of the Chicago *Tribune*. She then took her column over to the Chicago *Record-Herald*, whose editors allowed her the privilege of writing on any topic she chose.

The publicity all these activities attracted impelled Producer John Cort to put together another road show starring Lillian Russell in the certainty that the growing number of feminists in every city would pay off at the box office. According to a rumor floating around Broadway, possibly propagated by antifeminists, Lillian's husband had cabled George Bernard Shaw suggesting that the playwright concoct a libretto to the specifications of Lillian's mature personality. Shaw, the story went, had cabled in reply: WHO IS LILLIAN RUSSELL? Lillian was so annoyed by the canard that she was determined to prove that she wasn't in any sense a has-been, and under Cort's management she undertook a coast-to-coast tour with the Lillian Russell Feature Festival. Her supporting bill included William Farnum, the stage and film star, and the famous Chinese magician Ching Long Foo. The tour was successful enough to allow Lillian to announce, this time for sure, that she was retiring from the theater. Not so, as it turned out, but it was her penultimate appearance.

Perhaps her proudest moment that year came when she joined the greatest demonstration of the women's rights movement. Fifty thousand women, with bands playing and banners flying, marched up Fifth Avenue from Washington Arch at Washington Square to Central Park—whole battalions of stenographers, shopgirls, nurses, workers in the needlework trades, professional women, and a brigade of schoolteachers carrying blackboards chalked with slogans. The parade went on all afternoon and the rear ranks did not reach Central Park until after darkness fell. It was a shocking demonstration of female power and determination. Many of the males lining the route, with the wave of the future clearly visible, loosed volleys of boos and sent up heartfelt groans.

Leading the parade on a magnificent white horse was the young and beautiful Inez Milholland. Yet she did not steal the show. Marching along as a humble ranker, yet quickly recognized by her plumed hat and the stately walk which had carried her through so many performances on stage, was Lillian Russell. Masculine outrage was turned to respectful silence as The American Beauty strode past waving a sizable banner. "Even Lillian Russell, who was accustomed to riding in hansom cabs, walked the long route for the glory of womanhood," a journalist noted. That long walk of Lillian Russell's on an autumn day probably converted more dissident males than any number of suffragette speeches.

10

DECLINE AND FALL OF THE
GREAT GASTRONOME

DURING the several years before World War I the patron
saint of Broadway and its environs seemed to be Saint
Vitus, and his most fervent devotee was Diamond Jim Brady.
There is a theory of minor intellectual interest and no great
historical import that great wars are preceded by violent dance
crazes, a theory which held true for both world wars. Intimations of the coming of World War II could be studied in the
frenetic patterns of jitterbugging and the Big Apple. Before
World War I, the waltz gave way to the dances which were inspired by the new craze for ragtime music, a delirium which
started when a former waiter in a Chinese restaurant, Irving
Berlin, wrote "Alexander's Ragtime Band."

It was the beginning of the jazz era, accompanied by socio-
logical phenomena and a revolution in manners and morals,
which seemed to signify the complete breakaway of America as
a cultural appendage of Europe. Its repercussions would be
endless. Trivial and evanescent though it may have seemed at
the time, its influence on Western civilization would be incalculable, as significant in its way as the embarkation of the
American Expeditionary Force in 1917. Henceforth Europe
would ape America, instead of vice versa. From then on, per-

haps more importantly, the old morality lost its grip on the American people.

"Within twelve months," as a journalistic observer wrote, "jazz had upset New York, set a whole continent gyrating, temporarily revolutionized our social life generally and had even found its way to Europe and begun an assault upon the Orient . . . soon awkwardness and inability to tread a fancy measure lost caste as marks of distinction for captains of industry and self-made men. . . . An odd thing about the craze was that it attacked not only the young, but the middle-aged and the old. Grandfathers and grandmothers, lame and rheumatic though they might be, got up and danced. The first became fired with ambition to show the world that age was merely relative to years, and that, when it came to treading a measure, however remote its rhythm and speed from the square dance and the round waltz they had learned in girlhood, they could equal their own granddaughters in grace and vie with them in agility and endurance. So it was that soon white-topped heads began to peer roguishly and flirtatiously above manly shoulders on public dance floors." Even the stately Waldorf had to employ paid partners, "lounge lizards," as they were then called, gigolos later, to dance with elderly dowagers. "At the same time, it was not all comedy when one observed women of seventy or more . . . now frantically whirling and skipping over a dance floor in the arms of young men hired to hold them up and attend to the necessary navigation. . . ."

Not that the professional guardians of public morality were unaware of what was happening. Anthony Comstock, as the chief avenging angel of the New York Society for the Suppression of Vice, inveighed almost daily against the madness. Mayor William J. Gaynor of New York, otherwise a man of libertarian principles, called the wild new dances "lascivious orgies" and unavailingly tried to have them forbidden by statute; the legislators themselves were turkey-trotting all over the place when his call for action was sounded. A New York *Times* editorial stigmatized the turkey trot as a "phenomenon closely analogous to those dancing manias of the Middle Ages . . . to which victims of neurotic diathesis are susceptible."

It turned out that whole masses of people were unwittingly suffering from neurotic diathesis. The malady was epidemic at the Yale Junior Prom of 1913 when the lights of the ballroom were suddenly switched off and the thousand chaperones present were plunged into darkness and anxious confusion, the dance floor becoming a frenzy when the band began playing ragtime. The new dances encouraged women to become more daring in their dress, tight skirts appearing with slits to allow more athletic movement, and heels getting higher. The Pennsylvania Railroad threw itself behind the forces of morality by announcing that if a woman passenger slipped or fell on railroad property, the company would "take note of the style of her skirt and heels, of her age, and of the circumstances of her life, and will publish them." A generation which has accommodated itself to the mini-skirt and hot pants and to the mindbending of acid rock may find it difficult to believe, but in those years just before World War I the glimpse of a woman's calf on a windy street corner was a signal event for girl-watchers.

Diamond Jim Brady, happily unaware that he was participating in the early phases of a social, moral, and cultural revolution, was quick to join the madly capering throngs who danced the bunny hug, the camel walk, the kangaroo dip, and the turkey trot. If there was one thing he could not bear contemplating, even in his late fifties and in his deteriorating physical condition, it was not to keep up with the crowd. His portly figure was not the perfect visual embodiment of any kind of dancing, but like many fat men he was graceful enough to compete with the willowier types. Every night he went out on the town surrounded by a half dozen or more dancing partners, looking like a frivolous pasha abroad with part of his harem or, as one observer put it, an ocean liner being towed by a fleet of tugboats.

While Lillian Russell devoted her later years to social reform, politics, and other serious matters, her friend Brady seemed to grow giddier, more pleasure-bent with every gray hair that cropped out. The advice of his physicians that a more dignified pace might add years to his life was disregarded. There was one beneficial aspect of his career as a blimplike bacchant: the violent jigging and bending and dipping of the new dances meant the end of twelve-course dinners and provided a considerable amount of physical exercise.

Diamond Jim got into the swim of things immediately after the new dances were introduced at Louis Martin's café by a serpentine import from Paris named Maurice. In Paris he had introduced the adagio to polite society and reportedly had broken one female partner's neck while performing the Apache dance. The sleek and slightly sinister Maurice demonstrated the tango and the turkey trot to the patrons of Louis Martin's; about the same time Blossom Seeley was making herself famous in Lew Fields' production of *The Hen Pecks* with her "Toddlin' the Todolo" number, and a handsome young couple named Vernon and Irene Castle were appearing in the same show and being inspired to invent their syncopated routines by Miss Seeley's toddlin'. But initially Maurice was the high priest of the new dances. "All New York flocked to see him," as one social historian recorded, "waiting breathlessly for the climactic moment when his pretty blonde partner leaped astride his hips and, clinging to his waist with her bent knees, swung outward and away from his whirling body like a floating sash. Dowagers of the utmost social distinction sent him hundred-dollar bills, pleading that he come to their tables and offer to lead them through the paces of the tango or the turkey trot. Frequently they received nothing more for their money than a snub. This provocative rudeness increased his popularity with smart people. Besides, he was elegant, sophisticated, and he spoke, with equal fluency, both the French of the boulevards and the argot of the *apaches*. A romantic figure, certainly. There were so many piquant legends about his early life that nobody guessed the facts. He was not a Parisian *apache* or the illegitimate son of a French aristocrat, but merely a native New Yorker, born and bred in the slums. . . ."

Among the more successful petitioners of the sleek and slithery Maurice for instructions in the turkey trot and other esoteric maneuvers was Diamond Jim Brady. He outbid the dowagers and paid Maurice thousands of dollars for private lessons. Like many men of his heft, he was light on his feet, bobbing like a captive balloon to the hectic syncopation of the new and madder music. Mentally and chronologically, however, Brady was attuned to the statelier movements of the waltz, and his huge presence on the dance floor aroused a certain amount of amusement from onlookers, to whom he resembled a much-caparisoned circus elephant gone berserk. When the music began, he followed his partner to the exact center of the dance floor. He bobbed and weaved and jigged, more or less in rhythm with the ragtime, and all the time his moonlike face was gravely expressionless, his mouth pursed in a soundless whistle. At the same time his beringed hand kept fluttering up and down his partner's back. Maurice did an imitation of Brady capering through the turkey trot or the kangaroo dip which became the set piece of his act.

When Vernon and Irene Castle, having developed the "Castle Walk" to add a new dimension to the dance mania, became the pacesetters for fashionable and faddish New York, Brady paid out more thousands for private lessons to improve his style. The elegant and English-born Vernon Castle, who would be killed in action during the coming war, and his socialite bride were the top celebrities of the town. For fees of $100 an hour they attempted to instruct Brady in the intricacies of the new steps they popularized, not only the Castle Walk but the Grizzly Bear, the Lame Duck, the Half-in-Half, and the Innovation.

As one of their more faithful pupils, Brady attended the opening of the Castles' club, Sans Souci, which was located under the sidewalk in Times Square with the subway thundering away just behind a thin partition and only partly drowned out by the famous Jim Europe's Negro band. The decor was by Elsie de Wolfe, and Brady rubbed elbows at the opening with the Goulds and Harrimans, William Rhinelander Stewart, and Cornelius Vanderbilt with a large party. "Diamond Jim was a gay dancer," as Irene Castle remembered him. "He handled himself very well for so big a man and whistled the tune he was dancing to as he propelled his young charmer around the floor. When he danced with me he was very silent and his *joie de vivre* evaporated. I think he was either concentrating on his feet or felt conspicuous." Probably the latter. Brady was always awed by someone like the well-bred Irene Castle, who was brought up in a Westchester suburb.

On her part, Irene Castle found a certain disparity between Diamond Jim Brady in person and his legend. He was "always a disappointment to me," even his "very chunky yellow diamonds." The newspaper accounts of the Sans Souci opening included a "very charming little story about Diamond Jim and me. According to one teller of fairy tales, Diamond Jim asked me to dance and, after waltzing me around the floor, shyly presented me with a gift, a diamond-encrusted watch with a band of matching diamonds. Unfortunately it was not true."

To the jumpy tune of "Everybody's Doin' It, Doin' It, Doin' It" (Irving Berlin's celebration of the new dances), Jim Brady cavorted nightly in the Broadway cabarets and maintained his position, through strenuous effort, as the King of Night Life, as spectacular a figure as he had been in the nineties. He disported himself at the Casino de Paree, Maxim's, Bustanoby's, the Moulin Rouge, and Reisenweber's, the latter a place on Columbus Circle with four dance floors which was organized as a "club" under the title of the Association of United Friends and was allowed to stay open until dawn. He was also a familiar of Lee Schubert's Palais de Danse, the first New York nightclub, of the Jardin de Danse, on top of the New York Theater, and of Flo Ziegfeld's New Amsterdam Theater roof.

As always, Brady's method was that of conspicuous excess. He used the platoon system for maintaining a continuous supply of dancing partners who, since Jim insisted on flinging himself into every dance, tended to weary after a few hours. He always appeared with a half dozen girls of assorted types whom he paid twenty-five dollars and provided all the food and wine they wanted; apparently he also decked them out in furs and jewelry strictly on a loan basis. According to Irene Castle, he "had the reputation of only *lending* the finery to the 'lovelies' who went out with him. I've often wondered how he went about getting his finery back. Did he just pull the ermine wrap off their shoulders as they departed from his car to their front door, saying, 'Now, hurry, dear, so you won't catch cold'?" During the night he would summon reinforcements, a half dozen at a time, by telephone. It was a matter of considerable pride to him that he was able to dance so many young women off their feet.

To the sober-minded observer of his activities there was a fever flush, a desperation to all this determined gaiety. He knew that the state of his various organs did not forecast a long life. But at least his fondness for dancing kept him from brooding in his Eighty-sixth Street establishment, where he maintained two limousines, each with a crew of chauffeur and footman on day and night shifts, to keep him constantly mobile. His favorite dining place during this period was the Vanderbilt Crypt in the Vanderbilt Hotel, in which he owned a part interest. Frank Bacchi, the maître d' of the Vanderbilt Crypt, recalled in a newspaper interview many years after Brady died that he had cut down considerably on his consumption of food and orange juice. "First he'd had a couple of glasses of orange juice at the bar. Then he'd begin a meal with two dozen big oysters trimmed with crabs. And he'd enjoy the aroma of cooking while a chicken was being broiled over charcoal on the chef's wagon beside his table. With the chicken, he would have Virginia ham and mushrooms." A mere snack compared to the feastings of yesteryear.

In the year or two before World War I, with his rather touching yearning to be warmed by the often illusory glow of youth and celebrity, he attached himself to a couple of young dancers and their husbands, who served as replacements for a certain foursome he could only recall with an aching sense of loss. The girls were the Dolly Sisters, Jennie and Rosie, who were on the rise to theatrical fame. Jennie was married to Harry Fox, a vaudeville star, and Rosie to Jean Schwartz, a songwriter. To banish world-sickness, to revive his jaded interest in life, he played host to the sisters and their husbands in restaurants and at the theater. Knowing it would take more than the lifting of a few dinner checks to allow him to share part of their lives, he bought each of the sisters an automobile, a diamond chain, and a six-carat diamond ring. (In his will he left a chain of sixty-five pearls to Rosie and a scarf pin set containing twenty-two diamonds to her husband, and to Jennie a pearl ring containing a 130-grain pearl and eight diamonds weighing twenty-four carats and to her husband a ring set with fourteen diamonds.)

A few months before World War I broke out, he made his debut in what later became known as "filmland society," thus providing a social linkage between the old show business centered on Broadway and the new tributary headquartered in a Los Angeles suburb. One of those he entertained was Charlie Chaplin, the young English comedian who was beginning to make a name for himself in two-reelers. Brady had earlier entertained Chaplin at a party in his New York house, in the course of which Chaplin wearied of the revels and was found sleeping in Brady's gigantic bathtub.

Brady's headquarters in Los Angeles was the Alexandria Hotel downtown, where most of the producers and many of the stars lived, Hollywood then being only a place of work. His social entree evidently was provided by the Dolly Sisters, who had gone out to scout the possibility of appearing in the films.

In his autobiography Chaplin recalled attending a dinner given at the Alexandria by Brady and being slightly bewildered by the strange quintet made up of Brady, the Dolly sisters, and their husbands. His other guests included Carlotta Monterey, a brunette beauty who would become Eugene O'Neill's last wife; Lou Tellegen, who had been Sarah Bernhardt's leading man and was now lending his classic profile to the movies; Mack Sennett, the producer of film comedies; Nat Goodwin, the much-married actor; and two of the current darlings of the screen, Blanche Sweet and Mabel Normand. "The Dolly sisters were sensationally beautiful," as Chaplin would remember the dinner party. "The two of them, their husbands and Diamond Jim Brady were almost inseparable; their association was puzzling . . . Diamond Jim was a unique American character, who looked like a benign John Bull. That first night I could not believe my eyes, for he wore diamond cufflinks and studs in his shirtfront, each stone larger than a shilling. . . . A few nights later we dined at Nat Goodwin's Café on the [Santa Monica] pier, and this time Diamond Jim showed up with his emerald set, each stone the size of a small matchbox. At first I thought he was wearing them as a joke, and innocently asked if they were genuine. He said they were. 'But,' I said with astonishment, 'they are fabulous.' 'If you want to see beautiful emeralds, here,' he replied. He lifted his dress waistcoat, showing a belt the size of the Marquis of Queensberry's championship belt, completely covered with the largest emeralds I have ever seen. . . ."

His doctors were unable to slow him down, either at work or play. It was a mystery to them when he slept, because he was reported out dancing the night away and yet was putting in a full day at his desk in the offices on Cortlandt Street or commuting between New York and the Standard Steel Car Company's plant in Pittsburgh. He no longer went on the road but was a full-fledged tycoon.

Immediately after the war in Europe began, his workload and responsibilities were greatly increased. The Allies needed thousands of railway cars for their supply trains since war had become so weightily a matter of logistics. England and France were frantically calling on the American industries to balance the industrial might of the German empire and its satellites.

Most of Brady's fellow Irish-Americans were so anti-British that they tended to support the kaiser, particularly after the Easter Rebellion in Dublin was smashed. They supported the Irish republican underground with money and sympathy and regarded England's troubles as Ireland's good luck. If the kaiser and his armies managed to destroy British military power, the British would have to withdraw the occupation forces which had kept Ireland in subjugation for four centuries. Many of the longshoremen in the neighborhood where Brady was born and raised, the sons of the men who had patronized Brady's saloon, were conspiring with German-American plotters, Irish Socialist agitators who had recently slipped into the country, and German espionage agents to interfere with and sabotage the shipment of supplies to the Allied armies.

They did not find an ally, or even a sympathizer, in Diamond Jim Brady. He had got along fine with the Anglo-Saxon establishment and had always treasured the way he had been treated by the Fox family in England. And Jim had never considered himself an Irishman, but a 100-percent American.

If the United States policy was neutral in favor of Britain and France, that was good enough for Brady, who could hear only faint echoes of the lilting voices of his boyhood recounting how his parents' generation of Irish had been driven from their native island by the potato famine and the indifference of their British overlords. Furthermore, American policy of supplying the Allies but not their enemies was damned good for business. American factories were working around the clock to supply the orders from overseas, not least the Standard Steel Car Company, which was called upon to produce the freight cars which hauled munitions to the Atlantic ports.

Midway through the war Standard had to expand its facilities and even build a factory in France when it received an order for 38,000 freight cars from the French government. So much rolling stock had been captured in the first German offensives that France had to rebuild her railway net and float a special defense bond issue of $100,000,000 to handle the financing. Brady saw no reason why German manpower shouldn't make its contribution to the French war effort. The freight cars were shipped in sections from Pittsburgh and assembled at the French plant by German prisoners of war, the cheapest labor anyone could hope for.

As the unofficial and untitled chief executive of Standard Steel, Brady was involved in a constant swirl of activity, trips to Pittsburgh, negotiations with Allied procurement officers. His doctors begged him to cut down either his workload or his social life, and if neither of those his eating, but he genially rejected their warnings.

A protégé of Dr. Hugh Young, the Johns Hopkins surgeon who had saved his life, was detailed to keep a special watch over Brady. He was a Johns Hopkins graduate, Dr. Oswald Lowsley, who was a member of the staff at Bellevue Hospital. Young Dr. Lowsley gave Brady a weekly checkup and a weekly sermon, but without much effect on his patient's habits. "I managed to make him stop eating candy and sweet foods," Dr. Lowsley would recall later, "but that was as far as my influence over him extended."

His remonstrations on the value of moderation only drew Brady's reply, "You ain't going to make me stop eating. Hell, I've got to have some fun; I haven't much longer to live."

Brady gave a testimonial dinner for Dr. Hugh Young when the Brady Urological Institute was formally opened in 1915. It was held at the Vanderbilt Hotel, and the menu was composed of just those viands, richly sauced, which the many doctors present would *not* have prescribed for their host. As a newspaper account of the banquet described it, "The menu was distinguished by a sort of elegant simplicity as to dishes and gorgeous abundance as to the quantity of each. As a concession to Mr. Brady's terpsichorean tastes, the cover of the menu represented a dancing couple doing the tango. August Keller, the maître d'hotel, had for some time been making a list of the favorite dishes of Diamond Jim. So the dinner led off with gumbo jelly soup. Then came crab meat Creole. Next was asparagus of a size that would make the average gardener writhe with envy. Followed the *pièce de résistance*: two lambs roasted whole and borne in the fashion of the boar's head at old Yule festivals. Everybody got a piece. Hearts of lettuce salad with cheese followed by *Fraises* Melba, just strawberries with ice cream and raspberry sauce with little cakes and coffee completed the menu. . . ."

A year later it was evident that the great gastronome's career was coming to an end. He had lost his appetite, the weight was falling away from him, and he no longer summoned his platoons of dancing girls and whirled them off in his night limousine. Big Casino, the death card, had been dealt Diamond Jim Brady, according to the Broadway rumor.

In the spring of 1916, taking cognizance of the rumors, the New York Society of Restaurateurs decided to give a banquet for Brady, the best customer they ever had or would have. Jim appreciated the honor but dreaded making a speech. Finally he decided to compose a poem for the occasion, a sort of farewell ode to the Broadway which had been his playground for so many years. The New York *Times* covered the event and reported that "at one time it appeared that Brady would not be permitted to make his speech at all; but it was all due to a mistake of a waiter who did not realize the importance of the distinguished guest. The lights had been turned low to show a scene on the stage, but still a great illumination came from the rear of the room in the middle of the speaker's table. 'Turn out that light,' ordered someone. A waiter went back and reported that the light came from Brady's blazing diamonds."

Brady, his voice trembling with emotion, rose to deliver his poem. More fittingly, perhaps, his first and only literary effort might have paid tribute to Wall Street, where the money for his decades of high living came from, instead of the sector into which so much of it vanished. At any rate the following verses were the last words Broadway would hear from its biggest spender, a sentimental tribute which only that cynical collective, case-hardened from its years of trimming the suckers, could accept with a straight face:

Ah, boys—it's the same old Broadway
With its gayly glowing lights
That the bards have sung, since New York was young,
With the same old seductive sights.
It's the same White Way your daddies knew,
In their callow, youthful flights,
It's the same Broadway for me and you,
That keeps us out at nights.

It's the same Broadway where the world parades
The same old circus and clowns.
The same Broadway where jays and jades
Come searching for gold and renown.
It's the same Broadway where the nations play
On the Street of the Midnight Sun.
So, here's a toast—and let me say,
Old Broadway—there's only one.

Six months later Brady suffered an attack of gastric ulcers, serious enough for Dr. Hugh Young to come up from Baltimore and consult with other specialists on the advisability of surgery. They decided against operating, and Brady realized that the one thing he couldn't buy—time—was in short supply. In addition to the ulcers, he was suffering from angina pectoris, diabetes, and malfunctioning kidneys. He was paying the price for his years of massive indulgence, cheerfully on the whole. He was living up to the one and only rule in the Broadway code: Take your losses without griping.

Knowing that his life was measured in months, he decided to remove himself from the New York scene. But he refused to return to Johns Hopkins Hospital. He would meet his maker, "the man in the bright nightgown," on ground of his own choosing: Atlantic City. To moralists it may have seemed a curious choice for a man facing the final reckoning, since Atlantic City was the sin capital of the United States, the Las Vegas of the early decades of the century, the paradise of middle-class lechery.

Brady took a $1,000-a-week suite at the Shelburne Hotel, a huge apartment facing the ocean, and had a glass-enclosed veranda built around it from which, wrapped in rugs in a steamer chair, he could survey the winter-gray and stormy Atlantic.

Young Dr. Lowsley often came down from New York, more out of personal than professional concern, since Brady was constantly attended by other doctors and round-the-clock nurses. Brady was tearfully grateful; out of all that legion of friends he had professionally acquired through the years, the young physician was one of the few who made the trip to off-season Atlantic City. In his last months he occupied himself with plans for the establishment of the James Buchanan Brady Urological Pavilion at New York Hospital with the proviso that Dr. Lowsley be placed in charge.

He was placed on a strict diet and was constantly surveyed by specialists from New York and Baltimore, but there was nothing they could do but prolong his life a few weeks, a few days.

Early on the morning of April 13, 1917, with rain driving in from the Atlantic and drumming against the glass windows of the veranda, Jim Brady died in his sleep. No personal friend was present, though he had made a profession of winning friends and his loyalty and generosity toward them were undeniable.

A special train brought his body back to New York, where it lay in state the weekend of his death. Hundreds of people came to pay their respects, as the generic phrase has it, though there may have been mixed feelings in some of those who viewed the body. The bier was blanketed with orchids and expensive wreaths, but Brady would have approved of the fact that room was made for the small bouquets laid beside the coffin by newsboys whom he had befriended. Among many, no doubt, there was a natural curiosity about how much Jim Brady had left them in his will; there were not only all those millions he had accumulated but in the master bedroom upstairs a collection of jewelry appraised at slightly more than half a million dollars, including not only his thirty sets but a diamond-studded watch once worn by Napoleon Bonaparte, which he left to his old friend Jules Weiss, a diamond and pearl collar containing 422 pearls and 38 diamonds, a diamond and black opal brooch, eleven gold cigarette cases, eleven silver corn knives, twelve silver hat brushes, and a drawer full of gold watches. And most of those hopefuls would be disappointed. Except for a few friends remembered with bequests of cash or jewelry, and the provision made for his sister and her son, Brady's estate was left to various philanthropic enterprises. He did not endow a Lillian Russell Theater as a testimonial to a great and lasting friendship; both he and Lillian were too sensible for that sort of gesture. Instead he left $10,000 bequests to the New York Central Employees' Hospital, the Newsboys' Lodging House, the Roman Catholic Orphan Asylum, the Children's Aid Society, and the Actors' Fund of America. The residue was divided between the Johns Hopkins Hospital and the New York Hospital for furtherance of their research and treatment of urological disorders.

Thousands crowded the streets around St. Agnes' Roman Catholic Church on Forty-third near Lexington for the funeral on April 16, which preceded his burial in an ornate mausoleum at Greenwood Cemetery. Among the mourners were various railroad magnates and business associates and a delegation from the theater including De Wolf Hopper, Wilton Lackaye, and other prominent figures, as well as newsboys and waiters and Pullman porters and bellboys and others who knew him at his free-spending best.

And, of course, Lillian Russell. She wept when his coffin was lowered into the grave.

The usual religious and secular clichés accompanied that final descent, but it could be safely said that Jim Brady was an American original and no one would ever match his zest for getting and spending.

11

THE PRESIDENT'S
PLENIPOTENTIARY

ONE May night in 1915 a charity performance was given
at the Metropolitan Opera. Finally, briefly, yet triumphantly Lillian Russell attained her ambition of hearing herself cheered in an opera house. Stage and screen celebrities
were politely applauded as they walked on and took their bows.
But a respectful hush settled over the house when the master of
ceremonies, Henry E. Dixey, announced:

"Here comes the Queen!"

No one had to ask who "the Queen" was. Until her death it
would always be Lillian Russell. Instead of walking across the
stage from the wings, Lillian, with her majestic stroll, entered
from the rear of the house. The audience, by joint consent,
rose and stood in silence until she took her seat. A reporter
noted that she still had eyes "the color of lilacs after a rain."

It was solid evidence of her standing in the profession, if not
at the box office, and indication that she still had a role of some
kind to play in public life. And she would search diligently for
that role.

Two weeks before Diamond Jim Brady was buried the
United States had entered the World War. Unnoticed at the
time, like most such endings, the curtain thus fell on the pe-

riod which Brady and Russell, in the shorthand of social history, would epitomize for posterity.

But if Lillian Russell was converted into an anachronism by the social upheaval accompanying the First World War, she refused to demonstrate any awareness of the fact. Her determination to remain a public figure, glamorous if possible, still utterly visible if not, was undiminished. Out of all the thousands of women who worked and struggled for the right to vote, most of them without being garlanded with headlines, it was Lillian who would be chosen for the distinction of a high public office—the final reward of celebrity.

During the brief American engagement on the Western front, she contended mightily for the role of number-one female patriot. Elsie Janis and Mary Pickford and other young actresses may have outshone her with their beauty and fresher claim to fame, but Lillian managed to keep herself in the vanguard of homefront activities, and no one was more impressive at shaking a dainty fist at the kaiser across the seas.

Before Congress passed legislation introducing the military draft she flung herself into the recruiting program, appearing nightly before crowds in various Pennsylvania towns and urging young men to volunteer for the armed services. In Pittsburgh there was a Lillian Russell Recruiting Day, at which she delivered a stem-winder of a patriotic oration and persuaded scores of young men to step up and volunteer; each was given a tiny bejeweled American flag as his reward. One night she persuaded 259 men to enlist at McKeesport. Later she revealed the exaltation she felt in such endeavors, apparently without considering what might have happened to those men in combat, but her feelings in such matters were as simplistic as the UNCLE SAM WANTS YOU recruiting posters. "As I stepped upon the platform which was built in the middle of a public square," she wrote, "I saw before me about ten thousand people. It had started to rain and umbrellas were raised. I shouted: 'Men and women—our boys are knee-deep in mud in the trenches in

France, fighting for you and me.' Actually it would be months before the first AEF regiments would reach the forward lines, but hyperbole is not necessarily the lesser part of a patriotic endeavor. 'It's raining there,' she continued. 'Do those boys have umbrellas?' In five seconds every umbrella was down, and in less than five minutes the rain had stopped. The most emotional moments I ever experienced in my varied career were in those days, when we needed men. . . ."

The government rewarded her efforts by making her an honorary sergeant in the Marine Corps after she starred in a Liberty Bond rally at the Hippodrome in New York on October 18, 1917, before 5,000 persons gathered to marvel at what one newspaper called her "pulchritudinous" presence. After an eloquent demonstration of "pure patriotism," as the newspaper put it, she approvingly watched hundreds in the audience storm the stage to buy bonds.

There was no doubt of the sincerity of her passion, yet there was also the discernible element, inseparable from an actress' deepest instincts, of satisfying her dramatic urges by swaying large audiences.

As she wrote several years later, "I have had first nights of great successful operas and plays surrounded by an adoring audience and company and receiving the congratulations of friends, receiving wagonloads of flowers and jeweled presents, and I have been through all the emotions of sorrow and love; but the greatest moments (and they were many and varied) were when, after I had made a sincere and impassioned appeal for the boys to 'come to the call of Uncle Sam and enlist to fight for their old fathers, their mothers, sisters and sweethearts, and save them from the atrocious Germans,' I would see the onrush of lads who would fairly tear down the railings around the recruiting stand to come up to me and offer their lives for their country. There was never anything to compare with such moments."

She affirmed that she was deeply touched, late in the Liberty

Bond campaign, when some of the young men she had recruited were invalided out of the service and came back to help her sell bonds.

Lillian did manage to control her patriotism, however, when the opportunity arose for returning to the theater. Naturally, in announcing her return, she declared that providing entertainment in wartime was her patriotic duty; she also wanted to make it clear that she was not one of those tiresome old prima donnas who were forever making farewell tours and ached for signs they were still held in public favor. "I am not 'returning to the stage,' " she starchily informed the newspapers, "because I never retired from it and never intend to retire. Retirement from one's most useful occupation, one's most enjoyable activity, is a confession of decrepitude that my physical and mental condition abhors. It is true that I have had an interval of occupation away from the stage, but I have not been idling, for a large part of my time has been spent in doing my bit for our country and our soldiers. I feel that in these times of stress anything that contributes toward lightening the hearts of the people should be looked upon as worthwhile, and the stage is the place from which best to scatter sunshine."

She had, of course, announced her retirement almost two years before at the end of her coast-to-coast tour, but actresses cannot be held accountable in such matters. In any case, she was delighted to accept the offer to appear in what would later be called a cameo in Raymond Hitchcock's *Hitchy Koo*, which turned out to be a great success. She sang three songs, demonstrated few if any signs of decrepitude, and received an ovation on opening night. And then Lillian Russell's name went up in lights on Broadway for the last time the summer of 1918.

At a victory rally in November she appeared on the stage of the Palace in her honorary sergeant's uniform. Never before had the uniform of the United States Marine Corps bulged in so many unlikely places.

During the last several years of her life, her career taking a turn that would be incredible, if not impossible, in any other nation, Lillian Russell was a politician. Furthermore, she was associated with the national administration which most feminists would consider as malodorous with all the evils they charged to the male political animal: smoke-filled rooms in which conspiracies were hatched, high-level corruption, immoral goings-on, whiskey-guzzling, and cigar-chomping. Given the vote, as bitter-end masculinists might have observed, the American women promptly helped to elect one of the handsomest but also one of the most inept Presidents in history, Warren Gamaliel Harding of Ohio.

If there was an autumn of discontent in her life, it was the period between the end of the World War and the inauguration of Harding. There were no more summons from Broadway or any other sector of show business. There was no crusade with the emotional pull of women's suffrage to engage her interest. Her position as one of the rulers of Pittsburgh society was not demanding enough to use up her energy.

Some of her intense vitality was burned off in occasional speeches denouncing President Woodrow Wilson and his campaign to persuade the United States it must join the League of Nations. By now Lillian was violently Republican and regarded the pedantic Mr. Wilson as some kind of demon who would lead the country into a "godless" involvement with Europe's ancient quarrels. She made fiery speeches on the subject; an imposing figure on the platform with the heroic figure and imperious profile of a Roman matron imploring her menfolk to go out and chase the Visigoths off the city walls. She accompanied her husband to the Republicans' 1920 nominating convention in Chicago, which with strenuous effort finally managed to produce Senator Harding as their candidate. Among the several worthier candidates, Lillian had selected Senator Hiram W. Johnson of California as her choice for the nomination, but the dark horse Harding won through a deadlock among the other candidates. She was soon reconciled to the convention's choice.

"Will you go on the stump for Harding?" her husband asked.

"I will go for the Republican cause," she quoted herself as replying, in a rhetoric which was becoming as familiar to her as the overblown lyrics of an operetta, "for it needs every patriot in America, but I must meet Senator Harding and know him, and I must learn for myself whether I can make speeches for him."

Lillian and her husband were soon invited to meet the Hardings in his hometown of Marion, Ohio. One glimpse of his noble profile—no one ever *looked* more like a President than Warren G. Harding—and she became an enthusiastic follower. At luncheon she was placed on his right side, and "I was especially honored when Senator Harding said, 'Mrs. Moore, you will have to make a speech to about a thousand women who have seen you in your profession and who know you by your work.'" Lillian obediently went out and addressed the crowd gathered outside the Harding front porch.

At dinner Lillian again was placed on Senator Harding's right side and "he spoke quite intimately about his mother and a sister who had been a missionary out in India. I learned enough from that little chat to know that our President depends upon God's guidance for every day in his life."

Lillian was bewitched—what a leading man he would have made!—and agreed to hit the campaign trail for Harding's candidacy.

The Republican National Committee mapped out a tour which took her through fifteen states, and in the course of a month on the stump she made more than a hundred speeches, the keynote of most of them being an emotional denunciation of the League of Nations and the Democratic "plot" to involve America in more European conflicts. Campaigning was rigorous at times, such as when a bearded old gaffer stepped up to the platform in Chicago and announced that he had voted for Lincoln. He insisted on a kiss. Lillian kissed him on his furry cheek. "No," he protested, "not that way. I want a kiss on the lips, and by gosh I haven't forgotten how to yet either!" The newspaper accounts of her appearances in various Western cities indicated that she had star quality as a partisan orator.

Senator Harding was not only elected but demonstrated that he had a sense of gratitude (which is lovable in an ordinary citizen but often a fatal flaw in a politician). His appointments were colossally inappropriate, naming as his Secretary of Interior and watchdog over the naval oil reserves, for instance, the man who was notoriously the bedfellow of various oil magnates.

The plum which President Harding plucked off the tree of goodies for Lillian Russell was not in a class with his selection of Senator Albert B. Fall as Secretary of the Interior, but it was still an odd choice, if experience and knowledge are the desired criteria for a public servant. It came about largely because Lillian and her husband, frequently visiting Washington, were admitted to the inner circle of the Harding administration, the social ambience of which drew the contempt of the capital's aristocracy. If a later administration could be proclaimed as a reconstruction of Camelot, Harding's was a preview of Al Capp's Lower Slobbovia. The President's chief relaxation was gathering with his cronies and playing poker in an atmosphere redolent of illegal whiskey, Havana cigars, and casually arranged deals to loot the national resources. Avid card player though she was, Lillian was not mentioned in any of the contemporary chronicles as joining in the poker sessions herself, but her husband, Alexander Moore, was included in the withering comment of Mrs. Alice Roosevelt Longworth, daughter of Theodore Roosevelt and wife of the Speaker of the House: "No rumor could have exceeded the reality; the study was filled with cronies, Daugherty, Jess Smith, Alec Moore, and others, the air heavy with tobacco smoke, trays with bottles containing every imaginable brand of whiskey stood about, cards and poker chips ready at hand—a general atmosphere of waistcoat unbuttoned, feet on the desk, and spittoons alongside."

The capital was fairly shockproof regarding Presidential appointments by the fall of 1921, but there was still a raising of eyebrows when the White House announced that Mrs. Alexander Moore, better known as Lillian Russell, had been appointed Special Commissioner of Immigration and was being sent to Europe to study the immigration problem. The United States was then in a mood to slam its fabled "golden door." There was a postwar slump and a rise in unemployment, and consequently a clamor for revision of the laws which then permitted the entry of 350,000 aliens annually. In the past several years, too, there had been much agitation against alien minorities already in our midst. The Germans, and to a lesser extent the Irish, had been accused of having done their worst to sabotage American assistance to the Allies. Just after the war ended there was a stock headline on the nation's front pages: NEW ROUNDUP OF RADICALS. President Wilson's Attorney General A. Mitchell Palmer was a fanatical anti-Bolshevik and had arrested more than 6,000 foreign-born, whom he labeled dangerous aliens, and more than 1,000 of these had been deported with scant regard for whatever civil rights they possessed. Before that, there had been a bomb-throwing period in which foreign-born anarchists were plentifully involved. The national mood was that the country was endangered politically as well as economically by continued large-scale immigration.

In explaining his appointment of Lillian as a special agent of the government, Harding declared, with more than a touch of hyperbole, that such an attractive woman could coax and wheedle more information out of Europeans "than all the intelligence and diplomacy of the Government."

Lillian journeyed to Europe and spent several months investigating the conditions which impelled millions of Europeans to yearn for departure from their war-damaged countries, with large parts of Germany, France, Italy, Austria, and the Balkans devastated and disease rampant among the displaced and dispossessed.

She returned with opinions that could only please those who

wanted immigration slowed down to a trickle and an attitude in striking contrast to the liberal-humanitarianism of her crusading days when she was more interested in feeding the poor than protecting the established.

Her report to Secretary of Labor James Davis, she told reporters when her ship docked in New York, would be an amazingly effective corrective to all the humanitarian propaganda to which Americans had been subjected. "America is over propagandeered," she declared. "Stories of suffering humanity in Europe and oppression all have the dollar sign back of them. It is my own personal belief that there are organizations financed for the sole purpose of making money out of what they call 'humanity.' Many well-meaning people are hoodwinked by these parasites who are trying to bring to this country men and women who do not understand our language. It seems to me a crime that American boys have to wait until they are twenty-one to vote, when aliens, such as I saw abroad, can, within five years have the privileges our forefathers fought for. Our slogan should be America for the Americans."

Once again Lillian felt the warming and reassuring glow of publicity's spotlights. This time the whole nation was her audience and for the most part it approved of what she said.

Hoping to be called as a witness before the committee investigating suggested changes in the immigration laws, she memorialized Congress on her findings in the trip to Europe. Her lecture was received with a mixed reaction in the Senate, though that body was liberally populated by men who remembered Lillian Russell as the sexiest symbol of their youth. Still there were those who wondered just how well a musical comedy actress was qualified to expound on such an intricate problem.

Special Commissioner Russell informed the Congress that henceforth U.S. consuls abroad should give intelligence tests to all applicants for immigration and that consulates should be staffed with American physicians to make sure the diseased and unfit were weeded out. She continued:

249

The immigration of recent years has been from that class of people which arrests, rather than aids, the development of any nation. When I declare that most of those now seeking to come here have not any of the inspiration of the necessity of the early settlers from abroad, I am stating facts that impress everybody who makes any study of European conditions. The higher civilization of past ages, history teaches us, succumbed to such foreign invasions as now threaten us. It is against such a fate that America must protect itself, that the American Government must protect its people, including those of foreign birth or extraction who have loyally taken up the duties of American citizenship. I believe it would be a good thing for America if an immigration holiday of five years could be declared. But if we must keep the gates open, I would urge a new system by which the sifting process should be carried on abroad, so that none but those who, physically and mentally, would make valuable additions to our population would be permitted to board ship for America.

Senator Pat Harrison—though a Mississippi Democrat—rose on the Senate floor to quote lovingly a sentence from Lillian's report ("Alien infiltration wrecked Rome") and to chide the Republicans for failing to call Lillian before the investigating committee.

This touched off an acrimonious exchange, with Senator James Reed of Missouri rising to declare: "I want to inquire when Lillian Russell became an authority on the rise and fall of Rome. I will admit that she is an authority on matters theatrical and perhaps on cosmetics [this was an unchivalrous reference to Lillian Russell's Own Preparations, Inc., a beauty aid firm which had briefly flourished and then collapsed several years before], but I never knew until just now that she had entered the field of immigration."

Senator George Moses of New Hampshire hurled himself into the breach, shouting across the aisle at Senator Reed: "I rise to point out the incongruity of the Senator's criticism of Mrs. Moore. I think it highly undignified and most ungentlemanly."

The debate sputtered out with a few damp squibs of Senatorial humor.

By then Lillian Russell was back in Pittsburgh and fighting for her life. She had addressed the Society of Patriotic New Yorkers on the subject of closing the gates on immigration, then returned home late in May, 1922, in a state of collapse. On board the ship on which she returned from her European survey she had slipped and fallen, suffering internal injuries which she dismissed as trivial.

Possibly she refused to consult a doctor because of her earnest practice of the Christian Science faith. Eighteen years before Weber and Fields had to close down the Music Hall when she contracted tonsilitis and refused to be treated by a physician. Finally she yielded to the pleas of her fellow players, her producers, and her friends, not to mention a New York *Evening World* editorial that lectured her on her duty to the public and her profession. "Christian Science," the editorial added, somewhat cavalier about an individual's religious beliefs, "has never been known to remove a mole from a pretty cheek or to mend a broken leg, or to cure an attack of sickness that did not disappear when the patient first exercised the theory of mind over matter. In other words, Christian Science is a most excellent thing for those who suffer from something they haven't got."

When she returned to her Pittsburgh home seriously ill, however, she was placed under medical care, which was unavailing. On June 6, 1922, she died of what was reported in the newspapers as "a complication of diseases." Whatever they were, Lillian had kept them secret and carried on as best she could.

Certainly she went to her grave in the Allegheny Cemetery in Pittsburgh with the undiminished affection and gratitude of the theatrical profession. A few years earlier her fellow trouper Nat C. Goodwin had written in his memoirs that she had "the soul of a saint, the true spirit of comedy. . . . All through her

251

life she has endeavored only to obtain a home to enable her to bring her child up an honest woman. And these efforts have been as futile as her success as an artist has been assured. . . ."

And Alan Dale, the sometimes hypercritical newspaper drama critic, observed that "Everyone who knew her knew that her help was theirs merely for the asking. It is cruel to realize that Lillian Russell has passed on. She would never have grown old, and now she never can."

At President Harding's order she was buried with full military honors, with a floral centerpiece from the White House on her coffin. There were memorial services in many American cities. Few members of her profession had known such success, and none had worn it more gracefully.

12

DIM THE HOUSELIGHTS

THE legend of Broadway, which Lillian Russell and Diamond Jim Brady helped to create, must seem incomprehensible to those who visit the Times Square area today in search of the glamor it represented to their grandfathers. It is undergoing a transition in which office buildings replace the theaters and restaurants, and few landmarks have been preserved as a tribute to the past. Any residual sentimentality is leached out by the value of real estate on which high-rise buildings can be erected. There are still rubberneck buses, Father Duffy's statue, a plaque marking the site where Eugene O'Neill was born, but nighttime Broadway is a concourse taken over by prostitutes, panhandlers, muggers, cruising homosexuals, and transvestites.

The insular world of midtown Manhattan which Lillian Russell, Diamond Jim Brady, and their contemporaries inhabited only a little more than a half century ago has vanished with the hansom cabs and the restaurants with their crystal chandeliers and tapestried walls and the cabarets with their ragtime bands. No other city in the world destroys its past as quickly and ruthlessly as New York.

You could blame it all on the wreckers' ball and the jackhammers of greedy real estate tycoons, but even those agents of dubious progress can only attack a dying organism. If the old Broadway had been viable, had endured the competition of mechanized entertainment, it would still be blazing with light instead of crouching in the shadows of the skyscraper headquarters of the television networks a few avenues crosstown.

The old Broadway dimmed its house lights more than a half century ago, shortly after Brady's death and just before Lillian Russell's. You could fix the hour and the day when the world they knew was obliterated. That hour was struck at midnight on January 16, 1920, when the Eighteenth Amendment took effect and Prohibition began. Without being able to sell liquor, the restaurants and cafés and cabarets which Brady and Russell had patronized were forced to close their doors. Some tried to resist the law but were harried into bankruptcy by federal agents. Wrecking crews soon demolished Louis Martin's, Maxim's, Bustanoby's, Shanley's, Churchill's, Reisenweber's, even Rector's. Murray's Roman Gardens, which had been celebrated for its revolving dance floor and lavish decor, was taken over by Hubert's Museum and Flea Circus. The elegant old Knickerbocker Hotel at Broadway and Forty-second was converted into an office building. Before the decade was out, the old Waldorf-Astoria with its Peacock Alley and stately dining rooms was demolished to make way for the Empire State Building. Very soon the places where well-heeled people could eat and drink with leisurely elegance were replaced by establishments such as the Bombay Bicycle Club and a hundred places known simply as Tony's—speakeasies where booze could be tossed down furtively, swiftly, and at an untold amount of damage to internal organs. By 1929 there were 32,000 speakeasies in New York City, double the number of old-time saloons.

It is possible to look back on the time of Lillian Russell and Diamond Jim Brady with an unqualified regret and unabashed nostalgia. It is quite probable that Americans never had it so good as during the eighties, nineties, and the first fourteen years of the new century. Between the Civil War and the First World War the nation was at relative peace longer than any other time in its history, though a number of Indians, Spaniards, and Filipinos might have disputed that statement. The long peace was disrupted by the Spanish-American War, it is true, but that was over in a short time and at relatively low cost in blood and treasure; and most Americans were united in the self-righteous belief that they were bringing independence and prosperity to Cuba, the blessings of democracy and personal liberty to the people of the Philippines.

Brady and Russell, in their persons and the style of life they embodied, epitomized that period in the social sense, in the shorthand of journalism, in the popular mind. They were not *important* except as symbols; capitalism would have advanced in giant strides without Brady's invention of himself as the first supersalesman, and artistically Lillian Russell added little to theatrical history except an aptitude for commercializing sex appeal, a process on which Hollywood would infinitely elaborate, and of course her amazing ability to hit high C eight times in a performance. Together they embellished the art of consumption, not the noblest endeavor in the world as we look back on it from the viewpoint of our diminished and soon-to-be-overtaxed resources. With their twelve-course dinners, their gold-plated bicycles, their encrustation of personal jewelry, their private railroad cars, they represented the ultimate vulgarization of the Horatio Alger legend, if you want to take a harshly uncharitable view of their endeavors. Less harshly, it might be noted that they were exceedingly generous with their time and money, and the world was probably a better place for their having lived in it. Certainly it would have been less amusing if Brady had saved his money and built a dynasty in the sober fashion of his contemporaries, or if Lillian had foresworn her popular and commercial career and dedicated herself to the disciplines of grand opera.

They had come along at a time when there was a vast expansion of the national wealth and a zooming standard of living.

In the middle of the nineteenth century there were less than a score of millionaires in the whole country. But in 1892 the New York *Tribune* published a list of 4,047 men reputed to be millionaires. This new concentration of wealth—and more particularly the conspicuous spending of a Diamond Jim Brady and a number of his freewheeling contemporaries—contributed to a dislocation in the American psyche, the force of which was greater than the inspirational quality of the Horatio Alger-type propaganda.

The personal expenditures, the open enjoyment of the money they acquired, which Brady and Russell flaunted in their rather innocent fashion, was at first greatly admired by their contemporaries. They had made it on their own—Brady from bellhop to steel magnate, Russell from chorus girl to superstar. Their pursuit of the fleshly pleasures was a matter of emulation rather than envy.

Then something curdled the public admiration of conspicuous consumers—perhaps it was the periodic depressions, the agitations of the populists and more radical types, the slow growth of what became known as a social conscience. The Rockefellers and other shrewd types adopted what now might be called a low profile; they were in the dynasty business, in for the long haul, while such innocents as Diamond Jim Brady, Bet-a-Million Gates, Coal Oil Johnny, and other magnificoes regarded their takings with no more wary respect than a crapshooter raking in his pot. Thus by 1914 Walter Weyl was writing in *The New Democracy* that the public had adopted a new hostility toward the conspicuous enjoyment of wealth.

Weyl observed that there was an "increasing bitterness felt by a majority which is not worse but better off than before. This majority suffers not an absolute decline but a relatively slower growth. . . . Everywhere we meet the millionaire's good and evil works, and we seem to resent the one as much as the other. Our jogging horses are passed by their high-power automobiles. We are obliged to take their dust. . . . We are developing new types of destitutes—the automobileless, the Newportcottageless, the yachtless. The subtlest of luxuries become necessities, and their loss is bitterly resented. . . . The discontent of today reaches very high in the social scale. . . ."

Jim Brady put it more pungently when discussing his 20,000 diamonds and 6,000 other precious and semiprecious stones. "Them as has 'em, wears 'em." Them as hadn't, presumably, were privileged to admire their betters. His conscience, as an ex-underdog himself, was untroubled. He knew that while he was crunching through multiple courses at the Waldorf, down on Orchard Street in lower Manhattan a less fortunate fellow could fill himself, for thirteen cents, on a substantial dinner and a schooner of beer. The American abundance was spread around, not equally by any means, but plentifully enough to ease the faint qualms of those who worried about the poor.

He and Lillian Russell just happened to possess the appetites and capacities for the utmost public enjoyment of an age of opulence, of uninhibited ostentation, which would never return to America even in the most prosperous times.

NOTES ON SOURCES

The complete listing of most of the sources indicated below under their authors' surnames may be found in the Bibliography, which follows.

Introduction

The chorus of the "Lobsters! Rarebits!" song is quoted in O'Connor, *Hell's Kitchen*, 82.

John Jay Chapman's letter is quoted in Ziff's *The American 1890's*, 245. Chapman was the great-great-grandson of the first Chief Justice of the United States Supreme Court. Despite the optimism of the letter quoted, he also considered his age "tyrannous," with a tendency to demand of everyone "Perish or play the game."

James F. Muirhead comments on the quality of American democracy in Baedeker's *The United States*, 1893 edition, to which Muirhead contributed, and in his own *The Land of Contrasts*, 19–20.

A lively description of the Columbian Exposition may be found in Dedmon's *Fabulous Chicago*, 220–37.

1. Star Quality

Childhood and family background of Lillian Russell were derived from various sources: her autobiography, "Lillian Russell's Reminiscences," published serially in *Cosmopolitan*, February to September, 1922, inclusive; the *Iowa State Guide*; Dedmon's *Fabulous Chicago*, 236; Smith's *First Nights and First Editions, passim*. Smith attended grade school with Lillian and later collaborated on some of the productions in which she starred. Later she attended the Convent of the Sacred Heart, and perhaps it is worth noting that Mother Superior Gotherau issued this cautionary to her parents: "Nellie is talented, dangerously talented; she will require careful watching."

Her mother's activities in Chicago as a writer, social reformer, and feminist crusader are detailed in Dedmon's *Fabulous Chicago*, 236–37.

A somewhat reticent account of her first marriage and her discovery by Tony Pastor may be found in her "Reminiscences," *Cosmopolitan*, February, 1922. The serialized autobiography was never published in book form, perhaps because she died midway through its publication.

For Lillian's recollection of her family's musical talent and her decision to become an opera singer see her "Reminiscences," *Cosmopolitan*, February, 1922.

Marie Dressler remembered Charles Leonard's traveling long distances to catch his daughter's performances in her memoirs, *My Own Story*, 86.

Lillian's adventures during her first year in show business are detailed in Morell's *Lillian Russell: The Era of Plush, passim.*

Lillian's sympathy for and generosity toward her fellow troupers is amply documented in a number of memoirs, notably Dressler's *My Own Story*, Isman's *Weber and Fields*, Morehouse's *Matinee Tomorrow*, Hopper's *Reminiscences of De Wolf Hopper*, and other show-business chronicles.

The systematic looting of her pay envelope by her maid is described in Morehouse, *Matinee Tomorrow*, 210–11.

Her triumphs in San Francisco are detailed by Lewis, *Bay Window Bohemia*, 77, 118.

The story of the Russian naval officer's gift, her account of the gifts received from her anonymous elderly benefactor, her story of how she fell in love with Edward Solomon, and her difficulties over rehearsing for W. S. Gilbert, are told in Lillian's "Reminiscences," *Cosmopolitan*, March, 1922.

Circumstances surrounding the breakup of her marriage to Solomon are described in Dressler's *My Own Story*, 83–84.

Her association with Aronson as a star at the Casino Theater is discussed in Aronson's *Theatrical and Musical Memoirs*, 70–71.

Colonel William d'Alton Mann's career is engagingly described in Logan's *The Man Who Robbed the Robber Barons*.

Clarence Day's brief experience as a spear carrier in Lillian Russell's service is described in "Appearing with Lillian Russell," *Saturday Evening Post*, October 26, 1935.

The career of Lillian's friend Nellie Melba was most recently recorded by Wechsberg, *Red Plush and Black Velvet*.

Melba's warning on hitting high C too frequently was recounted by Lillian in her "Reminiscences," *Cosmopolitan*, April, 1922.

2. Were Any of Horatio Alger's Heroes Fat?

Geographic and social background of Brady's birthplace are from O'Connor, *Hell's Kitchen, passim,* as is the quotation from Fitz-James O'Brien.

The death of Brady's father and his troubles with his stepfather are from Morell, *Diamond Jim: The Life and Times of James Buchanan Brady, passim,* and *Literary Digest*, April 28, 1917.

Decline of morality in the Flash Age is set forth in O'Connor's *Hell's Kitchen* and *Valentine's Manual*, a unique documentary of New York in the Victorian age.

Brady described his defrauding of the German band in a New York *Sun* interview, March 10, 1911. In the interview he also indicated, of course, that it was his first and last essay in dishonest practice. This was probably true.

Brady's methods of salesmanship and his encounter with George Baer are taken from "The Greatest Capital Goods Salesman of Them All," *Fortune*, October, 1954. Careful research showed, according to the article, that Brady averaged about a million dollars a year in commissions during the later and more lucrative phase of his career.

The description of Harry Hill's music hall is from Ed Van Every, *Sins of New York*, 81–82.

Brady's feats at the table are given admiring attention in Beebe's *The Big Spenders*, 74–76; also in *Literary Digest*, April 28, 1917; Cleveland Amory, "God, Nell, Ain't It Grand," *Horizon*, Summer, 1964, and Arnold Gingrich, "Feast of the Season," *Esquire*, December, 1967.

Brady's success with the Fox undercarriage is detailed in *Fortune*, and Morell's *Diamond Jim*, 50–52.

3. "Princess Nicotine" and Signor Perugini

The description of social intrigue surrounding the opening of the Columbian Exposition is taken from Dedmon, *Fabulous Chicago*, 230–31, as is that of Lillian's rebuff by Chicago society, 236.

Amy Leslie's interview with Sandow was published by the Chicago *Daily News*, May 2, 1893.

Colonel Mann's comment on the "romance" between Lillian Russell and Sandow is in *Town Topics*, July 8, 1893.

Colonel Mann on Lillian's return to the Casino is found in *Town Topics*, September 11, 1893.

Marie Dressler's friendship with Lillian is related in her *My Own Story*, 83–84.

Lillian's successful effort to obtain a pay raise for Marie Dressler is described in her "Reminiscences," *Cosmopolitan*, March, 1922.

Marie Dressler delivered her opinion of Perugini's character in *My Own Story*, 95–98.

Lillian's announcement of her marriage appeared in the New York *Telegram*, January 2, 1894.

The breakup of Lillian's second marriage, from an admittedly biased viewpoint, was recorded by Miss Dressler in *My Own Story*, 88–91.

Perugini's attempt to throw Lillian out of a hotel room window is described in Dressler's *My Own Story*, 92.

Lillian's statement on her reasons for leaving Perugini was published in the New York *Herald*, June 8, 1894.

Perugini's reply to Lillian's charges is in *Tammany Times*, June 15, 1894. Perugini eventually obtained a divorce, in 1898, from the New Jersey Chancery Court. His complaint was largely based on the charge that Lillian stayed up all night playing poker and neglecting her domestic duties.

4. Lobster-Palace Royalty

Lloyd Morris' description of Broadway by night is taken from his *Incredible New York*, 259–60.

The habit of respectable women of going to Rector's incognito is observed by Crockett in *Peacocks on Parade*, 157–58. Crockett was a star reporter for the New York *Herald* during the era he describes so tellingly.

The restaurant background of the Rectors, father and son, is included in Rogers and Weston, *Carnival Crossroads*, 109–13.

Lucius Beebe's observations on the mores of the lobster-palace set is from *The Big Spenders*, 70.

Oscar Tschirky recalled his first glimpse of Lillian Russell for Schriftgeisser's *Oscar of the Waldorf*, 34–35.

Brady's own account of his style at the table is quoted in Morris, *Incredible New York*, 263.

Lillian's adventures in London and with English royalty are recounted in her "Reminiscences," *Cosmopolitan*, April, 1922.

Nellie Melba's warning to Lillian against invading the operatic competition is recorded in Lillian's "Reminiscences," *Cosmopolitan*, April, 1922.

The incident of the man committing suicide in Niagara Falls over Lillian's rejection was reported in the New York *Morning Telegraph*, May 31, 1901.

Brady's historic automobile journey down Fifth Avenue is related in Morris, *Incredible New York*, 212–13.

Subsequent events in New York's automotive history are included in

Lord, *The Good Years*, 115–17. Lillian Russell also became fascinated by the automobile during its early years. She liked to roar down Long Island roads in her custom-built, chauffeur-driven "Red Dragon," which had cost her $30,000. On July 14, 1902, she was arrested for speeding by the police of Freeport, Long Island.

The ambience of the first Waldorf-Astoria and the sort of people who patronized it are described in James R. McCarthy's *Peacoch Alley*, Crockett's *Peacocks on Parade*, and Schriftgeisser's *Oscar of the Waldorf*.

Judge Gary's rejection as a candidate for Bet-a-Million Gates' poker table is related in Crockett, *Peacocks on Parade*, 125–26.

Quotation in footnote on the million-dollar baccarat session is from Crockett, *Peacocks on Parade*, 127.

The newspaperman's description of the Waldorf during Horse Show Week is from Crockett, *Peacocks on Parade*, 127.

The ad-lib concoction of Cantaloupe à la Lillian Russell was recalled by Oscar Tschirky in Schriftgeisser's *Oscar of the Waldorf*, 128.

5. On a Bicycle Built for Three

Lillian Russell's impressive measurements were provided by an undated newspaper clipping in the Robinson Locke Scrapbook Collection of the New York Public Library's theatrical section at Lincoln Center.

Oscar Tschirky's recollection of Brady's attempt at dieting is in Schriftgeisser, *Oscar of the Waldorf*, 38.

An account of the amazing grip the bicycling fad had on the public is in Morris' *Incredible New York*, *passim*.

Marie Dressler's recollection of "two plump girls" on their bicycles is from *My Own Story*, 82.

Brady's gold-plating of his bicycles is described by Beebe in *The Big Spenders*, 77–78.

The workings of the Brady Beneficent Society are explored by Amory, *The Last Resorts*, 432.

Brady's deal to corner the output of the Boston candy factory is detailed in Beebe, *The Big Spenders*, 77.

De Wolf Hopper's ruminations on the decline of comic opera and the rise of the musical comedy are contained in *Reminiscences of De Wolf Hopper*, 155–56.

Details of Lillian's German tour are recaptured in her "Reminiscences," *Cosmopolitan*, June, 1922.

The meeting of Brady and Edna McCauley and its consequences are related by Morell, *Diamond Jim*, 134–37.

Brady's encounter with the life-style of Count Boni de Castellane is described in O'Connor, *Gould's Millions*, *passim*.

6. A Summer in the Seraglio

The menu at Saratoga's United States Hotel is included in Bradley's *Such Was Saratoga*, 203.

Lillian described her antics with her "farm flirts" in her "Reminiscences," *Cosmopolitan*, August, 1922. She recalled that she regarded Blanche Bates—later, as Cigaret, the star of Ouida's *Under Two Flags*—as "another sister."

Saratoga's colorful history is delineated in Bradley's *Such Was Saratoga*, *passim*, and Amory's *The Last Resorts*, 244–45.

The background and career of Weber and Fields are provided by Felix Isman, their stage manager for many years, in his memoirs, *Weber and Fields*.

The opening of *The Girls from Maxim's* is described in Isman's *Weber and Fields*, 255–58.

William Randolph Hearst's worshipful attendance at the Music Hall and his admiration for Lillian Russell are conveyed by W. A. Swanberg in *Citizen Hearst*, 178–79.

John Heywood's poem hymning Lillian's beauty was published by the New York *Telegram*, October 18, 1899.

Brady's jewelry collection is itemized and assayed in Beebe, *The Big Spenders*, 74–75. In the *Fortune* article it was noted that Brady acquired a total of about 20,000 diamonds in his lifetime, with a value estimated at $2,000,000—and that he often wore $250,000 worth without ever requiring the services of a bodyguard. Only an out-of-town crook, ignorant of Brady's influence with the police, would have attempted to lift them.

Brady's tongue-in-cheek interview on the virtues of sartorial discretion was published in the New York *Telegram*, May 7, 1909.

Background of Bet-a-Million Gates is taken from Warshow's *Bet-a-Million-Gates*, *passim*.

Gates' acquisition of an art collection is related in Crockett, *Peacocks on Parade*, 91.

The Gates-Brady raid on J. P. Morgan's railroad interests is explored in detail in Warshow, *Bet-a-Million Gates*, 80–88.

Brady's method of entertaining is observed by Crockett, *Peacocks on Parade*, 311, 313.

Brady's career as a racing stable owner and his party to celebrate his retirement from the track are described in Beebe, *The Big Spenders*, 79–80.

Details of Brady as friend of Stanford White and guest of honor at White's Jack Horner party are from Langford's *The Murder of Stanford White*, *passim*.

Jacques Bustanoby's recollection of the eating contest between Brady and Russell is included in an interview with the New York *Mirror*, August 10, 1931.

Brady's epic bout at the breakfast table is recorded by Cobb in his autobiography, *Exit Laughing*, 361–63.

7. A Famous Foursome Breaks Up

The development of a rift between Weber and Fields is described by Isman in *Weber and Fields*, 287. Same source for details of the company's Western tour.

Sam Bernard's proof that Lillian once wore purple tights is recalled by Edward B. Marks in his memoirs, *They All Had Glamour*, 77.

The closing of the Weberfields company and its last night on Broadway were reported by the New York *Herald* and the New York *Sun*, May 30, 1904.

De Wolf Hopper's memory of the idyllic relations between members of the Weberfields company is quoted in Isman, *Weber and Fields*, 271.

Adverse comment on Lillian's use of the "arts preservative" is from the New York *Sun*, December 27, 1904.

The breakup of Lillian and Jesse Lewisohn, Brady and Edna McCauley are described by Morell, *Lillian Russell*, 251–53.

Beebe's survey of Brady's feeding habits is included in his *The Big Spenders*, 79.

George Rector's comments on the same subject are contained in his memoirs, *The Girl from Rector's*, 16–19.

Wilson Mizner's association with Brady and Russell, as well as his amazing career, is explored in the late Alva Johnston's lively chronicle of a remarkable family, *The Legendary Mizners*.

8. L'Affaire Sole Marguery: A Spy Story

How the recipe for sole Marguery was lifted from a Parisian restaurant is recalled by the culprit himself, George Rector, in *The Girl from Rector's*, 37–41. While working as a busboy-spy at the Café Marguery, young Rector also acquired the recipe for an elegant sauce Bordelaise. He also picked up a sense of the discipline maintained backstage in Parisian restaurants: "The slightest swerve from ancestral routine was punished with reduction to the ranks."

The Weberfields revival, and Lillian's role in it, is recounted by Isman in *Weber and Fields*, 310–12.

Enrico Caruso's comment on the relative rewards of low comedy and grand opera are found in Isman's *Weber and Fields*, 313.

Brady's illness, eventually traced to his enormous consumption of orange juice and orangeade, is related by his friend Harry B. Smith in *First Nights and First Editions*, 191–92.

Dr. Young's recollection of Brady's gratitude for removing his kidney stone is quoted by Morell, *Diamond Jim*, 246.

Interview with Brady and report of his recovery and return to New York are from the New York *World*, August 28, 1912.

9. Lillian Russell for President—or Something

Background to the women's suffrage movement is drawn from Holbrook's *Dreamers of the American Dream*, 213–23.

Details of Lillian's marriage to Alexander Moore are from the Pittsburgh *Post*, June 12, 1912, and the Pittsburgh *Leader*, June 13, 1912. In her "Reminiscences," *Cosmopolitan*, September, 1922, Lillian recorded the happiness of her fourth and last marriage. She also recalled that Fay Templeton, her ex-colleague, who had also married a Pittsburgh businessman, was present at the wedding and how they laughed over two graduates of the knockabout Weberfields troupe marrying respectable Pittsburghers.

Lillian's statement on women's suffrage was published by the Chicago *Inter-Ocean*, September 22, 1911.

The social historian quoted on Lillian's role in the suffrage movement is Lord, *The Good Years*, 278.

Lillian's maternal tribulations are variously recorded in the New York *Evening World*, August 25, 1903; Ann Fields, "When Lillian Russell Was Glamour Queen," *Coronet*, May, 1951; and the New York *Journal*, August 27, 1901.

Dorothy's defense of her mother was published in *Life*, November 19, 1951.

The state of the cinematic art when Lillian made her film debut may be studied in Crowther's *The Lion's Share*, 27–28.

Lillian's appearance in *Wildfire* and her effect on Lewis Selznick's shaky financial position are elaborated in Thomas' *Selznick*, 21–22. Selznick had organized the World Film Company with the idea of presenting Broadway successes with their original stars under the slogan "Features Made from Well Known Plays by Well Known Players." In addition to Russell and Barrymore, he also signed Lew Fields for *Old Dutch*, Alice Brady and Holbrook Blinn for *The Boss*, and Wilton Lackaye for *Trilby*.

10. Decline and Fall of the Great Gastronome

The pre-World War I dance craze and its effects on New York's manners and morals may be studied at greater length in Churchill's *The Great White Way*, 254–57, and Morris' *Incredible New York*, 320–21.

The journalistic observer alarmed by the effects of the frenetic dances on the elderly is Crockett, *Peacocks on Parade*, 306–8.

The social historian quoted on Maurice as the high priest of the new dances is Morris, *Incredible New York*, 320.

Brady's style as an elephantine dancing partner is recalled by Irene Castle in *Castles in the Air*, 92–93.

The interview with Frank Bacchi was published in the New York *Herald Tribune*, May 10, 1951.

Charlie Chaplin's recollections of Brady as a Hollywood host are in his *My Autobiography*, 156–57.

The banquet given for Dr. Young by Brady is described in the New York *World*, May 17, 1915.

The New York restaurateurs' dinner for Brady was covered by the New York *Times*, April 4, 1916.

Brady's death and funeral were reported by the New York *Times, Sun, World*, and *Tribune*, April 13–17, 1917, and *Literary Digest*, April 28, 1917.

11. The President's Plenipotentiary

Lillian's appearance at the Metropolitan Opera benefit is related in Ann Fields' "When Lillian Russell Was Glamour Queen," *Coronet*, May, 1951.

Her own account of her wartime activities is included in her "Reminiscences," *Cosmopolitan*, September, 1922.

Her appearance at the New York Liberty Bond rally was covered by the New York Morning *Telegraph*, October 19, 1917.

Her campaigning for Harding is detailed in "Reminiscences," *Cosmopolitan*, September, 1922.

Mrs. Alice Roosevelt Longworth's comment on President Harding's poker-playing circle is quoted by Francis Russell, *The Shadow of Blooming Grove*, 448.

Lillian's activities as a special immigration commissioner are recorded by *Literary Digest*, April 22, 1922.

Her refusal to seek medical aid while appearing with Weber and Fields was reported by the New York *World*, September 30, 1903.

Her death and funeral were covered by the New York *Times, Herald*, and *World*, June 6–7, 1922. Nat Goodwin's tribute is quoted from his memoirs, *Nat Goodwin's Book*, 122.

12. Dim the Houselights

The dire immediate effects of Prohibition on New York and the rest of the country are graphically told by Allsop in *The Bootleggers and Their Era* and Sinclair in *Prohibition: The Era of Excess*.

The New York *Tribune* published its list of American millionaires on November 2, 1892.

Walter Weyl's observations on the "new destitutes" are quoted in Richard Hofstadter, *The Age of Reform*, 146–47.

BIBLIOGRAPHY

BOOKS

Adams, Henry, *The Education of Henry Adams*. Boston, 1918.
Allsop, Kenneth, *The Bootleggers and Their Era*. New York, 1961.
Amory, Cleveland, *The Last Resorts*. New York, 1952.
Aronson, Rudolph, *Theatrical and Musical Memoirs*. New York, 1913.
Baedeker, Karl, ed., *The United States*. Leipzig, 1893.
Beebe, Lucius, *The Big Spenders*. New York, 1961.
Blum, Daniel, *A Pictorial History of the American Theater*. Philadelphia, 1960.
Bradley, Hugh, *Such Was Saratoga*. New York, 1940.
Castle, Irene, with Duncan, Bob and Wanda, *Castles in the Air*. New York, 1958.
Chaplin, Charles, *My Autobiography*. New York, 1964.
Churchill, Allen, *The Great White Way*. New York, 1962.
Cobb, Irvin S., *Exit Laughing*. Indianapolis, 1941.
Crockett, Albert Stevens, *Peacocks on Parade*. New York, 1931.
Crowther, Bosley, *The Lion's Share*. New York, 1957.
Dedmon, Emmett, *Fabulous Chicago*. New York, 1953.
Dressler, Marie, with Harrington, Mildred, *My Own Story*. Boston, 1934.
Goodwin, Nat C., *Nat Goodwin's Book*. Boston, 1914.
Hofstadter, Richard, *The Age of Reform*. New York, 1955.
Holbrook, Stewart, *Dreamers of the American Dream*. New York, 1957.
Hopper, De Wolf, with Stout, Wesley W., *Reminiscences of De Wolf Hopper*. New York, 1927.

Isman, Felix, *Weber and Fields.* New York, 1924.

Johnston, Alva, *The Legendary Mizners.* New York, 1952.

Kirkland, Alexander, *Rector's Gay Nineties Cookbook.* New York 1949.

Langford, Gerald, *The Murder of Stanford White.* Indianapolis, 1962.

Lewis, Oscar, *Bay Window Bohemia.* New York, 1956.

Logan, Andy, *The Man Who Robbed the Robber Barons.* New York, 1965.

Lord, Walter, *The Good Years.* New York, 1960.

Marks, Edward B., *They All Had Glamour.* New York, 1944.

McCarthy, James R., *Peacocks on Parade.* New York, 1948.

Morehouse, Ward, *Matinee Tomorrow.* New York, 1949.

Morell, Parker, *Diamond Jim: The Life and Times of James Buchanan Brady.* New York, 1934.

—— *Lillian Russell: The Era of Plush.* New York, 1940.

Morris, Lloyd, *Incredible New York.* New York, 1951.

Muirhead, James F., *The Land of Contrasts.* London, 1898.

O'Connor, Richard, *Gould's Millions.* New York, 1962.

—— *Hell's Kitchen.* Philadelphia, 1958.

Rector, George, *The Girl from Rector's.* New York, 1927.

Rogers, W. G., and Weston, Mildred, *Carnival Crossroads.* New York, 1960.

Russell, Francis, *The Shadow of Blooming Grove: Warren G. Harding and His Times.* New York, 1968.

Schriftgeisser, Karl, *Oscar of the Waldorf.* New York, 1945.

Sinclair, Andrew, *Prohibition: The Era of Excess.* Boston, 1962.

Smith, Harry B., *First Nights and First Editions.* Boston, 1931.

Thomas, Bob, *Selznick.* New York, 1970.

Valentine, Alan, *1913: America Between Two Worlds.* New York, 1962.

Van Every, Ed, *Signs of New York.* New York, 1891.

Warshow, Robert I., *Bet-a-Million Gates.* New York, 1932.

Wechsburg, Joseph, *Red Plush and Black Velvet.* Boston, 1961.

Ziff, Larzer, *The American 1890's.* New York, 1966.

MAGAZINES

Esquire, December, 1967.

Horizon, Summer, 1964.

New York Times Magazine, December 3, 1961.

Opera, February 10, 1962.

Fortune, October, 1954.

Life, November 19, 1951, and December 10, 1951.

Saturday Evening Post, October 26, 1935, and April 15, 1922.

Bibliography

Étude, July, 1934.
Literary Digest, April 22, 1922, and April 28, 1917.
Cosmopolitan, December, 1905, and February to October, 1922.
Munsey's, December, 1903.
Harper's Weekly, March 22, 1902, and December 17, 1904.

The author is especially indebted to Robert Woodward and Sue Wight of the Bangor Public Library for assistance in research. For similar reasons he is also grateful to the staffs of the New York Newspaper Library, the theatrical and musical collections at the Lincoln Center Branch of the New York Public Library, the Athenaeum in Boston, and the New York Historical Society's library.

273

INDEX

INDEX

Index

49, 174–75; career, 33–51, 136–40, 156–63, 182–84, 187–90, 202–4, 218–23; crusader for women's rights movement, 212–14, 215, 221–22, 223; criticism of, 125–26, 189–90; daughter, 25–26, 39, 50, 195, 217–18; death, 251–52; early success, 24–33; European tour, 137–40; friendship with "Diamond Jim" Brady, 13–14, 81, 87–88, 101, 108–11, 123, 148, 156, 193–95, 210, 215, 218, 219, 239; generosity, 28, 32; Harding election campaign and, 245–47; horse racing enthusiast, 84–85, 149, 155–56; illnesses, 251; lawsuits, 35, 38, 41, 111, 139, 199; lecture tours, 215–16; liaison with Jesse Lewisohn, 144–45, 149, 151, 153, 171, 179, 183, 184–86; marriages, 25–26, 34–40, 92–101, 210, 212–14; motion-picture career, 219–21; operatic aspiration, 24, 113–14; overweight problem, 125–27, 129, 154, 174; parents, 17–21; personal appearance, 23–24, 32; salary, 33, 45, 47–48, 136, 158, 160, 187; Saratoga summer, 147–56; Special Commissioner of Immigration, 248–51; syndicated columnist, 215, 217, 222; World War I activities, 242–44.
Rutland Hotel, New York, 132
Ryan, Paddy, 74
Ryan, Thomas Fortune, 168, 204

Saint-Gaudens, Augustus, 10
St. James Hotel, New York, 57–58, 59, 61
Sandow the Strongman, 86–87
San Francisco, Calif., 30–31
Sans Souci club, New York, 229–30

Saratoga, N.Y., 147–56
Savoy Hotel, New York, 106
Savoy Theater, London, 38
Scheff, Fritzi, 64
Schneider, Hippolyte, 115
Schoen Pressed Steel Company, 152
Schubert, Lee, 230
Schumann-Heink, Ernestine, 50, 163
Schwartz, Jean, 232
Scotty, Death Valley, 198–99
Seeley, Blossom, 228
Selznick, Lewis J., 220
Senn, Walter, 25
Sennett, Mack, 233
Shanley's lobster palace, New York, 106
Shattuck, Truly, 157
Shaw, George Bernard, 157, 222
Shelburne Hotel, Atlantic City, N.J., 238
Sherman, William T., 42
Sherman Act, 121
Sherman Silver Purchase Act, 81
Sherry, Louis, 160
Shubert, Sam, 199, 201
Siddons, Mrs. Scott, 188
Sinn, William, 24
Slade, Herbert, 74
Smith, Harry B., 112–13
Smith, Jess, 247
Smith, Robert, 163
Snake Charmer, The, 31
Soissons, C. S. de, 11
Solomon, Dorothy, 39, 50, 195, 217–18
Solomon, Edward, 34–40, 98
Sorcerer, The (Gilbert & Sullivan), 33
Sothern, E. H., 31
Southern Railway Company, 167
Spanish-American War, 255
Speakeasies, 254